IMAGES
of America

Gold Beach and South Curry County

On the Cover: Ferries were used to traverse the Rogue River; the first ferry was built and used by Mr. Bagnell for transportation from the North Bank Road across to the South Bank Road. It is known as Jerrys Flat Road today. The county replaced the Bagnell ferry with a new motorized ferry that transported the cars, buggies, and equipment from old Roosevelt Highway or the North Bank Road to the Wedderburn Loop or Bailey Road. (Curry Historical Society.)

IMAGES
of America

GOLD BEACH AND SOUTH CURRY COUNTY

Meryl Boice

ARCADIA
PUBLISHING

ISBN 978-0-7385-9615-0

Published by Arcadia Publishing
Charleston, South Carolina

Printed in the United States of America

Library of Congress Control Number: 2012940830

For all general information, please contact Arcadia Publishing:
Telephone 843-853-2070
Fax 843-853-0044
E-mail sales@arcadiapublishing.com
For customer service and orders:
Toll-Free 1-888-313-2665

Visit us on the Internet at www.arcadiapublishing.com

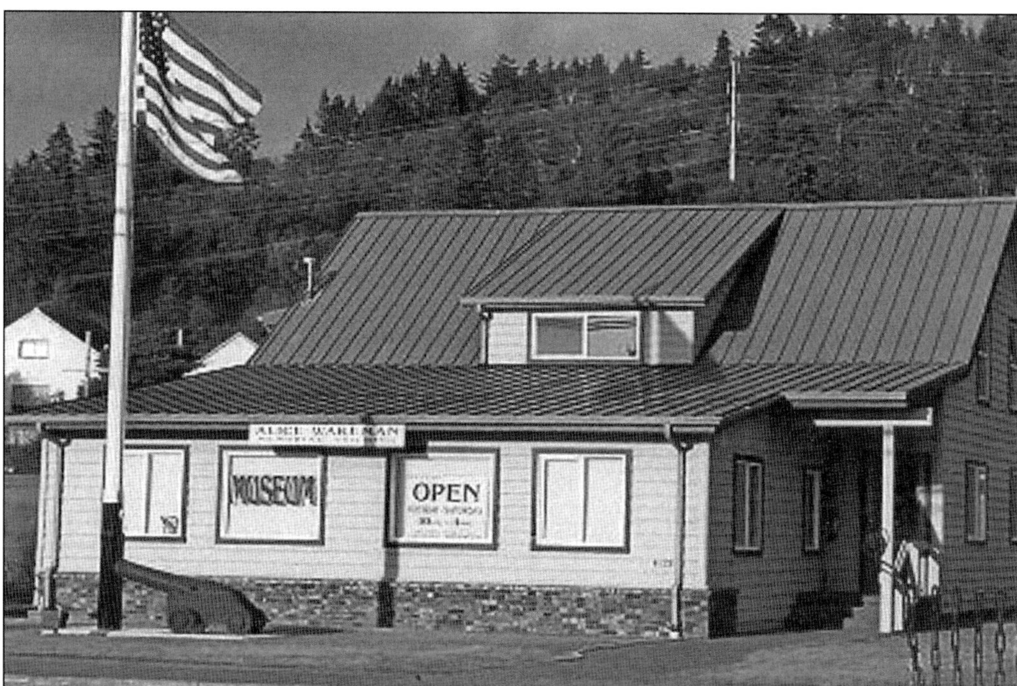

The Curry Historical Society was first organized in 1974 with a small building on the north end of the fairgrounds. In the winter, there were problems when it rained hard, as the building had a leaking situation. In the year 2002, with a grant written by P.J. Estlund, the society was able to obtain a building just across Highway 101 from the fairgrounds and transform it into a wonderful museum. Visitors who drop in have given the society many compliments as to the museum's openness and well-done exhibits. An annex was built for outside exhibits in 2011. (CHS.)

Contents

ACKNOWLEDGMENTS

I want to thank the Curry Historical Society (CHS) and Museum for the use of pictures for this book. Without these, the book would not be available. I also want to thank Walt Schroeder, who offered pictures to use in the book as well as his wealth of information. Thanks to all who were supportive of me.

Introduction

Gold Beach sits up higher than the ocean and Rogue River, so those fortunate to live close to town have an opportunity to see the changes in the ocean and the Rogue, whose headwaters are located at Crater Lake. Heading west, it meanders and curves around bends and is occasionally bounded on both sides by high canyons. Dropping over rapids and receiving the intake of little creeks on both the north and south, it meets with the Illinois River at Agness and flows on until it reaches the ocean. The town of Gold Beach is small but peaceful for those who look for the positives of living in such a place.

Residents who have lived here for many years love the ocean but do not see the area the same way some of the visitors do. The beauty of the area lies in the ocean, which always changes. High above the large expanse of the sea are beautiful sunsets, with no two ever alike. The mighty Rogue River at times flows with tranquility into a calm tide of the ocean, while other times it is met with huge waves crashing over the jetties and the rocks with the spray of the high breakers. During their yearly journey, huge whales play in the surf or the mouth of the river. Very often, it is a mother and her calf.

Fishermen cast from the bank or wait in their boats for the lucky strike of a large salmon, each striving to land the biggest one. With the beginning of salmon season, the boats line up side by side and become what is known as a "hogline" at the mouth of the river. The wildlife and varied species of birds flying overhead give outstanding beauty to this quaint little town.

Gold Beach maintains a more relaxed lifestyle compared to the hustle and bustle and bumper-to-bumper traffic of large cities. The big city is a fun place to visit and shop in, but the fast, congested traffic year-round would be a major change in Gold Beach's daily life. Once, a visitor wrote that this truly was a magical place, "where the sun rays dance on the waves and streaks of silver shimmer against the cobalt blue of the water."

At night, the moonlight casts a phosphorous glow on the rippled waves along the beaches that stretch out for long distances. Visible are little sea animals that skirt over the sand when the tide is out. It is fun to search for agates, colored rocks, seashells, or just the right piece of driftwood; occasionally, sand dollars, which represent the Easter story, can be found.

On the north side of the river is the small town of Wedderburn, which at an earlier era was larger than Gold Beach. It was founded by R.D. Hume, who built the first salmon cannery. He also built a can-making factory, a pea-canning facility, and hotels; started three different weekly newspapers, a fish hatchery, a racetrack, and a sawmill; and owned all the land on the north bank, from the mouth of the Rogue River up several miles. In 1935, the state passed a law halting commercial netting of the salmon and opened it up for sportfishing. This was the beginning of the famous hogline at the mouth of the river.

Today, the trip up the Rogue River can be made by car on the north bank of the river, but the road ends at Illahe, about five miles above Agness. Travel farther is done by passenger jet boats or private boats, which can travel upriver as far as 52 miles from the mouth. The scenery is magnificent. Along the way, one may see a graceful deer seeking a drink from a crystal stream or at the river's edge. Black bears will often meander or frolic along the riverbanks. High up in the treetops are many osprey nests with their owners flying overhead, caring for their young. Farther up the river, a bald eagle might be spotted or a pair resting on tree limbs; eagles mate for life. To watch an eagle soaring up higher and higher is exciting.

The woodlands stand in their glory with little cascading streams and tumbling falls flowing into the river. A short distance up the river stands a lonely cabin; the only things that seem to guard it are the fir trees, strong and tall.

There are several lodges on the river to accommodate the jet boat passengers, hikers, and drift trips. Paradise Lodge has a small airstrip for planes that want to fly in and use its facilities. In the fall, the downriver fishing trips bring happy fishermen with their fishing gear, all ready to rehash the day's trip.

Previous to the miners and early pioneers who first arrived in Curry County, Native Americans lived here and were part of designated tribes. Several large villages from Coos County to the state line had been established. The tribes had a simple life and survived off hunting wild animals, fishing salmon and steelhead from the river, harvesting seafood from the ocean, and utilizing the natural foods on the forest floor. They used animal skins for clothing, and some used it for their teepees, while others built shelters out of lumber. Their houses were constructed by setting walls down in a deep ditch and piling dirt around all four sides to keep out the cold. A hole was cut in the roof to allow the smoke to filter out.

They would cut a log, level the top, and set a carefully monitored fire in the middle to burn it down to an opening. They would then hone it out to make a dugout canoe for access to the river. The women would weave their baskets so tight that they could boil water in them with a stone in the center to cook their food. They were very knowledgeable and were survivors.

When the miners first appeared to work their claims, they used many varied types of machinery to mine the beaches. As the gold became less on the beaches, they soon traveled up the river to mine the banks and little inlets that flowed into the Rogue River. Soon, the water became muddy from the different mining implements, which caused the destruction of the natural foods for the Native Americans. Because of this as well as the poor treatment of their women by a few miners, the Indians felt the need to protect their way of life and turned into a war party.

When the battle cry sounded, the miners who were still beach mining quickly built a fort for protection on the north side of the river about a half-mile from the mouth. It was built at the edge of the ocean with a walkway across a moat around the fort to prevent the war party from entering. It was called the Miner's Fort. The 1856 Indian war continued until the pioneers in the fort were saved by the military, and after several skirmishes, the Native Americans were finally rounded up and transported to a reservation on the Siletz River, farther up the coast.

Slowly, the local pioneers rebuilt their homes that the Indians had burned and destroyed and started over by rebuilding a larger and better town.

What a delight it is to look at the ocean and river and see what visitors view. Beauty is always found if we look for it. Yes, God created everything well and lovely; this is what is found on the southern Oregon coast.

Today, some of the families in Agness are descendants of some of the earlier tribes that lived there. Every year, they have a big powwow in memory of their roots. They live a quiet life and are a wonderful group of people.

One

Gold Beach, the Special Town

Many years before the new highways, Gold Beach, Oregon, was a frontier town. When the highways and bridges were completed, the state became a haven for the tourists, and today, there is much to offer, especially in Gold Beach and Curry County. There are guided sportfishing and passenger jet boat trips that travel upriver as far as Agness or onto the Blossom Bar. The boating season runs from May through October. These are the two main attractions today.

The lovely, well-maintained motels and restaurant accommodations are an added attraction for the visitors. People are able to walk the beaches, camp in surrounding areas, hike various trails, and simply sightsee. There are plenty of RV parks for those driving motor homes or pulling trailers, and the airport can handle fairly large planes.

There is so much history here, and if visitors are interested, the museum is worth spending time in viewing the living history of the past.

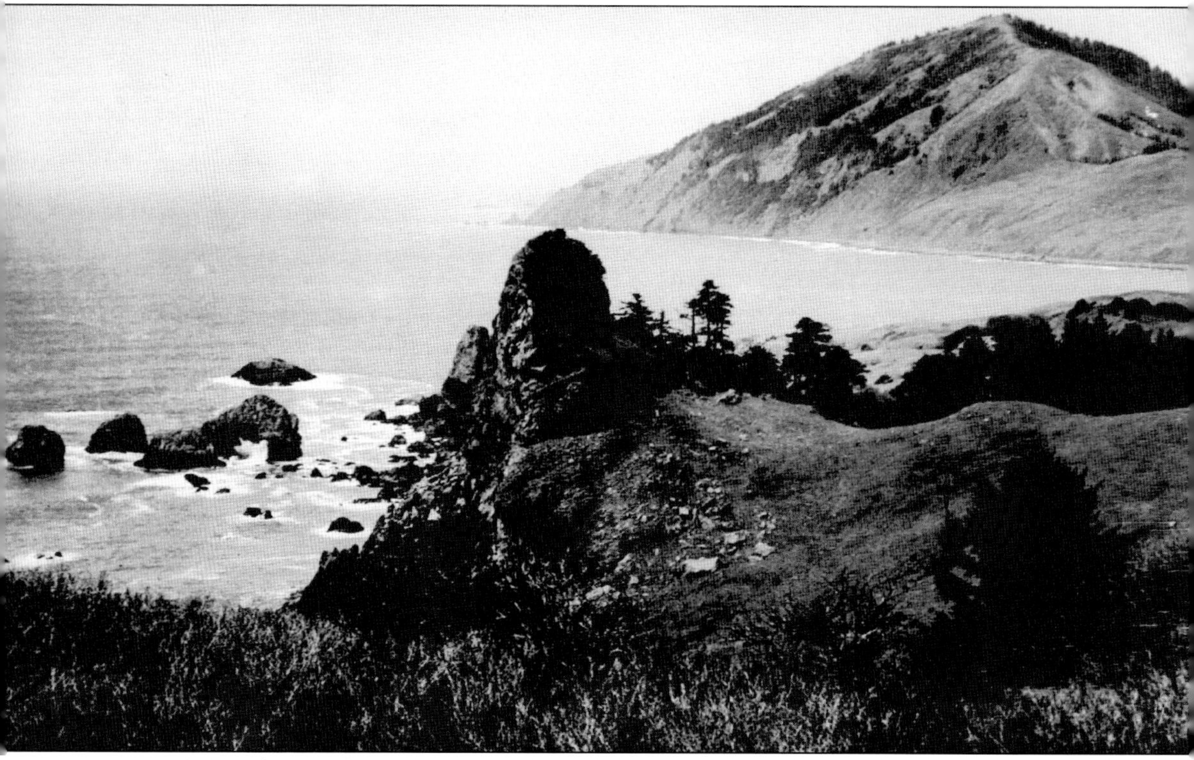

Located 20 miles north of Gold Beach, Humbug Mountain, at 1,748 feet high, is the highest mountain overlooking the Pacific Ocean in Curry County. There are taller mountains in the Kalmiopsis Wilderness, but this mountain is on the coast. It rises just above Highway 101. The highway passes through Brushes Creek and follows the shoreline of the ocean to Port Orford. The hiking trail that goes from the base to the top of Humbug offers one of the most fantastic views from all three directions. The base of the mountain is located on the shore of the Pacific Ocean. Its original name was Sugarloaf Mountain. (CHS.)

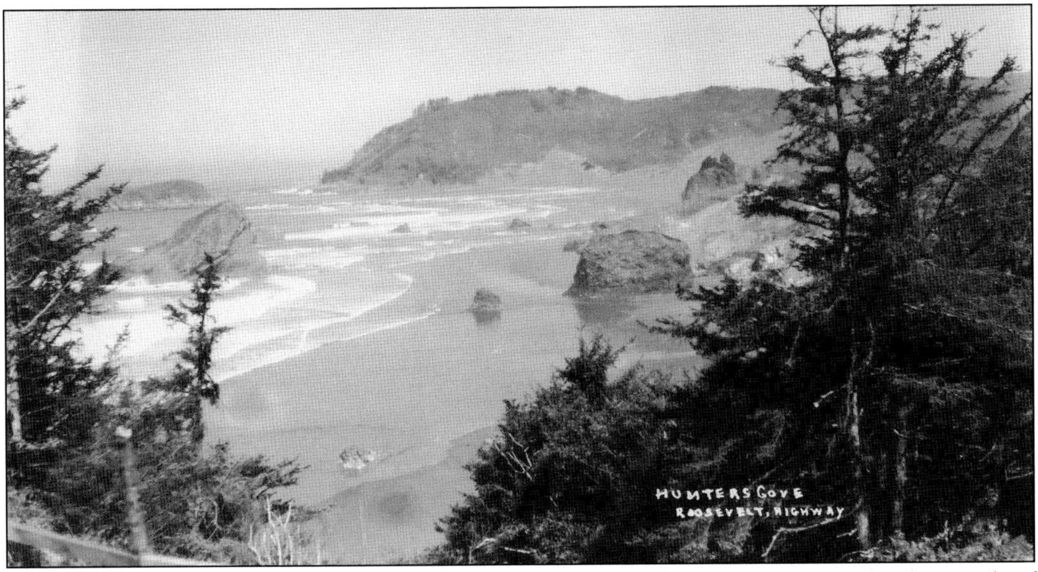

Hunters Cove is at Meyers Creek and just south of Cape Sebastian. Hunters Island is south of the cove. In the early days, hunting sea otters was a big industry. Those engaged in this business used small boats for cruising along the coast. During bad weather, they took protection in the cove. Today, beaches surround Hunters Cove, making it a pleasant area for walks. It is also a fun place to wade in the surf or look for souvenirs. In the evening, many enjoy roasting hotdogs and marshmallows in campfires, watching the moon come up and cast its glow on the waves, and listening to the surf pounding or gently lapping the shore. (CHS.)

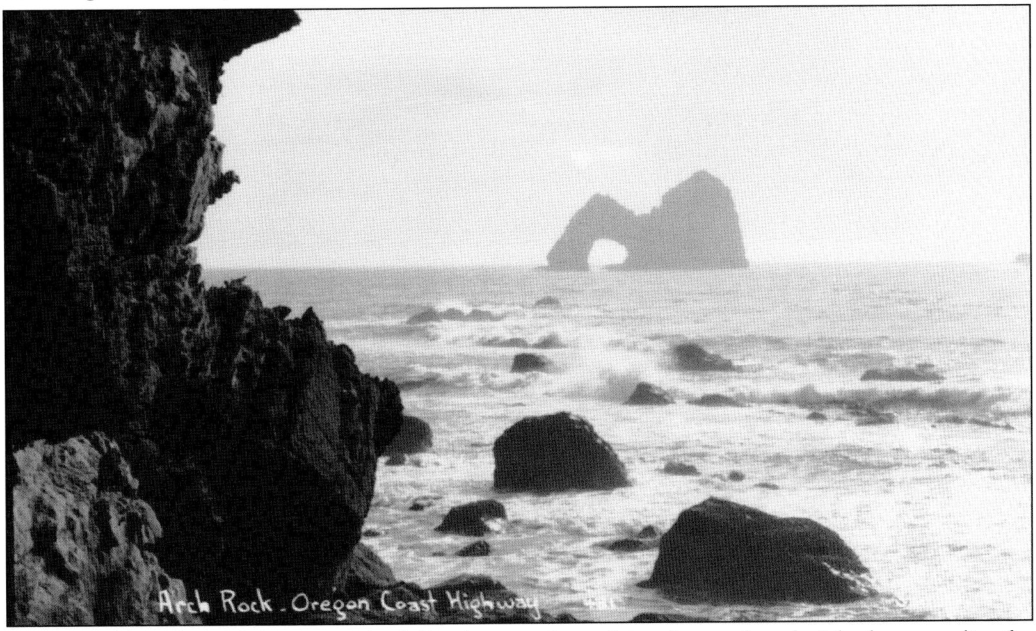

Before the building of the ports, Arch Rock was where ships dropped and picked up supplies for farmers and the locals at Pistol River. They would take their wagons to the entrance of the ocean at Arch Rock and row out to the ships, get their goods, row back, and load their wagons. Besides their needed products, they stocked the ships with meat, butter, fruit, produce, cheese, milk, and other products to sell. (CHS.)

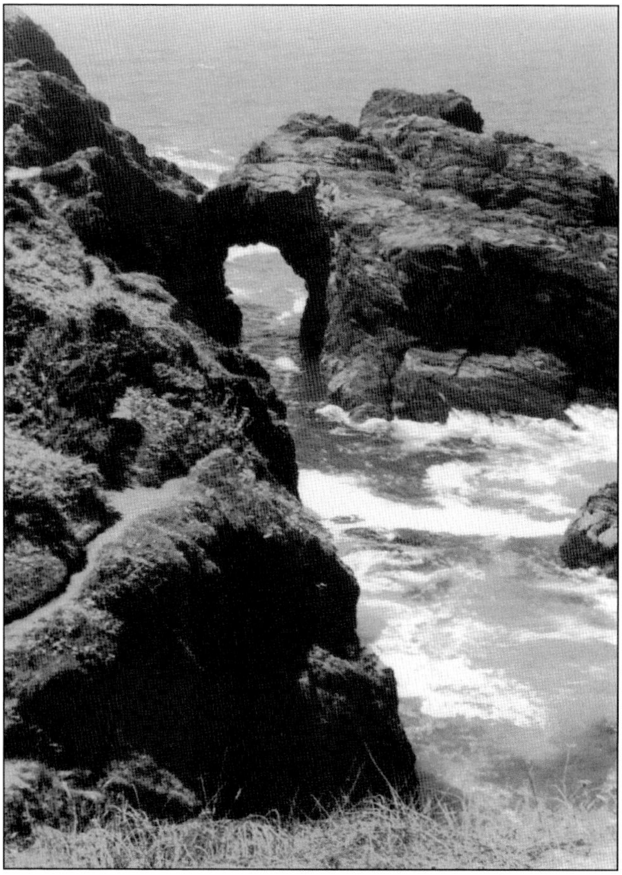

Just a little past Arch Rock on Highway 101, there is a posted sign that notes where the rocks are formed to show a natural bridge, and the parks system has built a trail to where it sits. It is a special view of the ocean, and it is spectacular how its natural beauty stands out. (CHS.)

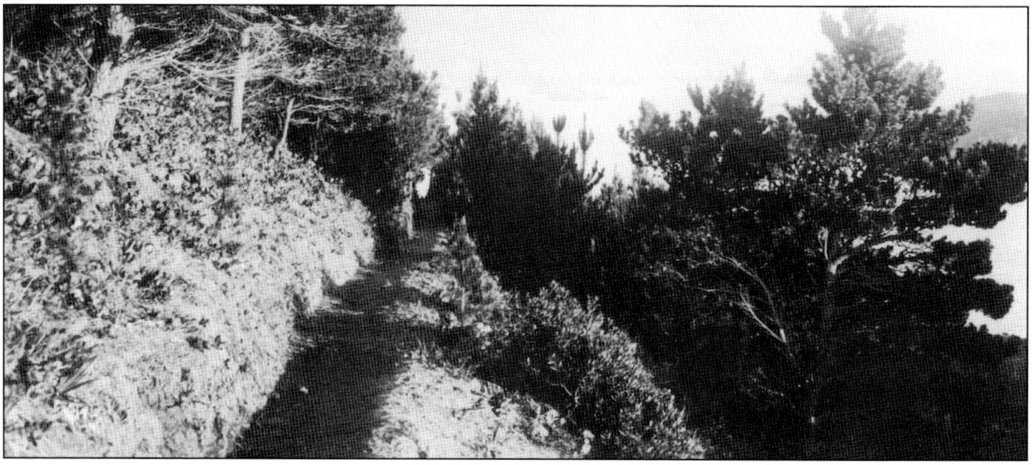

This trail leads to the ocean and beach from the Cape Sebastian lookout. It is a fairly steep trail, but worth the hike for all the beautiful scenery. The natural wildflowers pop up with each season, and the view at the top is incredible. On a clear day, photographers can capture the town of Port Orford to the north and as far south as the Crescent City Lighthouse. The road that goes to the top veers to the right off of Highway 101 about eight miles south. At the top, a sightseer can go right for one viewpoint or turn left to reach the viewpoint to the south, which is where the trail starts. (CHS.)

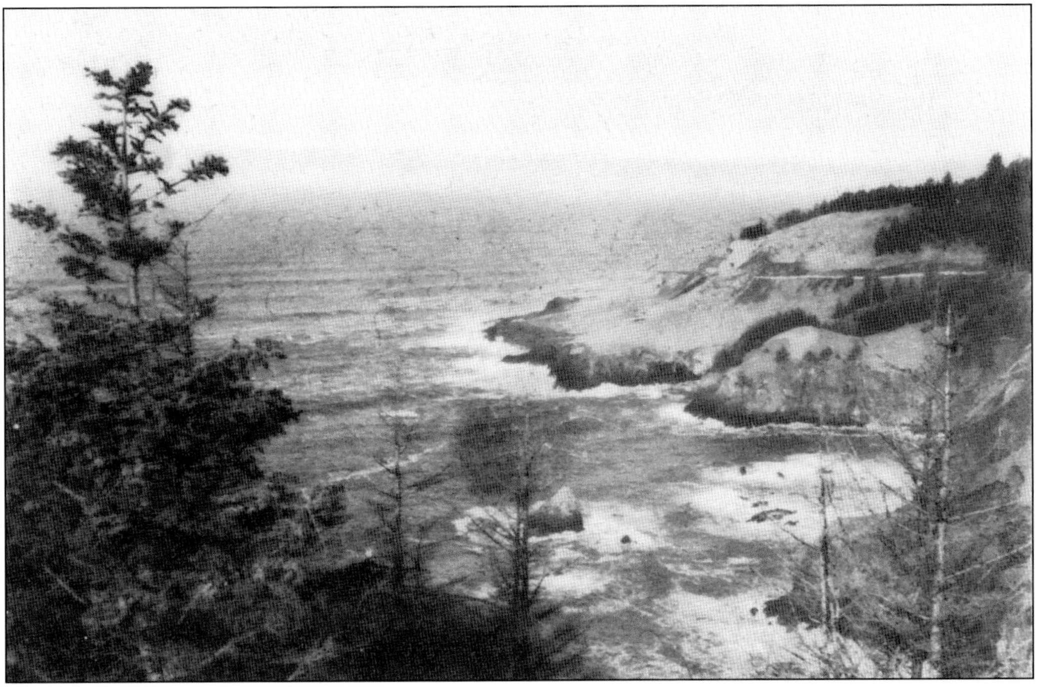

These are views of the ocean from the trail between Gold Beach and Brookings. There are special turnoffs from the highway to other viewpoints, such as the natural bridge, House Rock, Whales Head, and others that show the beauty of the ever-changing ocean. For photographers, it is worthwhile to find the trail for hiking or to spend time at each viewpoint from Port Orford to Harbor. (Both, CHS.)

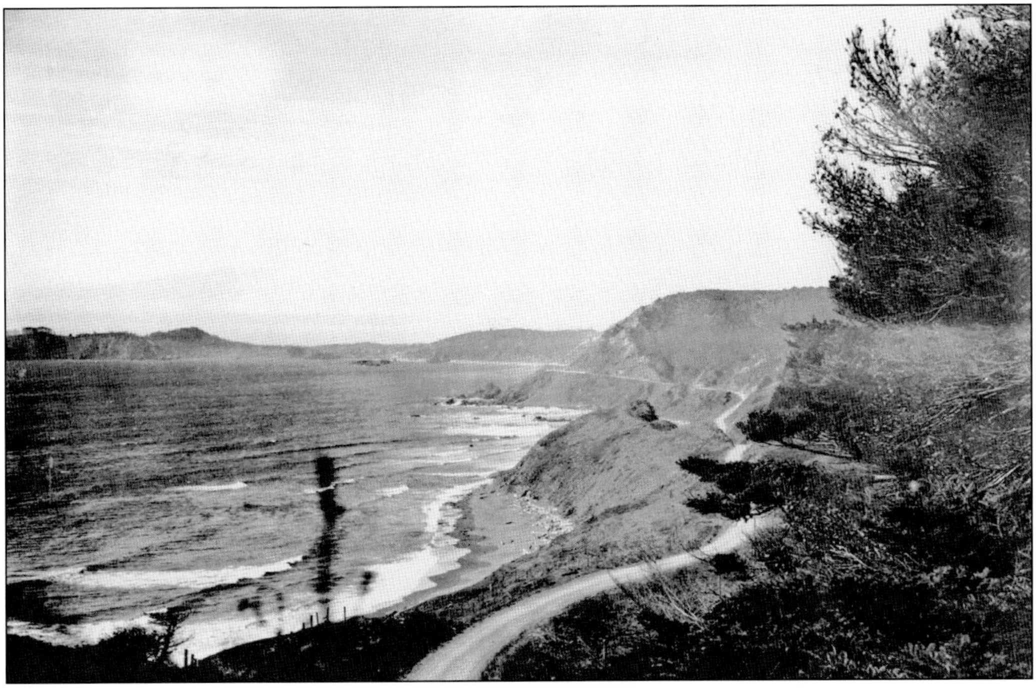

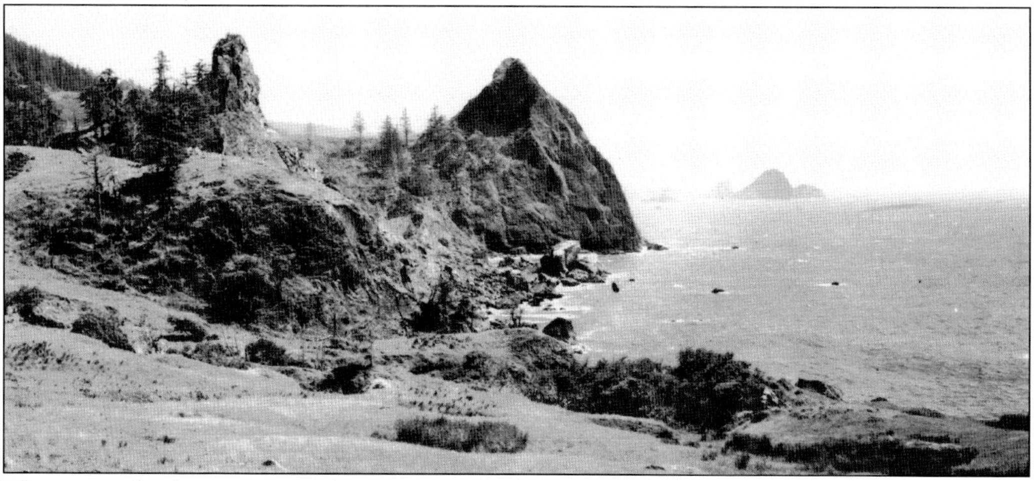

The area today known as Frankport was referred to in the earlier era as the Three Sisters. The three large rocks were used as a natural harbor for loading ships with logs and for exporting and importing supplies to and from San Francisco. A tram was used to transport tan oak to the waiting ships. Tan oak had many uses, especially for making leather. When the tan oak was no longer plentiful, long fir logs were transported. As there were no roads, a small town had been founded with a hotel and post office by a few working families, who named it Corbin. When the two companies that used it for exporting left, Sauce Bros. Tug Co. bought the land, and as far as it is known, they still own the land that connects with the Three Sisters. They have not reactivated the harbor for many years. The town of Corbin had disbanded when the tan oak company left the area. It was later that that Frankport was used for the making of illegal moonshine: the bootleggers utilized the back caves that were only reachable at certain very low tides. The last entry of the port was by a small boat full of drugs that ran aground on the beach. The crew was arrested, but the mothership was never located. (CHS.)

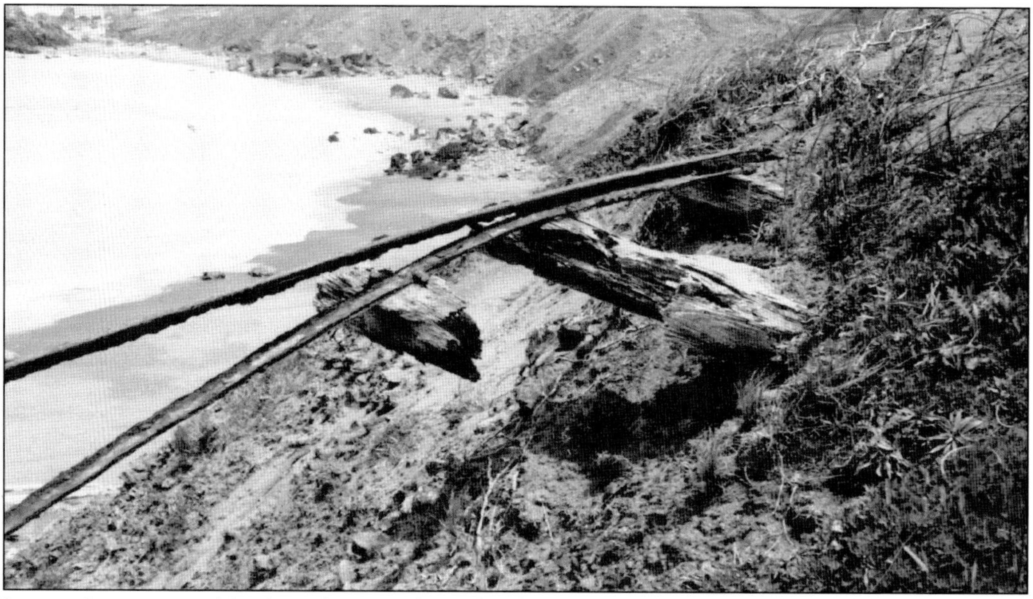

Located in a natural harbor, the tram brought the tan oak and later fir logs down to be placed onto the ships for delivery to San Francisco and also helped unload the imports from the ships for the pioneers. (CHS.)

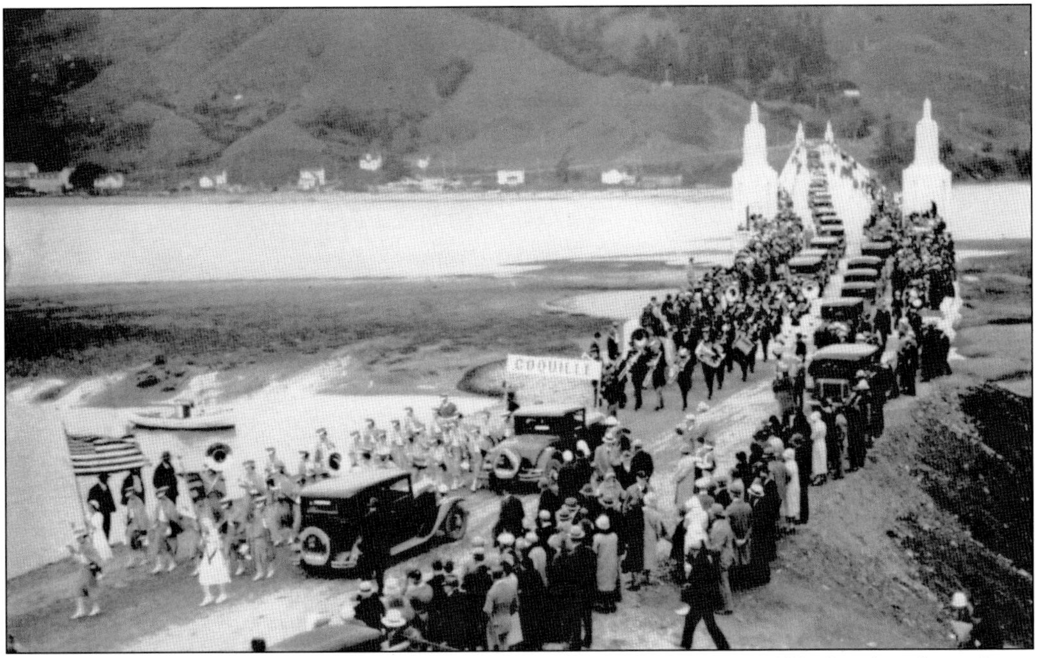

The first cars on the Isaac Lee Patterson Bridge are seen on May 28, 1932. On that day, a large ceremony was held for the opening of the bridge. Gov. Charles H. Martin and Judge Allen Boice were present for the cutting of the ribbon. At the White House in Washington, DC, Vice Pres. Charles Curtis pressed a gold telegraph key signaling to the world that the Rogue River bridge was open. (CHS.)

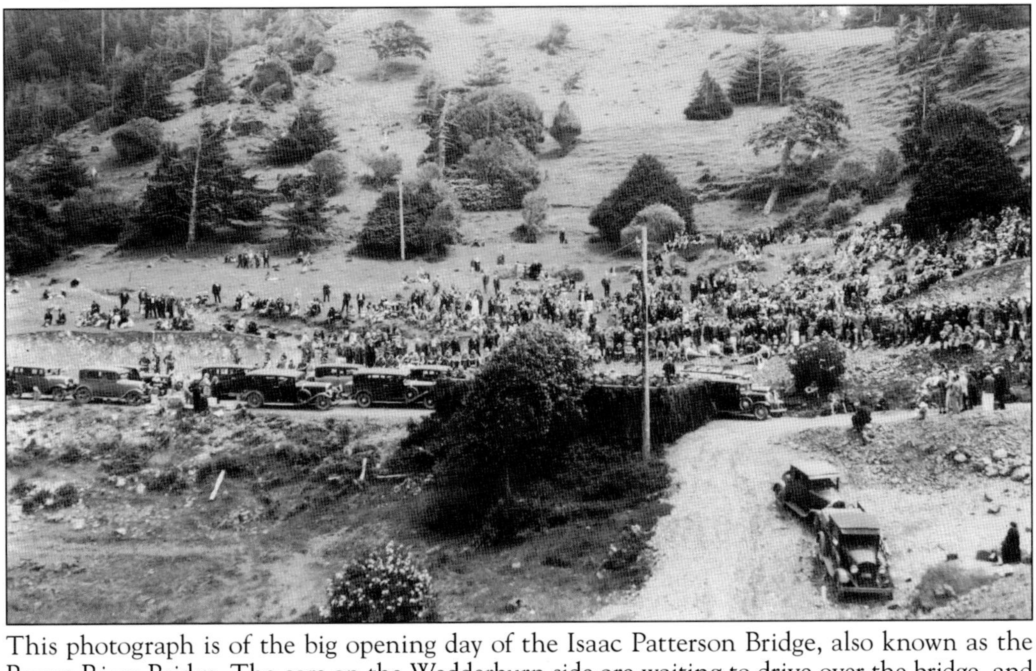

This photograph is of the big opening day of the Isaac Patterson Bridge, also known as the Rogue River Bridge. The cars on the Wedderburn side are waiting to drive over the bridge, and the crowd, located on the north end of the bridge, is excited for the speeches and the cutting of the ribbon. (CHS.)

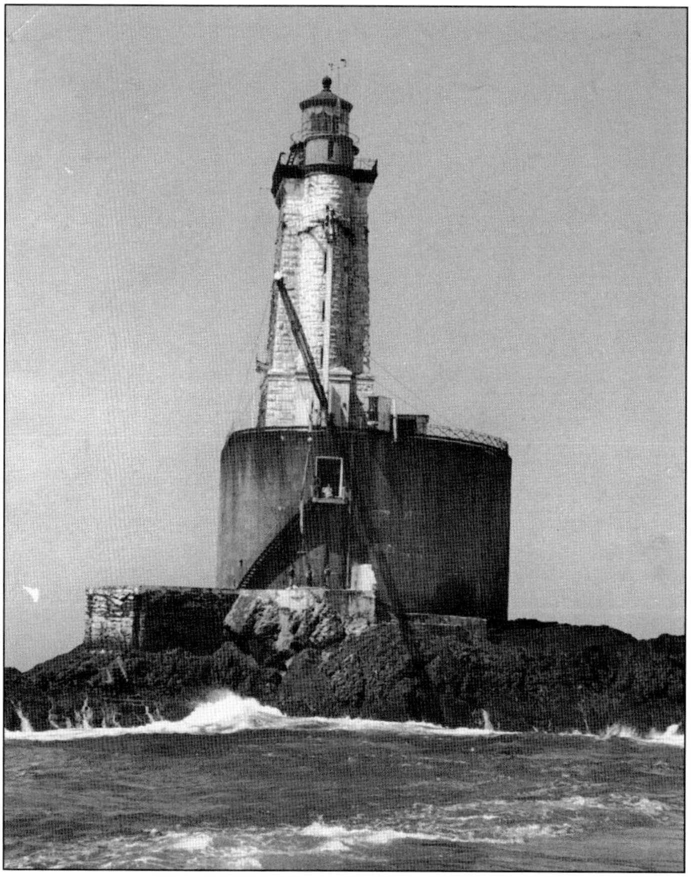

The St. George Lighthouse is found on the Oregon-California state line. Helicopter rides are available to fly around the lighthouse. It is a landmark that is worth seeing off the coastline of Brookings and Crescent City. (CHS.)

Cape Blanco at Sixes is between Port Orford and Bandon. One can drive out to the lighthouse and visit the buildings. There is a good campground on the road out to the lighthouse. (CHS.)

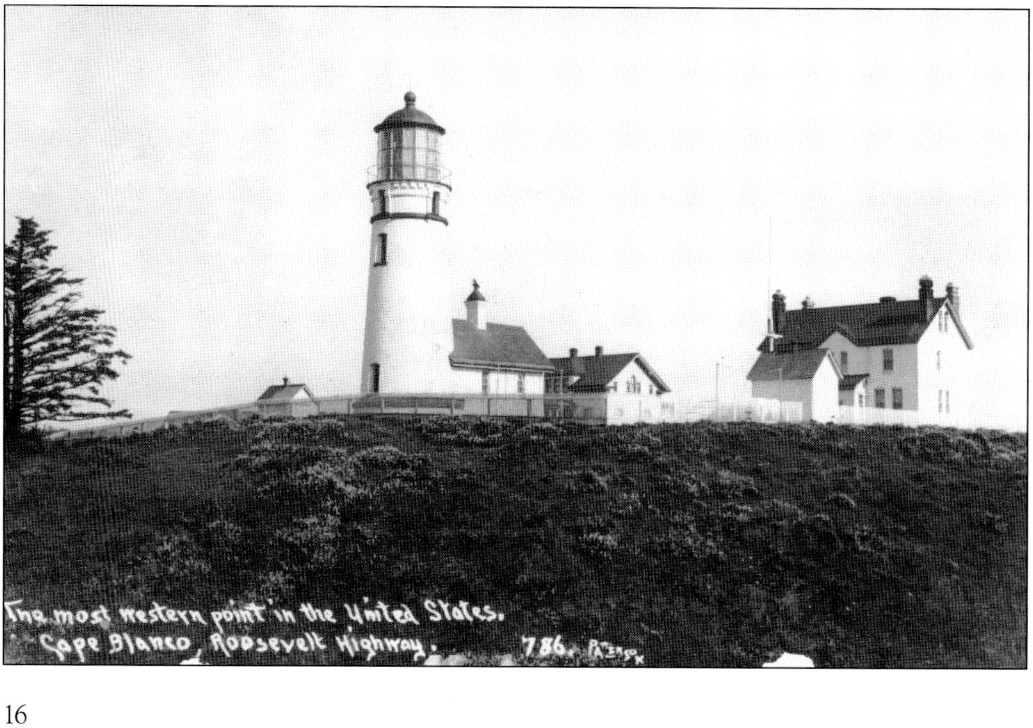

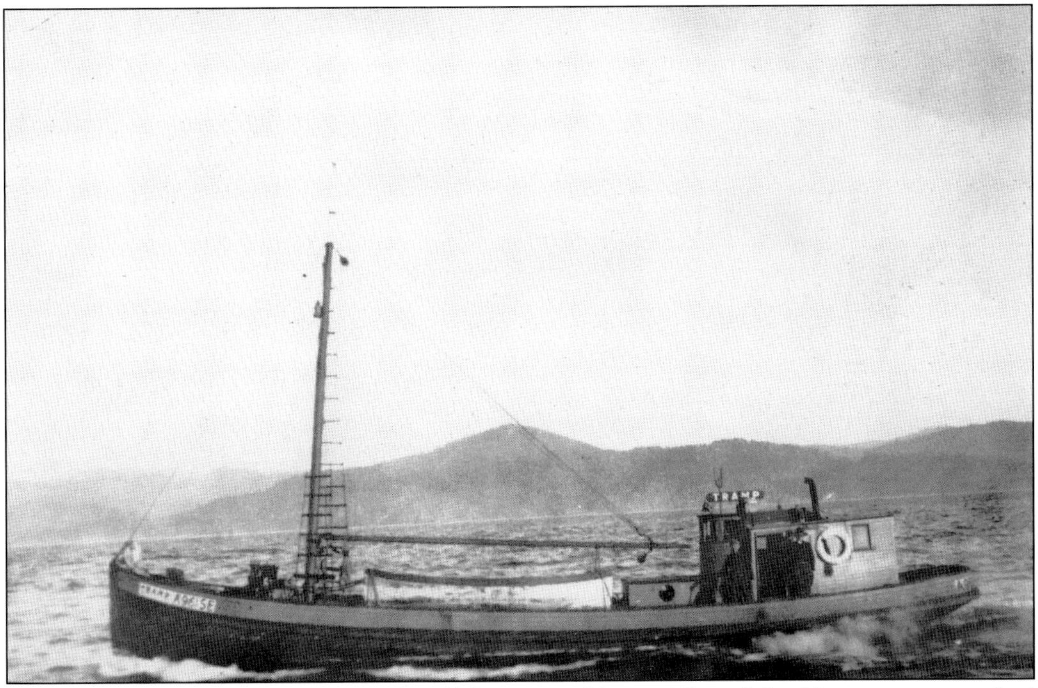

This image is of one of the shipwrecks off the coast of Curry. Named the *Tramp*, it was wrecked in 1919. Oftentimes, wreckers or crewmembers could move many of the supplies off the ship before the boat sank. If the ship were close enough to the breakers, the crew would make it to shore. (CHS.)

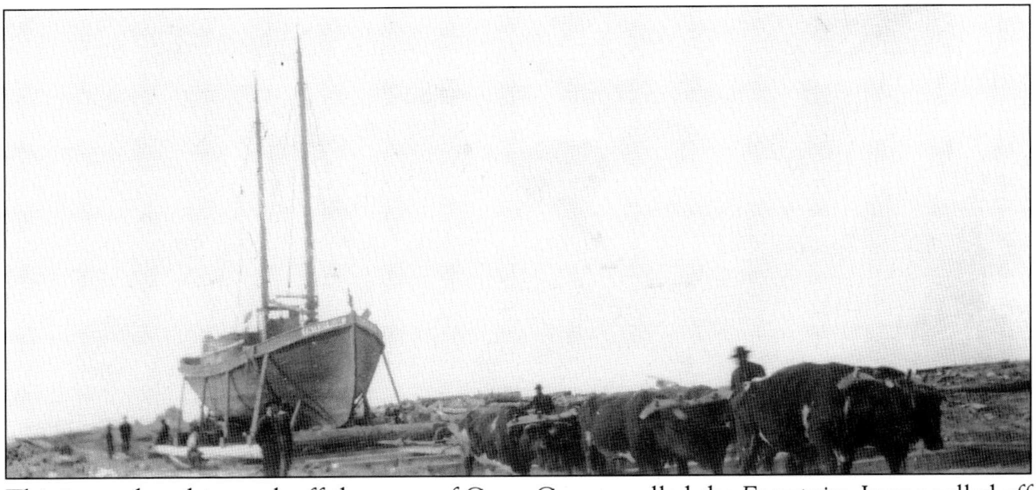

This is another shipwreck off the coast of Curry County called the *Enterprize*. It was pulled off the reef with oxen, thus saving all the cargo aboard. (CHS.)

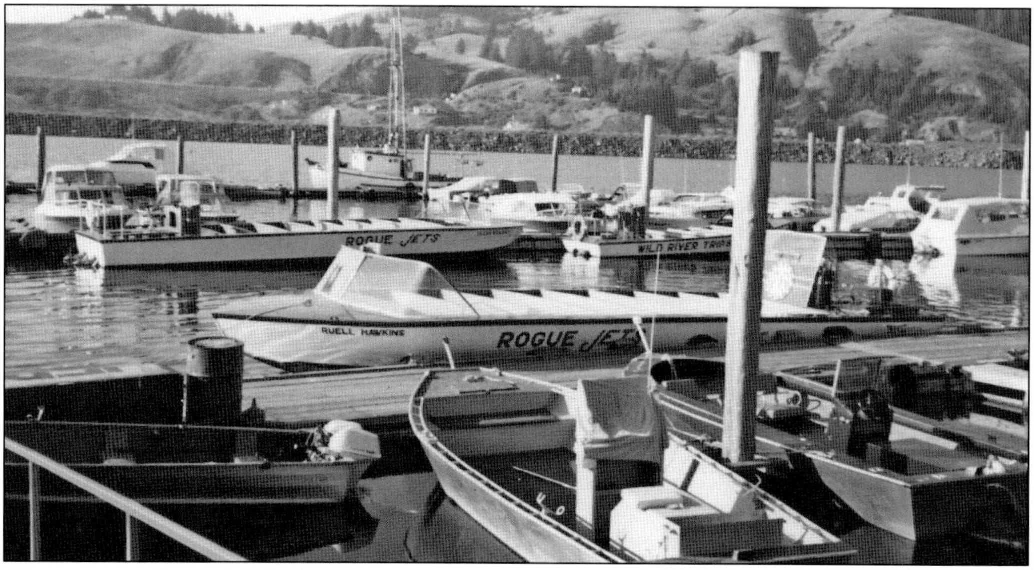

The company Rogue Jets helps promote tourism by transporting some passengers up Rogue River for round-trip lunches and by dropping others off for overnight stays at the lodges. There are three round-trips, the 64-mile, the 80-mile, and the 104-mile, that are available daily from May 1 to late October. The McNair family now owns Jerry's Rogue Jets and Mail Boats. This, along with guided sportfishing trips, helps to support the motels, restaurants, and other businesses, especially during the summer. (CHS.)

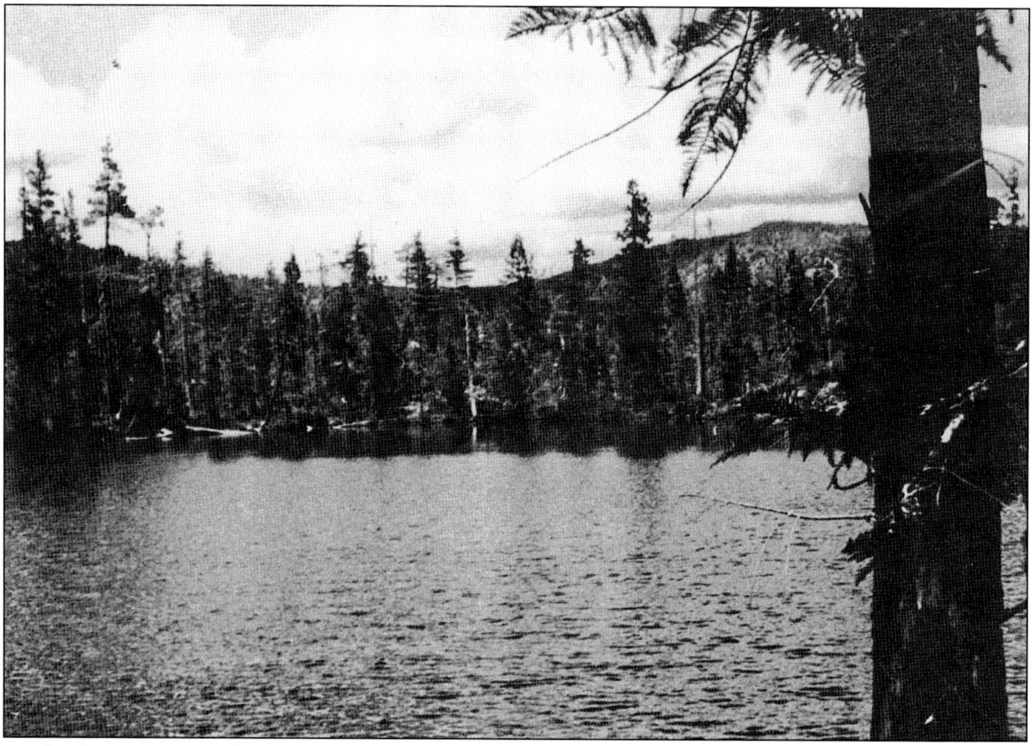

In the lower part of the Kalmiopsis Wilderness, there are several lakes. This is a breathtaking photograph of the one of the lakes. It is worth the hike to see some of them. (CHS.)

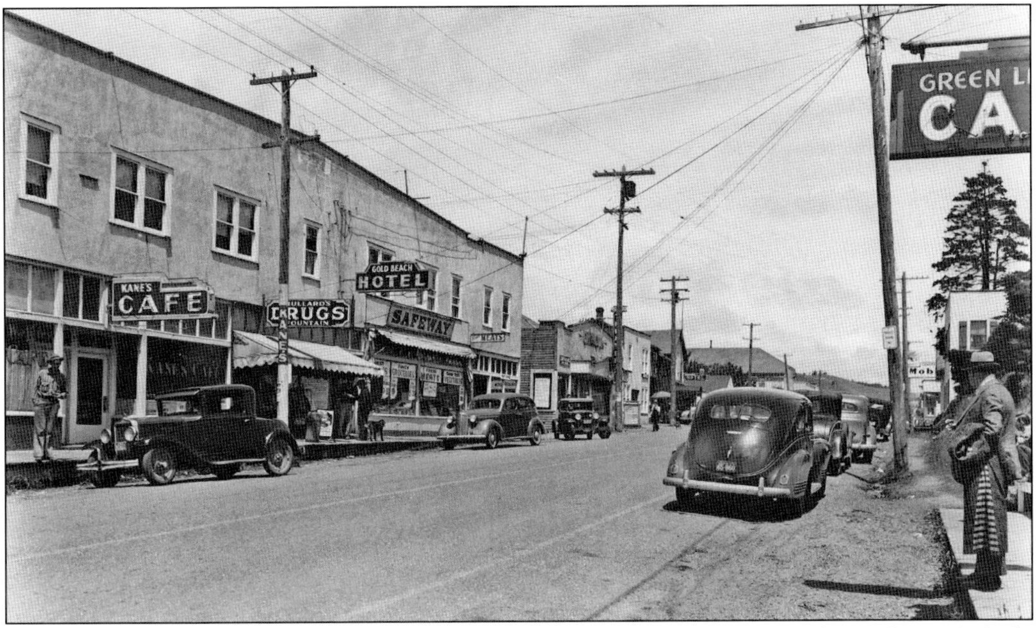

This is the Hickock Hotel, also known as the Gold Beach Hotel, in 1939. It housed Kane's Café, Bullard's Drugs, Safeway, and Christian's meat market. To the left, not seen, were the theater and Ethel's Café. Directly across the street were the Green Lantern Café and the Shell station. The hotel was condemned and had to be torn down around 1989. The theater and Ethel's Café burned down in 1995. (CHS.)

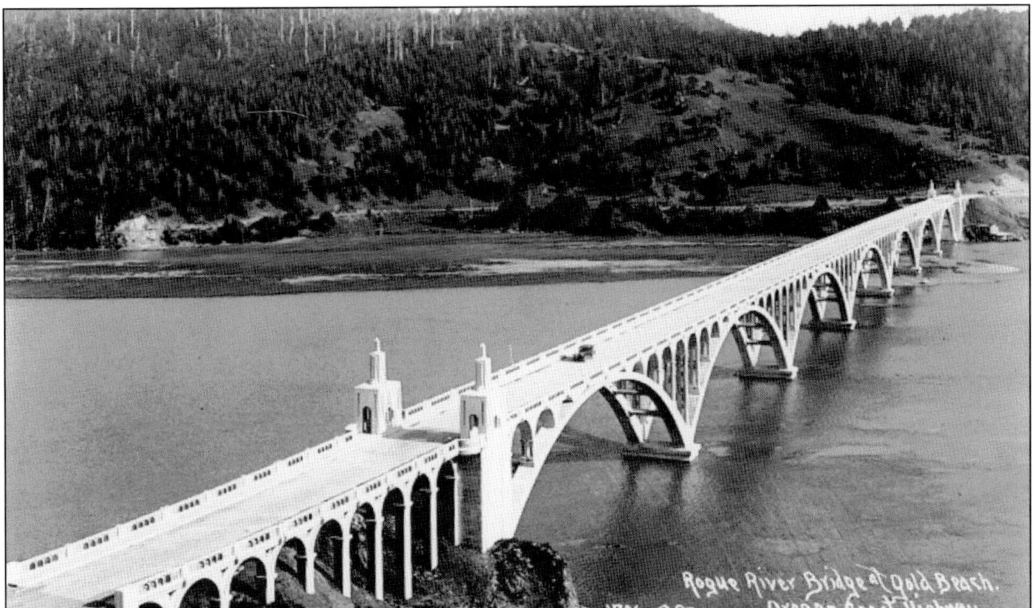

The Isaac Lee Patterson Bridge is also referred to as the Rogue River Bridge. Taken through the trees, this view is from Jerrys Flat Road on the south bank of the river. When the bridge was built and dedicated in 1932, it was known as the most beautiful bridge built at that time in Oregon. At the present, there are lights shining along each arch, making it a warm and inviting sight to see when returning home at night. (CHS.)

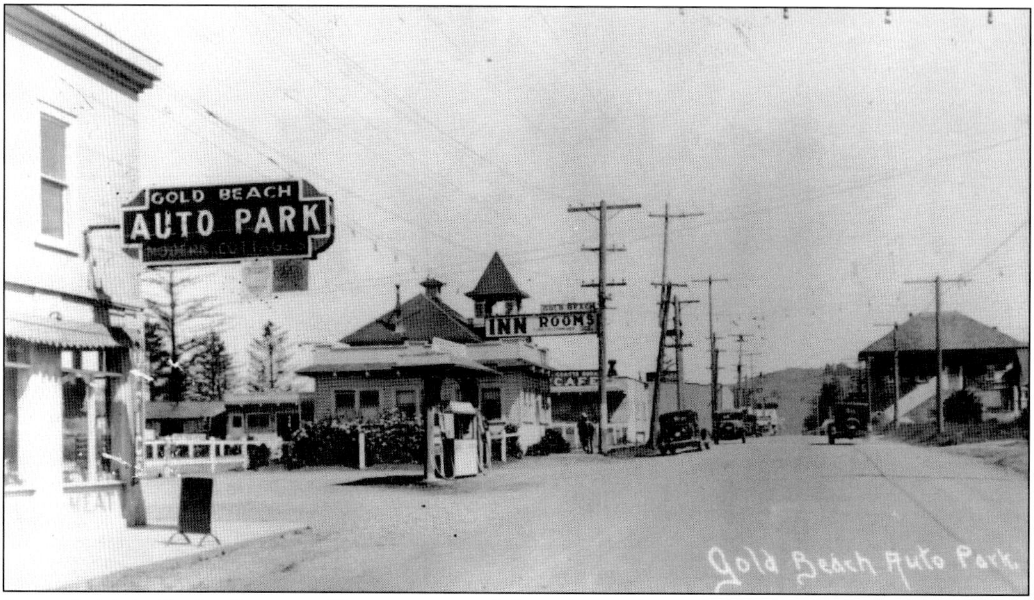

James Leith built the first motel/auto camp on Main Street that offered cabins with kitchens and fireplaces. He owned a market next door for needed supplies, such as food, drinks, snacks, and general merchandise. He had previously built a light plant, and it brought lights to his cabins, a bakery, a Standard Oil station, a bus depot, a Laundromat, and a café, which were all found in a single complex. (CHS.)

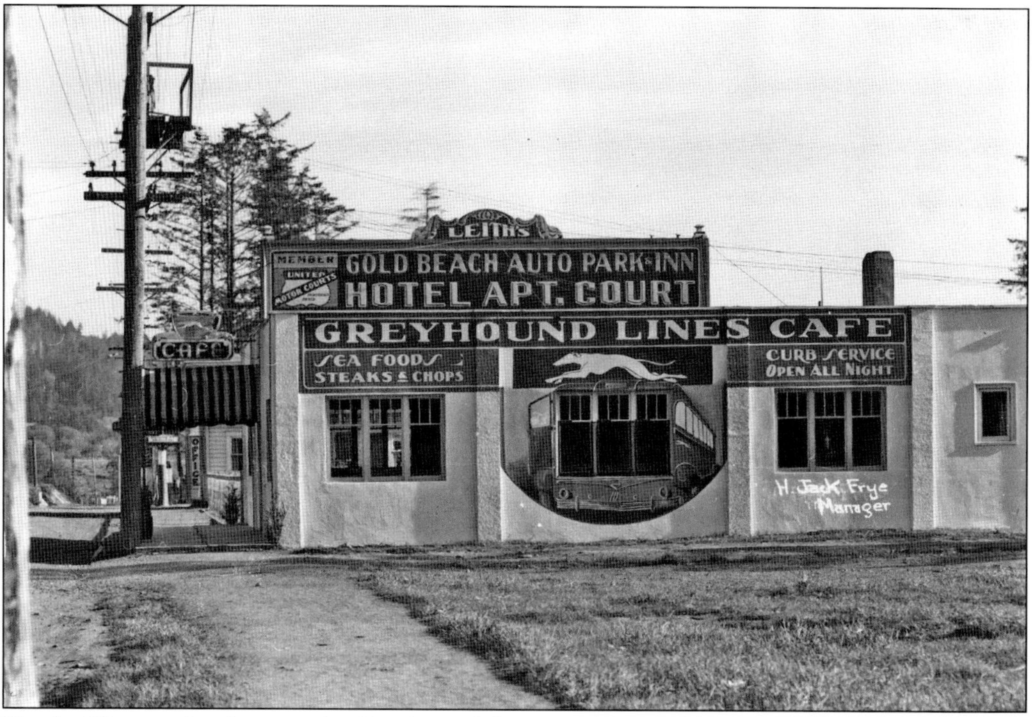

The building in this frame is the Greyhound depot, constructed by Jim Leith as part of his auto camp, store, café, cabins, gas pumps, and electric light plant. He was a man who did very well during the early days of Gold Beach. (Paradise collection.)

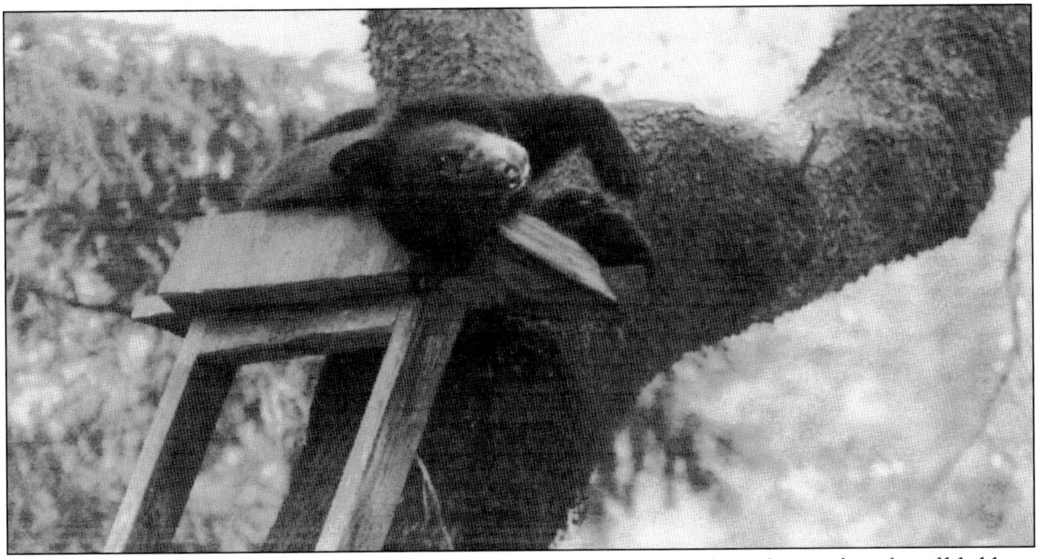

One morning at Paradise Lodge, a little hungry ragtag cub landed on the roof, and staff fed him a small amount of food and hoped to keep him there until the passenger boats came. However, he jumped off the roof, almost landing on the two boys working there, and ran up a tree. He stayed in the tree, and a ladder was quickly built at the base of the tree, with a platform being constructed later at the top of the ladder. When the boat passengers arrived, they were delighted. Visitors threw their chicken bones to Paradise Pete, which he inhaled. He received quite an excited reaction from the boat passengers. When he was full, he had his own zoo of people and entertained them. After a few days of coming everyday at noon, he started staying in the tree at night on his platform. The next summer, he came for a while but then no more. Employees and guests suspected that he had met the same fate as his mother. (Paradise collection.)

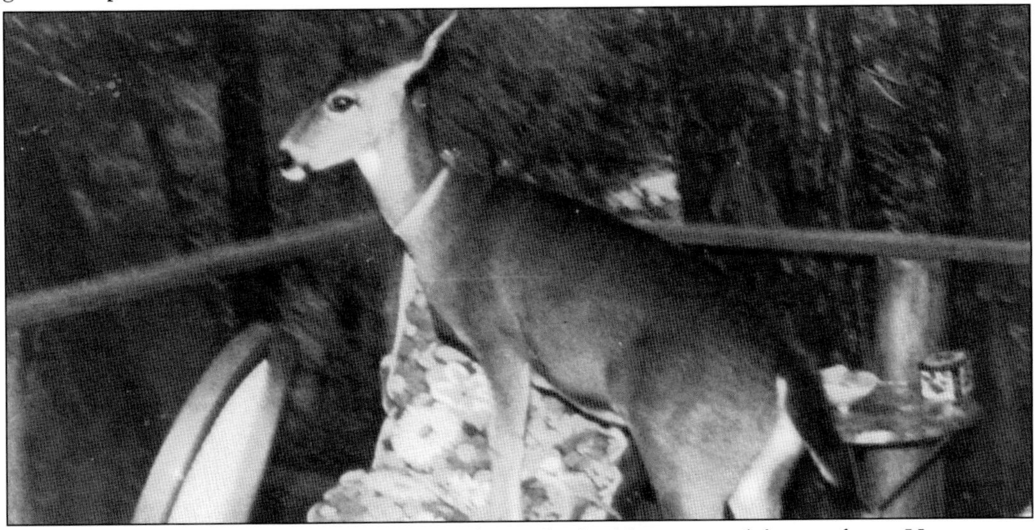

Mort was Paradise Lodge's motherless pet deer, who had been raised from a fawn. He was sure that he was a dog and could do anything the cats and dogs could do. Whenever Meryl Boice went outside, he followed her everywhere with the other animals. He always knew that lunch was ready when the boats came, so just before noon, he would put his front feet on the deck bench and look downriver, waiting for the boats to arrive. If the boats were late, he would go down to the docks to meet the passengers, who would happily greet him. (Paradise collection.)

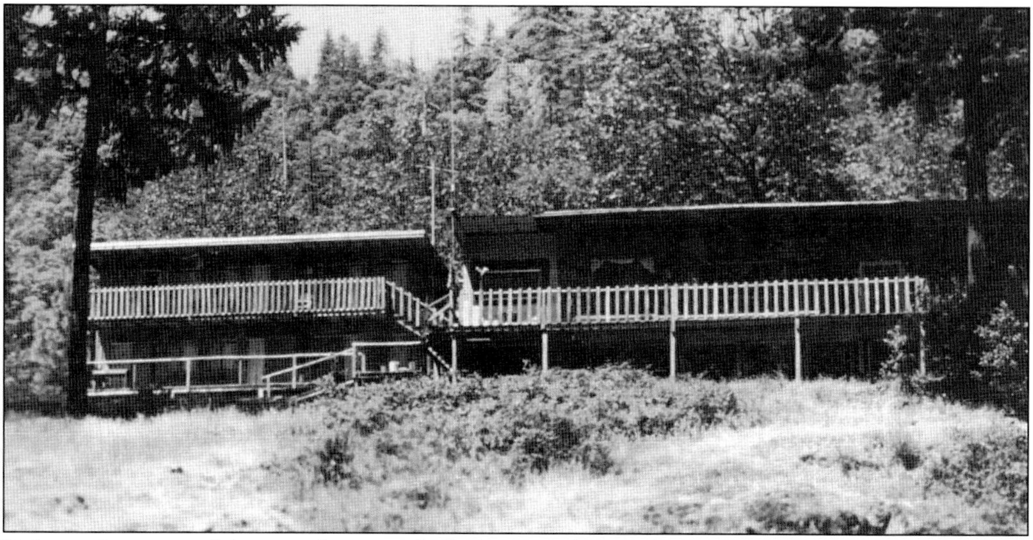

Before it became a fishing-and-overnight lodge, Paradise Lodge was first a village for the Rogue River Native Americans, but after the 1856 Indian war, the Native Americans were transported to the reservation on the Siletz River. Following this, Hathaway Jones owned Paradise Lodge. He sold it to the Pettinger family for farming, and John Pettinger sold it to Deak and Louise Miller. They invested in the property and made it into the first fishing lodge. In 1972, Allen and Meryl Boice purchased the lodge to make it not only a fishing lodge but also an overnight stop for the boat passengers. The lodge was also open for meals to accommodate the hikers, rafters, and those aboard the planes that landed on the small airstrip behind the lodge. The Boices ran the lodge until 1983, when they sold it to their son Court Boice, who owned a company that offered whitewater boat trips, running passengers on the 104-mile round-trip to the lodge and back. (Paradise collection.)

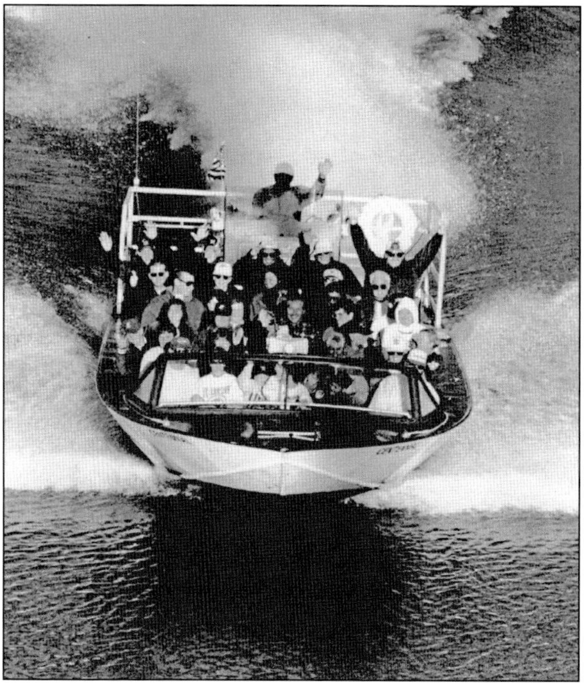

Court Boice's company, which offered whitewater boat trips, was the first to take a big 40-passenger boat up Rogue River on the 104-mile round-trip. Paradise Lodge hosted the passengers for lunch, and many chose to stay overnight. During the next few years, Jerry's Rogue Jets and Mail Boats followed suit and made not only the 64-mile and the 80-mile round-trips but also the 104-mile round-trip. (CHS.)

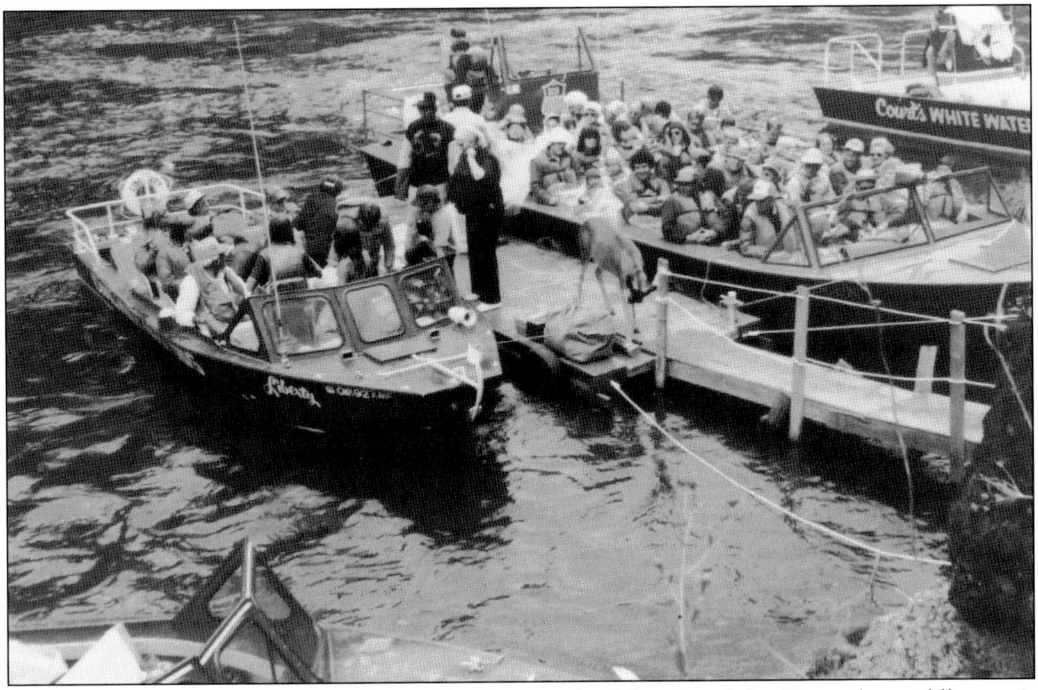

Pictured here are the three boat lines. The boat to the left is Jerry's Jet Boat, the middle one is the Mail Boat, and the one at right is Court's White Water Trips. The passengers are embarking for lunch, and of course Mort the pet deer is standing on the ramp waiting to greet the guests. After dinner, the guests can hike the grounds and airstrip and even soak their feet on a hot day in Paradise Creek. (Paradise collection.)

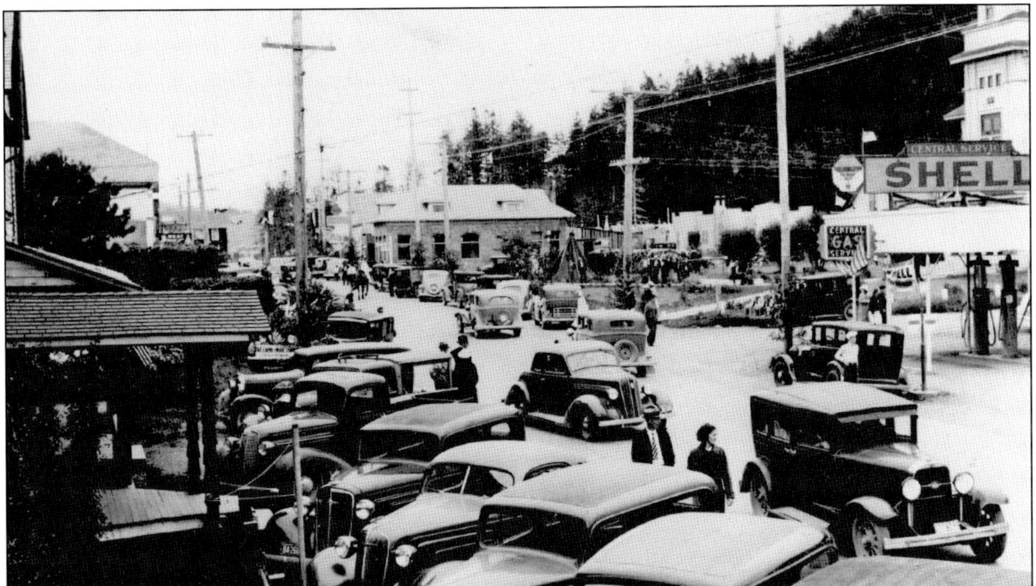

In 1937, cars parked on sidewalks, and often, pedestrians walked in the streets. The streets were narrow, and when the cars parked facing the sidewalk, there was no room left to safely walk the wooden sidewalks. (CHS.)

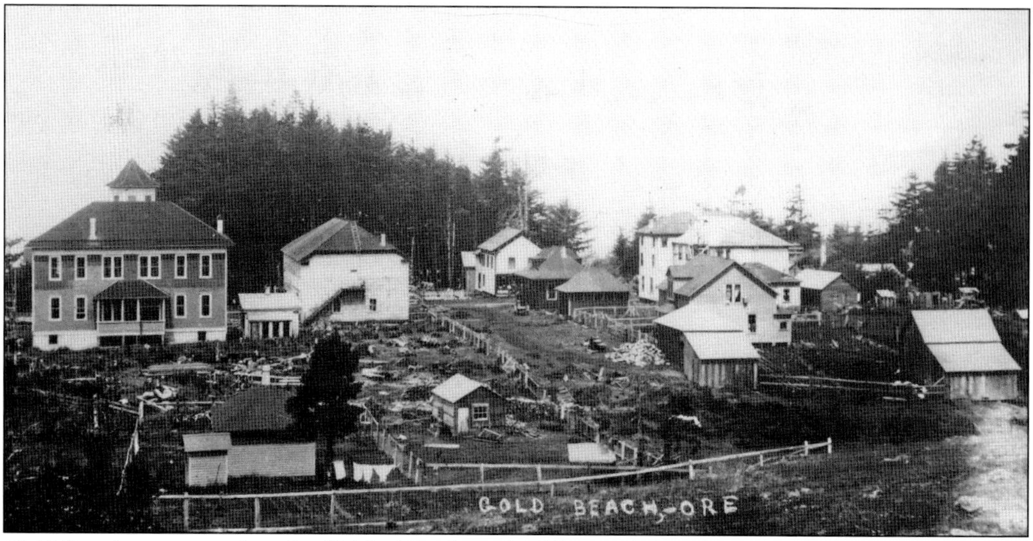

Gold Beach is pictured in the 1900s. The large building at left is the courthouse with an outside jail. Bullhide Moore's Peoples store is next to it. Across the street is the 1870 courthouse, which was made into a hardware store. Below it are, from left to right, the bank, Bullhide Moore's house in front of the Bishel Hotel, W. Kirk's house, Ash Moore's house, Y. Henry's house, and William Tolman's house. Tolman served as sheriff. The hotel, bank, and hardware store burned down in 1919. The bank was soon replaced and in time housed the *Curry County Reporter.* The smaller buildings were outbuildings. (Dick Guthrie collection.)

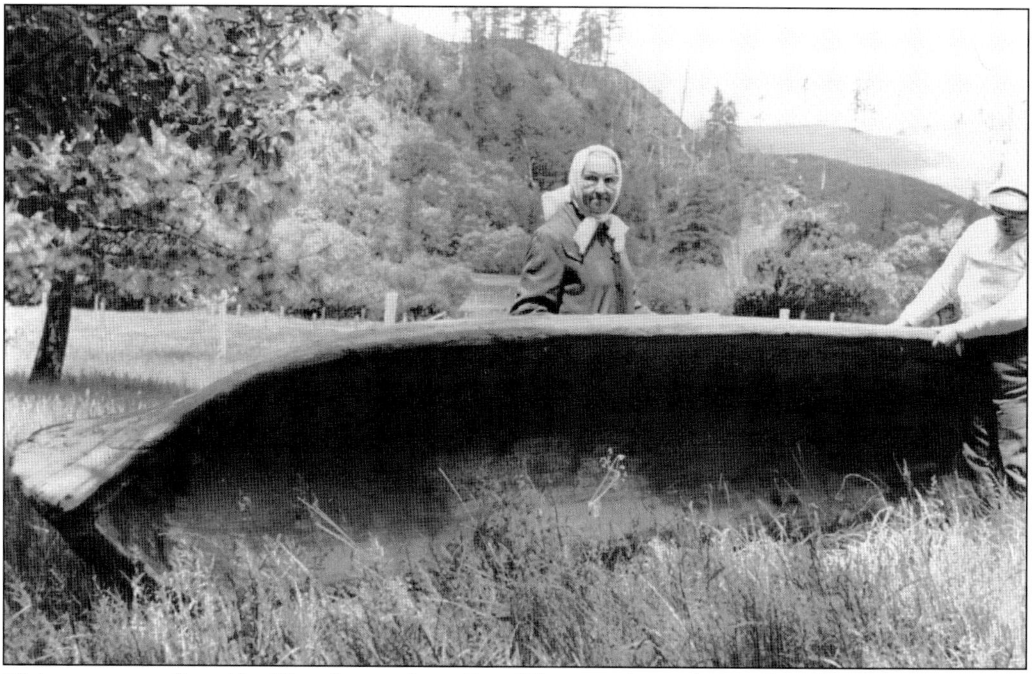

This canoe was found by Elma Ismert from Pistol River and was donated to the Curry Historical Society. It is now found in an exhibit in the annex. It most likely was made by one of the Klamath Indian tribes. Constructed for use in the Pistol River and ocean, it is very stable and still in good shape. (CHS.)

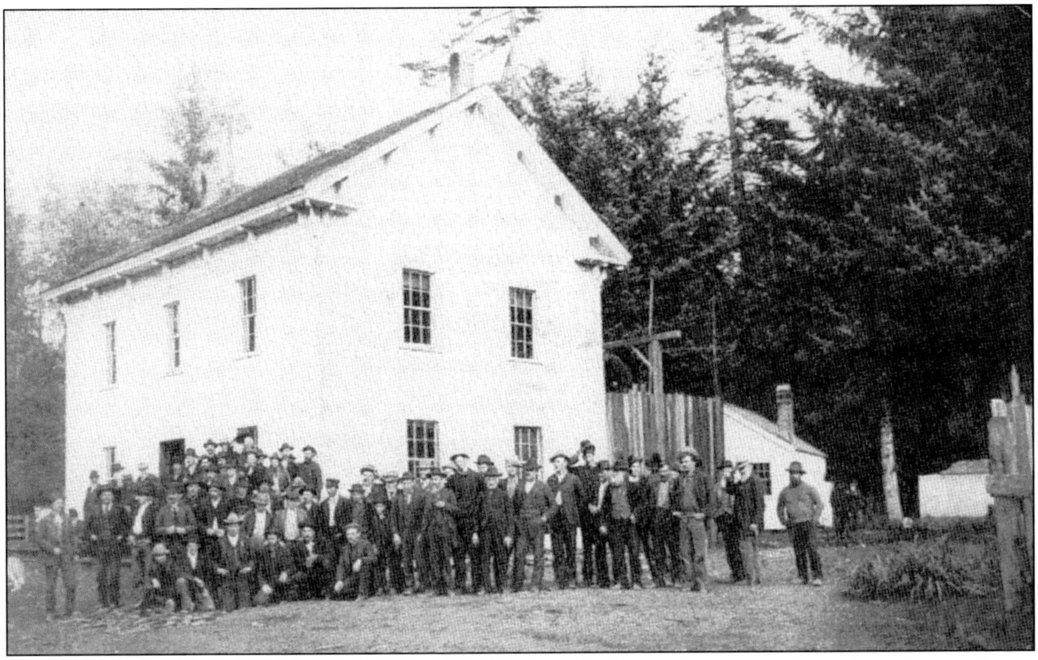

The first courthouse was built in 1870. This photograph shows the group of men standing in front of the courthouse. They are waiting to witness the only legal hanging in Curry County. This courthouse was finally replaced with a larger courthouse, built in 1912. (CHS.)

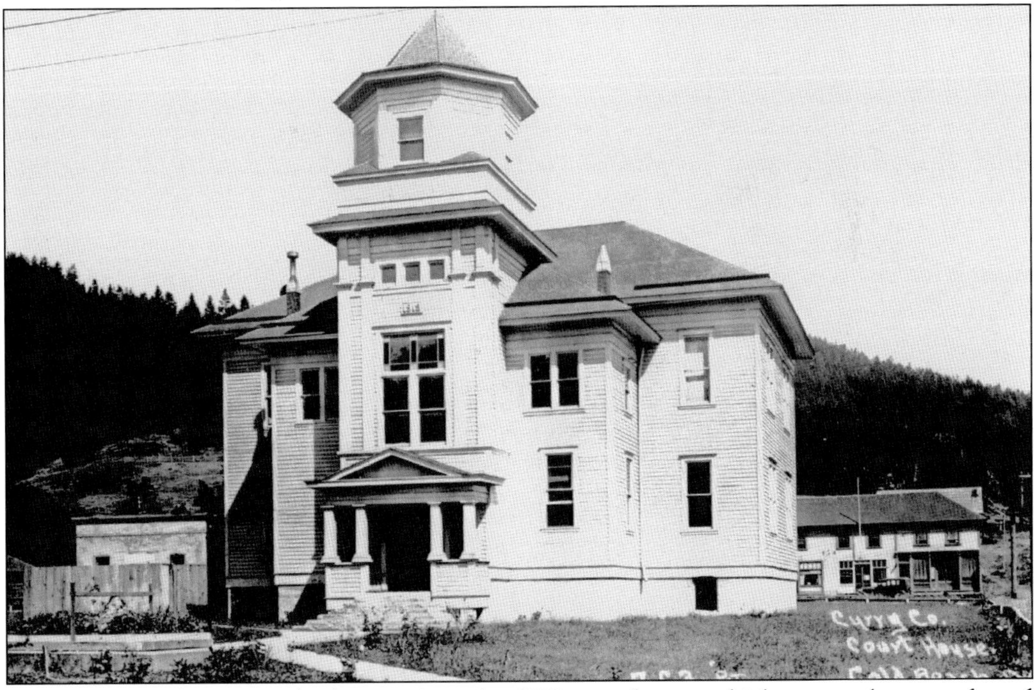

The 1912 courthouse was built to replace the 1870 courthouse, which was no longer safe and was condemned. It was sold and moved across the street and made into a hardware store. The merchandise available included horse and mule harnessing, farm implements, seed, hay, and all types supplies for farmers. (CHS.)

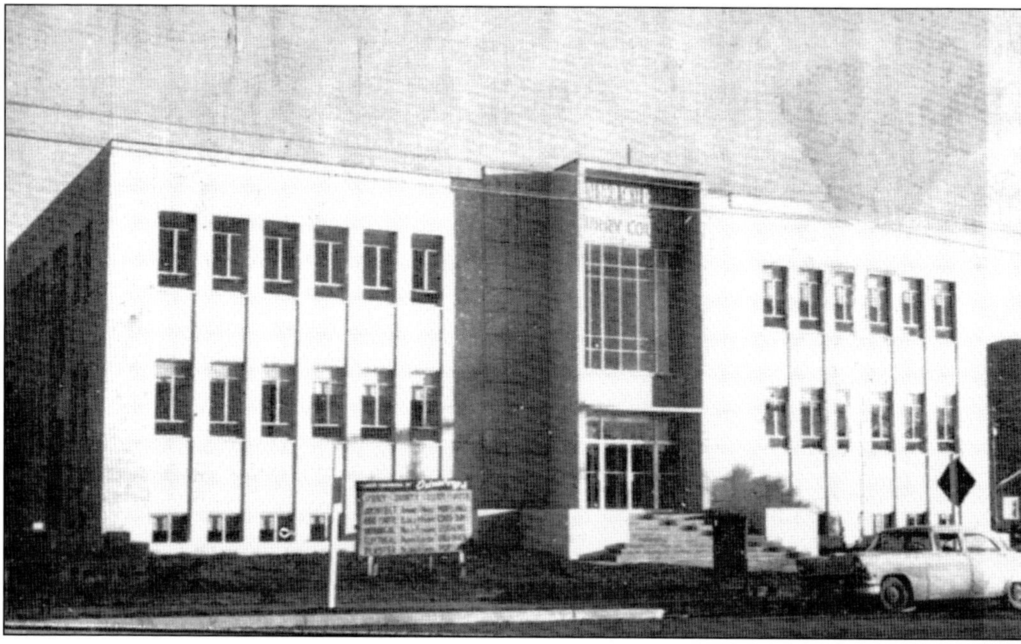

Shown here, the present-day courthouse was built in 1958 because the 1912 courthouse needed so much upkeep. It was no longer large enough to maintain all that was necessary to continue on with the larger population and was condemned. At that time, a new jail also needed to be constructed. (CHS.)

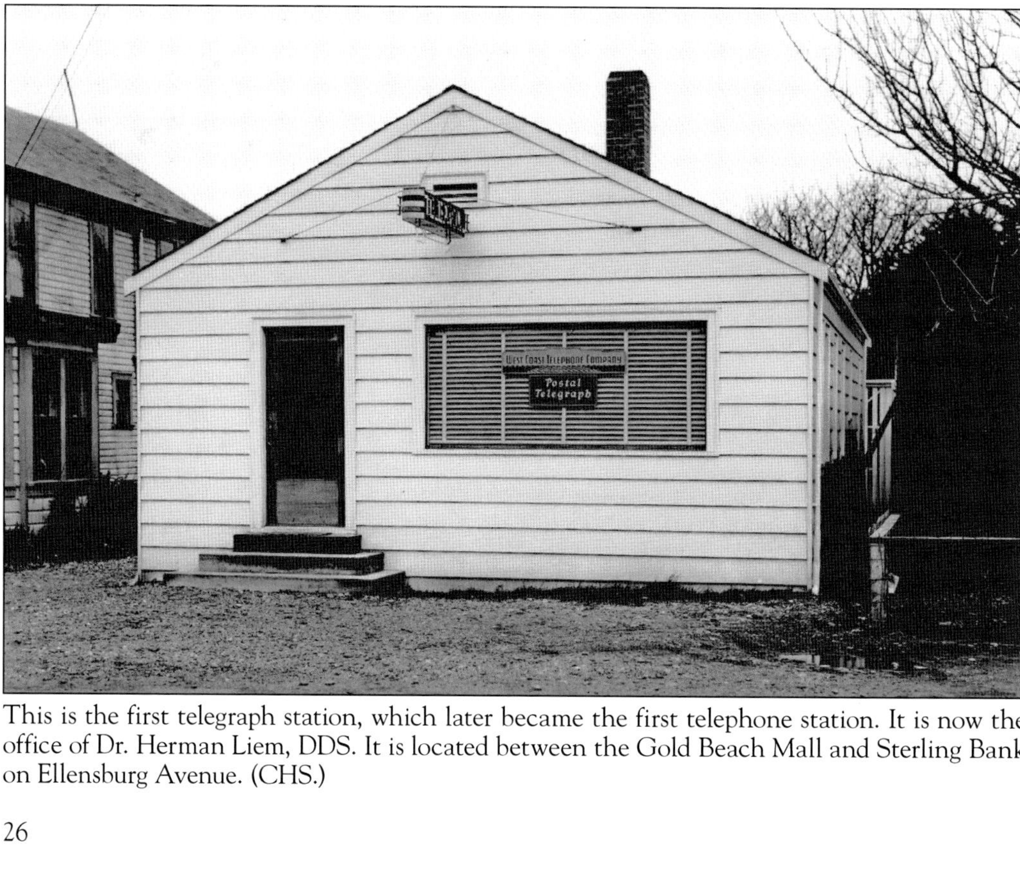

This is the first telegraph station, which later became the first telephone station. It is now the office of Dr. Herman Liem, DDS. It is located between the Gold Beach Mall and Sterling Bank on Ellensburg Avenue. (CHS.)

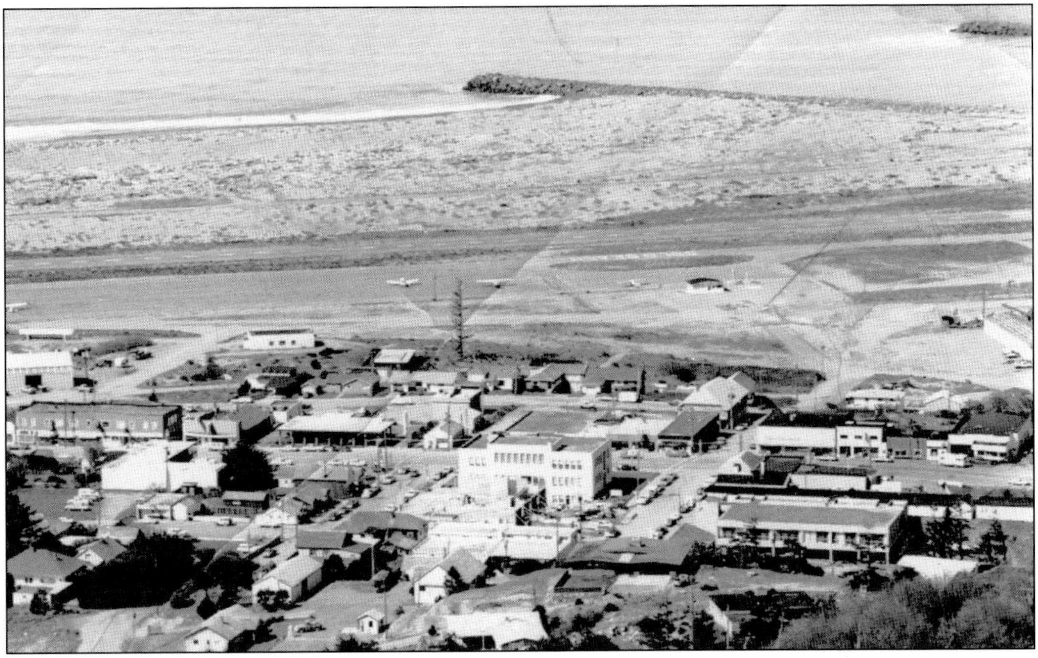

This aerial view shows the mouth of the Rogue River shortly after the jetties were built. The photograph shows the growth of the town in 1972. The construction of the jetties opened the mouth of the river to larger commercial fishing boats. They were able to deliver salmon, bottom fish, and crabs. (CHS.)

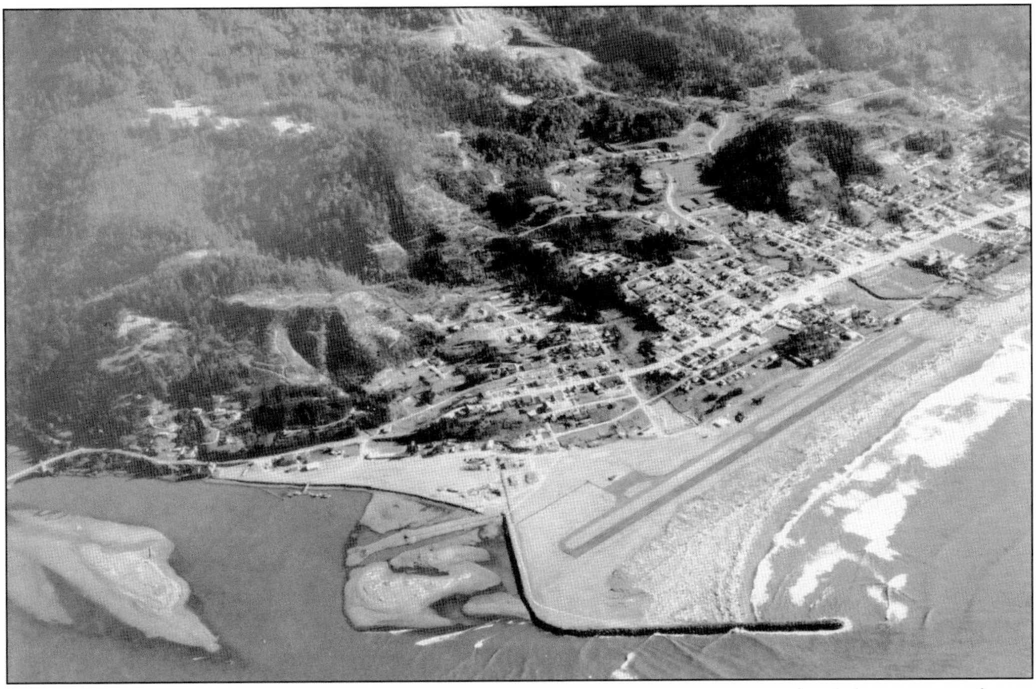

This aerial view shows the extended airstrip that runs nearly to the mouth of the river. It shows a better view of the town as it looks today. The mountains close to town stop it from spreading out to the east. (CHS.)

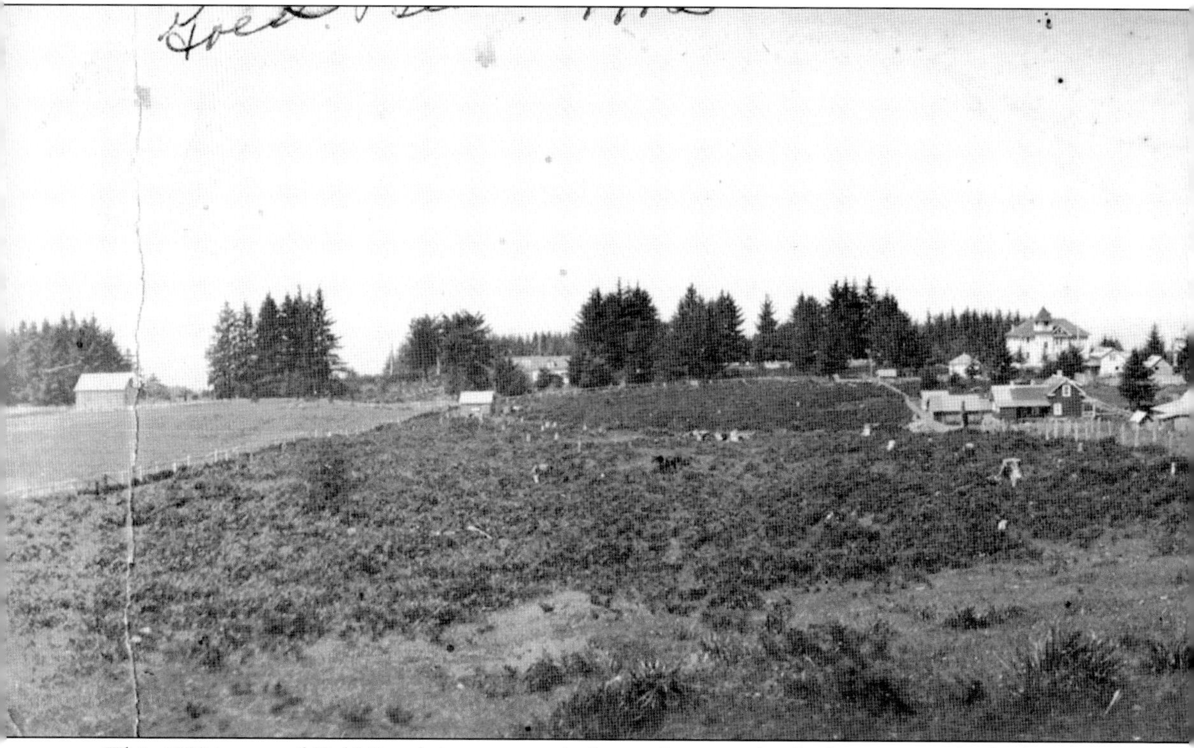

This 1912 image of Gold Beach is composed of two photographs. It shows not only the businesses

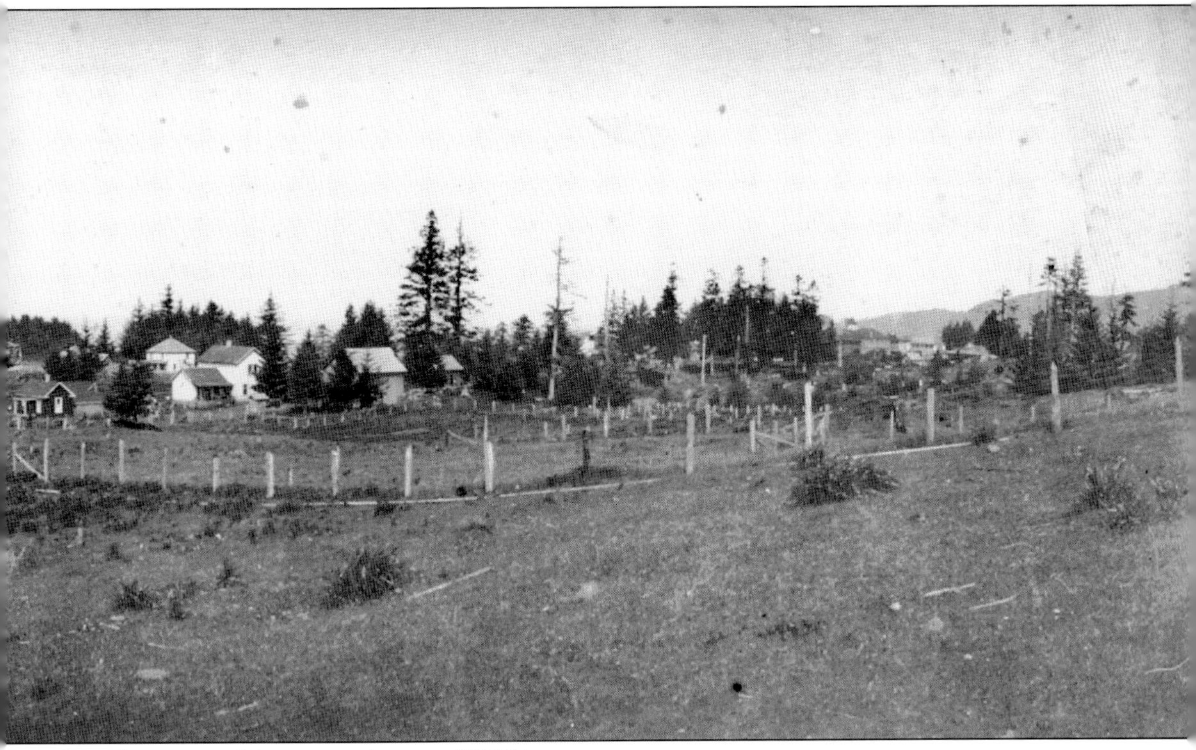

but also some of the private homes. (CHS.)

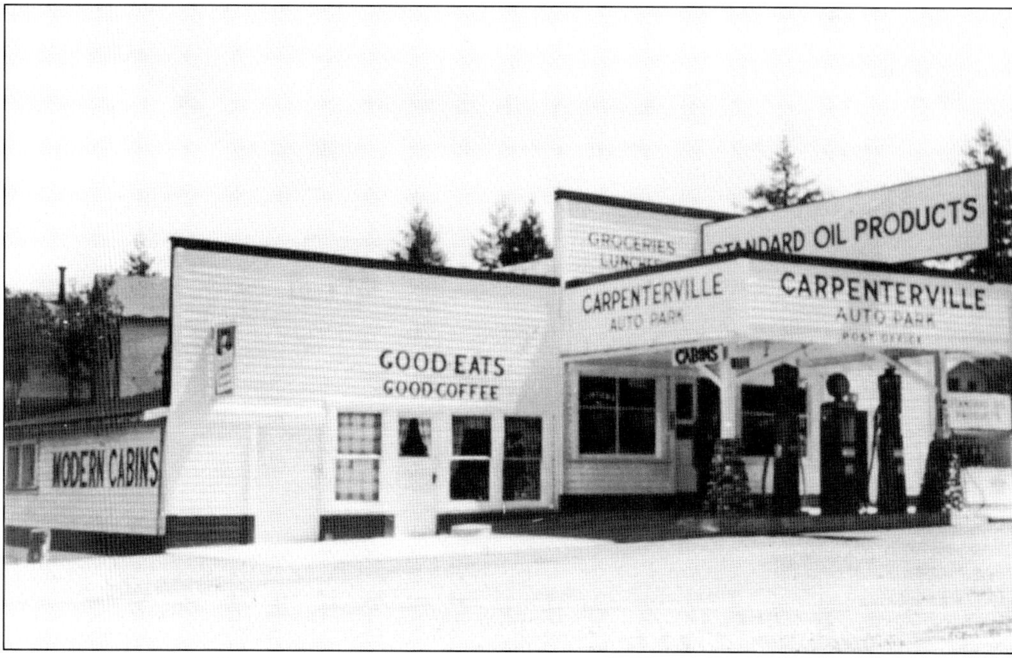

During the early 1920s, the Roosevelt Highway circled up over Carpenterville Road, and there, the Carpenter family built a store, gas pumps, and cabins open for lodging. Later on, a lodge was built at the top of Carpenterville and was known as the Skyline Lodge and Restaurant. The area where it was built had a view that was incomparable. When Highway 101 was built, it cut off some of the communities, like Carpenterville. The lodge was eventually torn down. (CHS.)

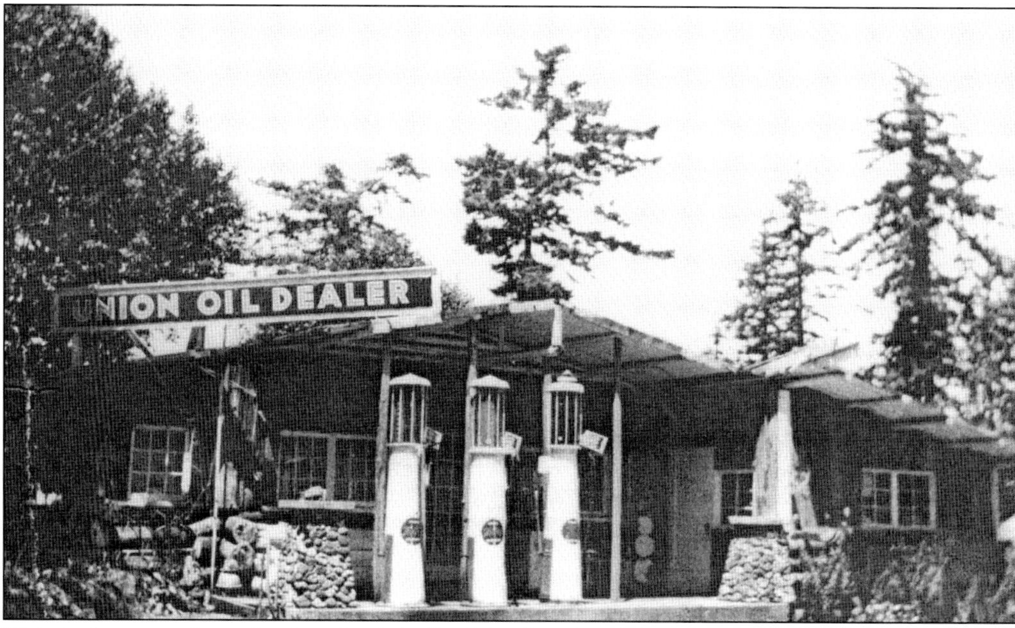

This is the second set of cabins built by Joe Meade, who also became a dealer for the Union Oil Company, which provided oil for the varied gasoline stations. When Highway 101 was built, the Union Oil dealership moved to the Shell station south of Main Street that was owned by Howard Hauschildt. (CHS.)

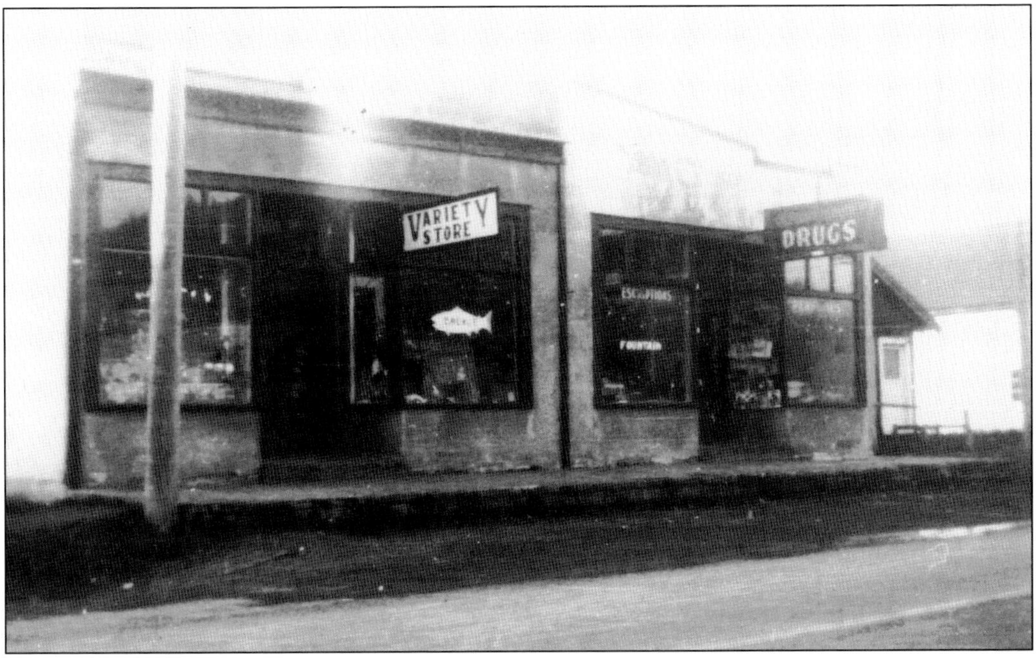

For many years, Evelyn Moore owned this store and was able to crowd merchandise in every corner. Truly, she owned a variety store, and if anyone needed anything, he or she could go to Moore's Variety Store and usually find what was needed. If fishing boots were needed, she had them; she also had children's clothing, crafts, cooking implements, and sewing implements. Store patrons would rave about it, often encouraging tourists to find and visit her store. (CHS.)

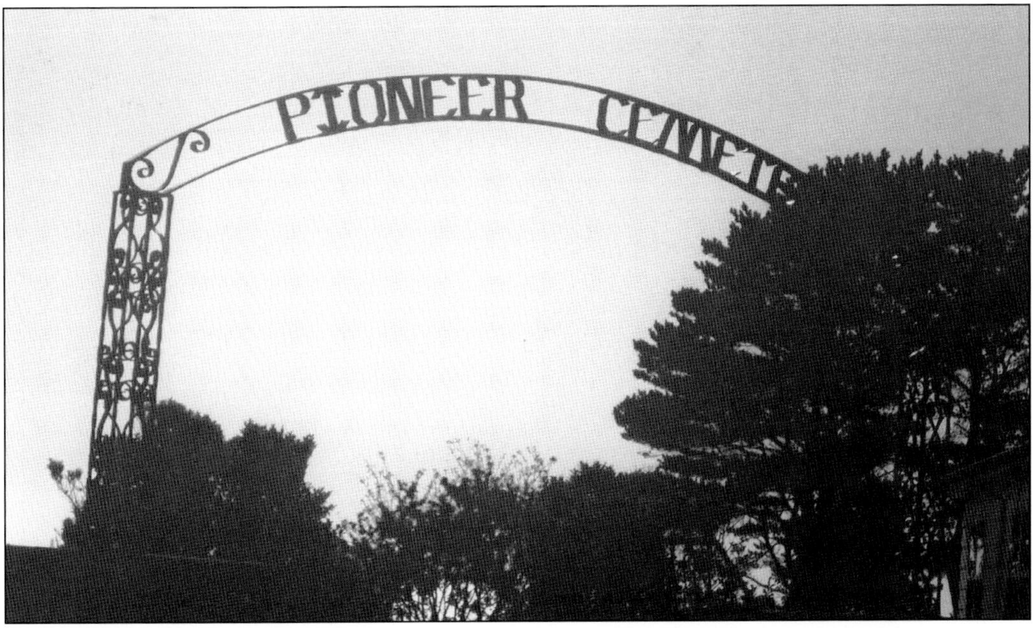

Early settlers, some of whom arrived via wagon train, are buried at the Pioneer Cemetery, which is located just behind the Presbyterian church. Laurel German greatly researched the cemetery and has written about it in a small book titled *Renderings*. The Curry Historical Society has presented three cemetery plays honoring many who are buried there. (CHS.)

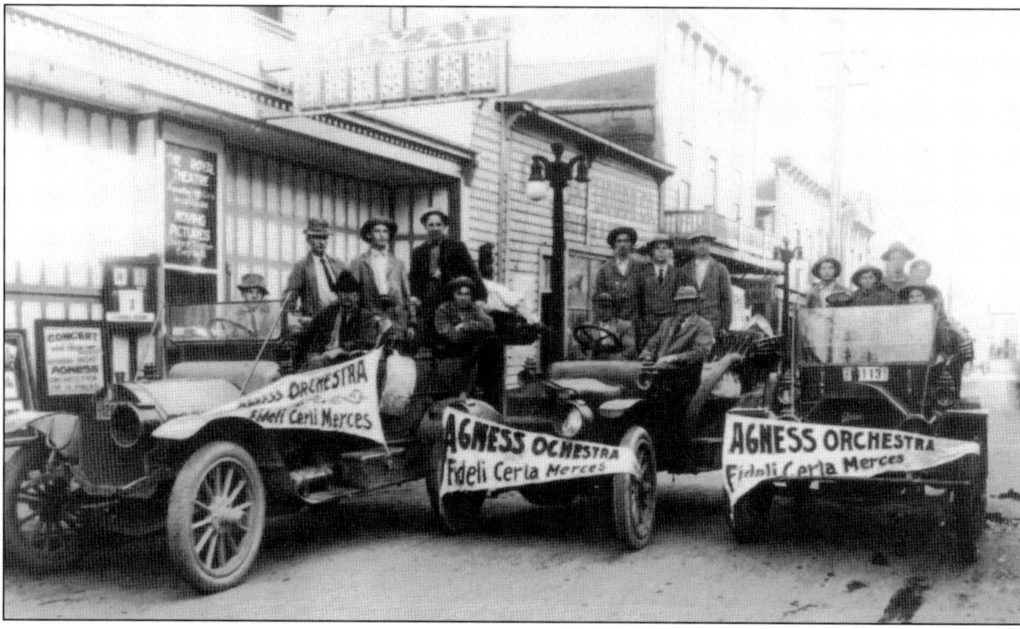

This is a picture of the Agness Orchestra, which is in line for the Curry County Fair Parade. During the early 1900s, every town had its own community band that proudly played at community happenings and any parades that were planned. (CHS.)

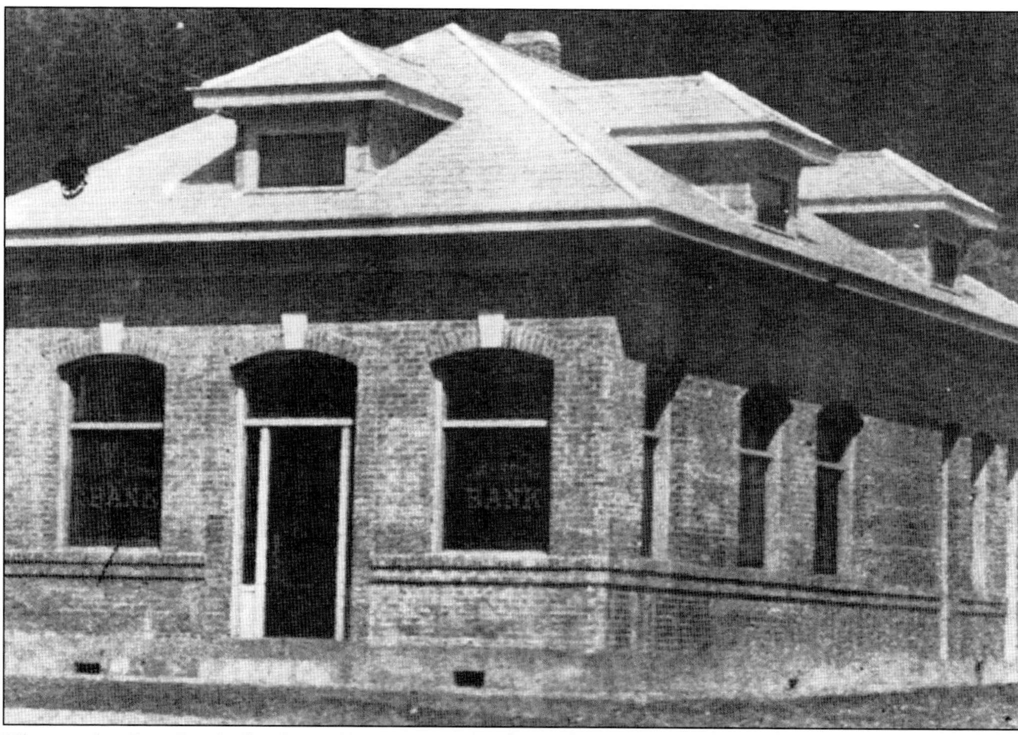

This is the first bank, built in 1912. It was built at the same time that the second courthouse was erected. The bank was first the Gold Beach Bank, then the First National Bank, and later became the home of the *Curry County Reporter* newspaper. (CHS.)

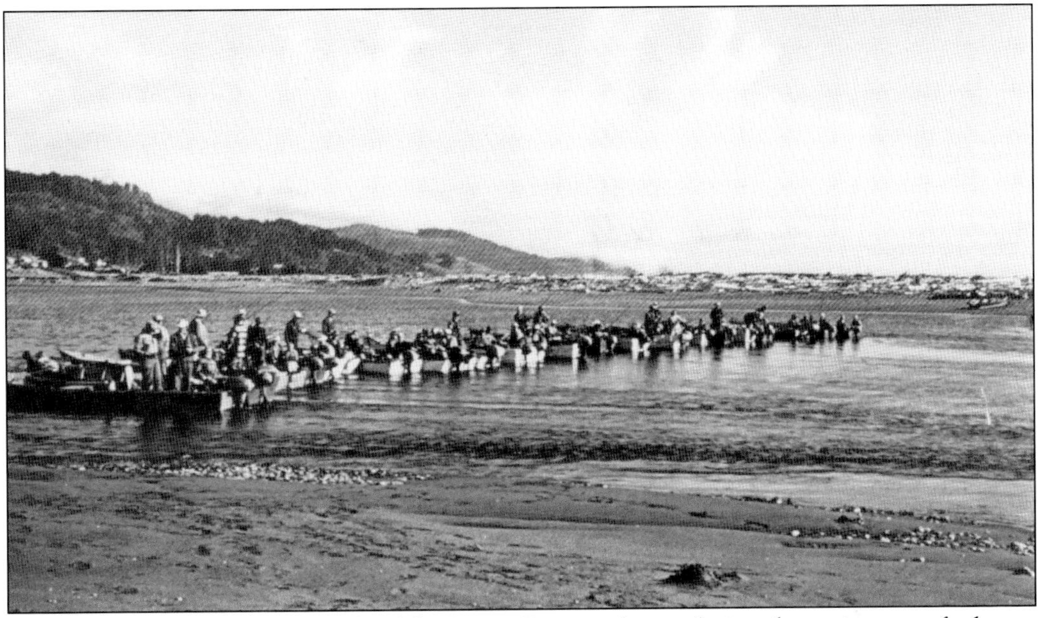

The famous hogline at the mouth of the Rogue River is shown during the spring run of salmon. The boats all line up together in a wide line so that they can catch more when the salmon come back into the river to spawn. This photograph was taken before 1952. (CHS.)

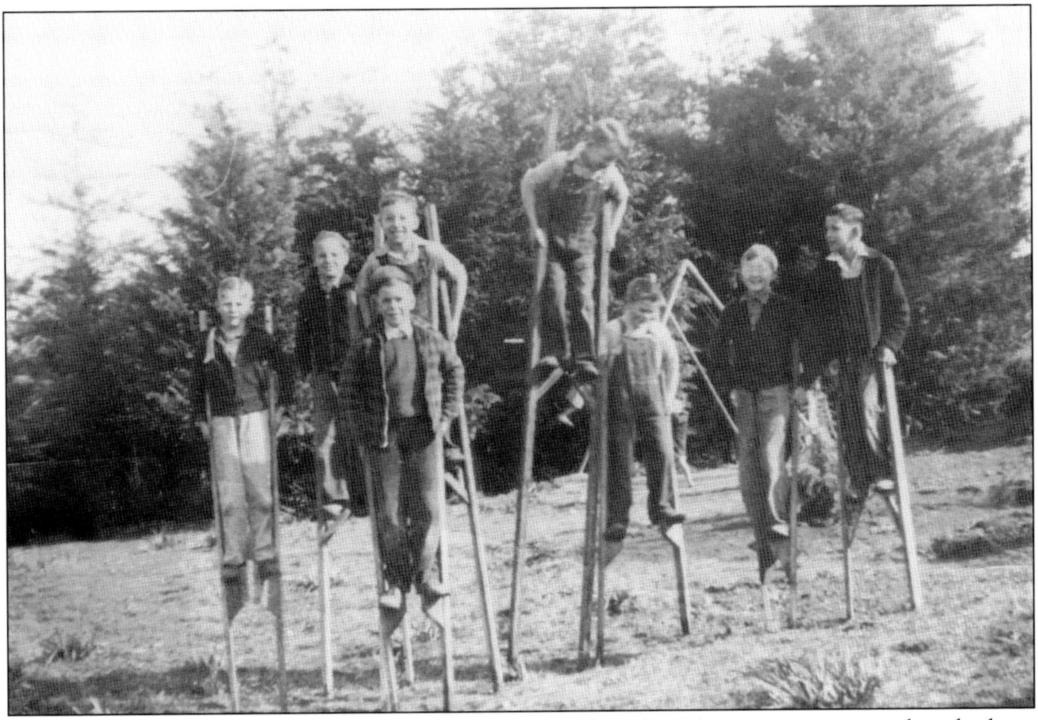

A group of eight young boys is having fun on homemade stilts. This was an activity that the boys enjoyed. Sixty years later, the boys reunited in the same location where they had spent so many fun hours together. (Paradise collection.)

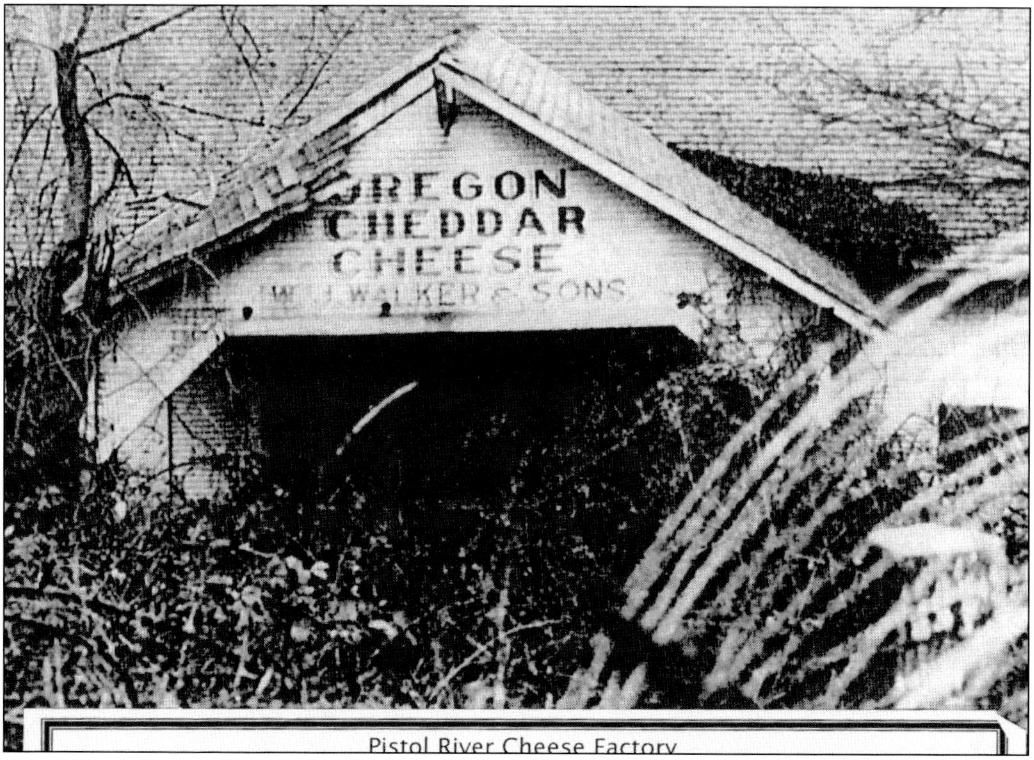

Pistol River Cheese Factory was built and owned by Will Walker and managed by Jay, his son. They also ran the Pistol River Store and post office. There was a line of six cabins for rent. The family owned a large cattle-and-sheep ranch for generations. The Walker children, when grown and married, settled on land close by. Pistol River ran through the property into the ocean. (CHS.)

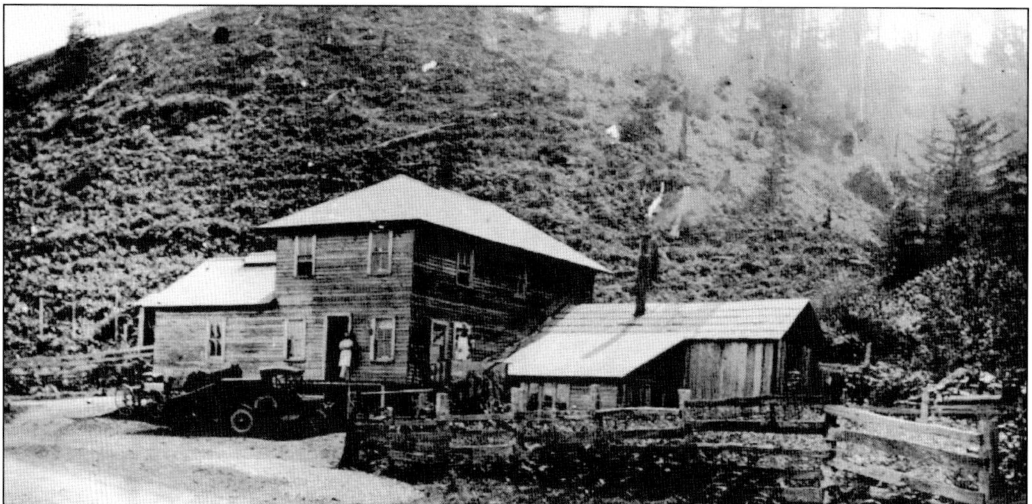

In the early 1920s, there was a cheese factory located on Euchre Creek. It received the cream from the local dairy farms to make cheese and was used as a teaching unit for other farmers who were looking for an outlet for their dairies farther away. The next closest cheese factory was at Pistol River. (CHS.)

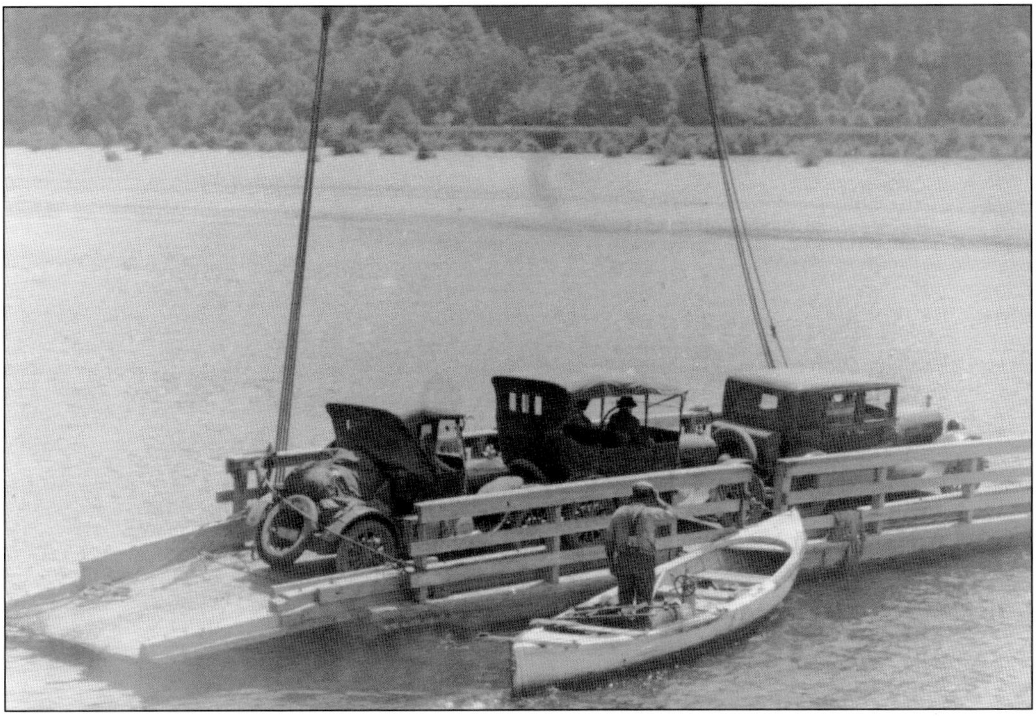

Before the bridge was built, ferries were used to traverse the river; the first ferry was built and used by Mr. Bagnell. It was used for transportation from the North Bank Road across to the South Bank Road. It is known as Jerrys Flat Road today. Soon, the county replaced the Bagnell ferry with a new motorized ferry that transported the cars, buggies, and equipment from old Roosevelt Highway or the North Bank Road to the Wedderburn Loop or Bailey Road. The cars loaded onto this ferry are at the beachfront of Scott's Lodge. A gasoline motor, instead of the original way of propelling the old ferry, propelled this one. (CHS.)

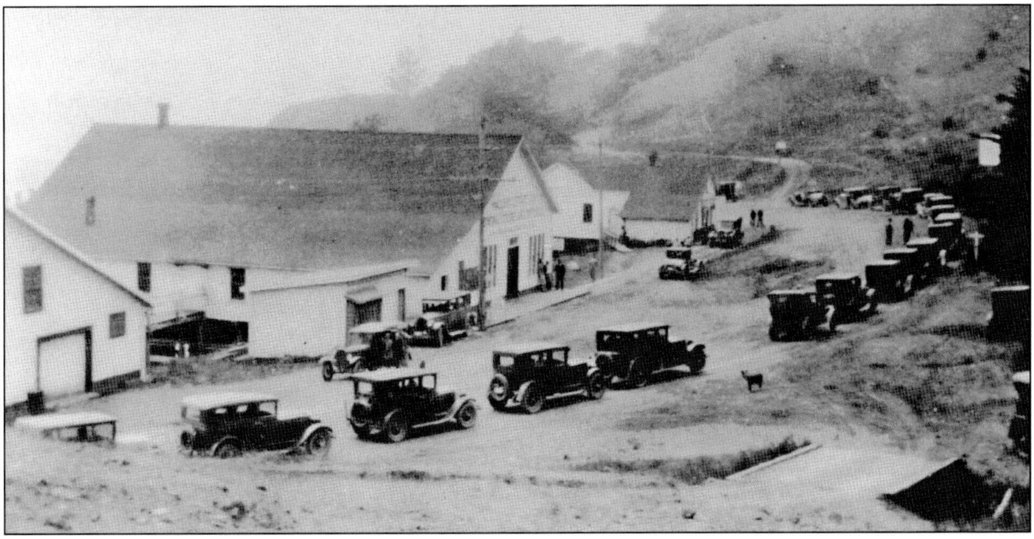

This is a follow-up picture of the cars waiting in line to be transported to the south side of the Rogue River on the new ferry that was leaving the beachfront of Scott's Lodge; they turned to the river just off the Bailey Beach Road. (CHS.)

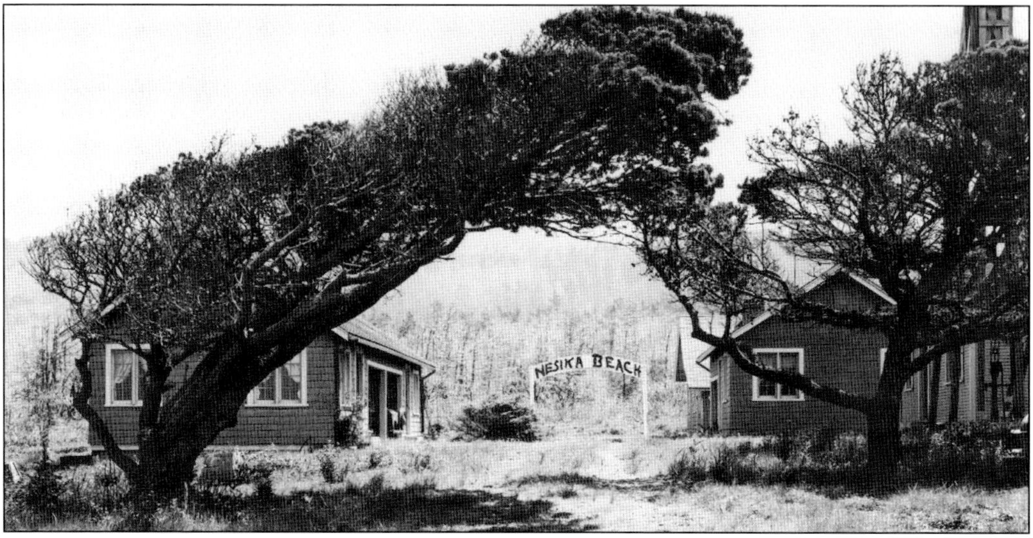

This is another small community, located about eight miles north of Gold Beach, named Nesika Beach. It had a post office, grocery store, and gas pumps in this time. It is where the Ophir Grange was built. In the early 1900s, several small towns organized a grange hall, and it was set up where the farmers could manage the cost of their supplies and wares. (CHS.)

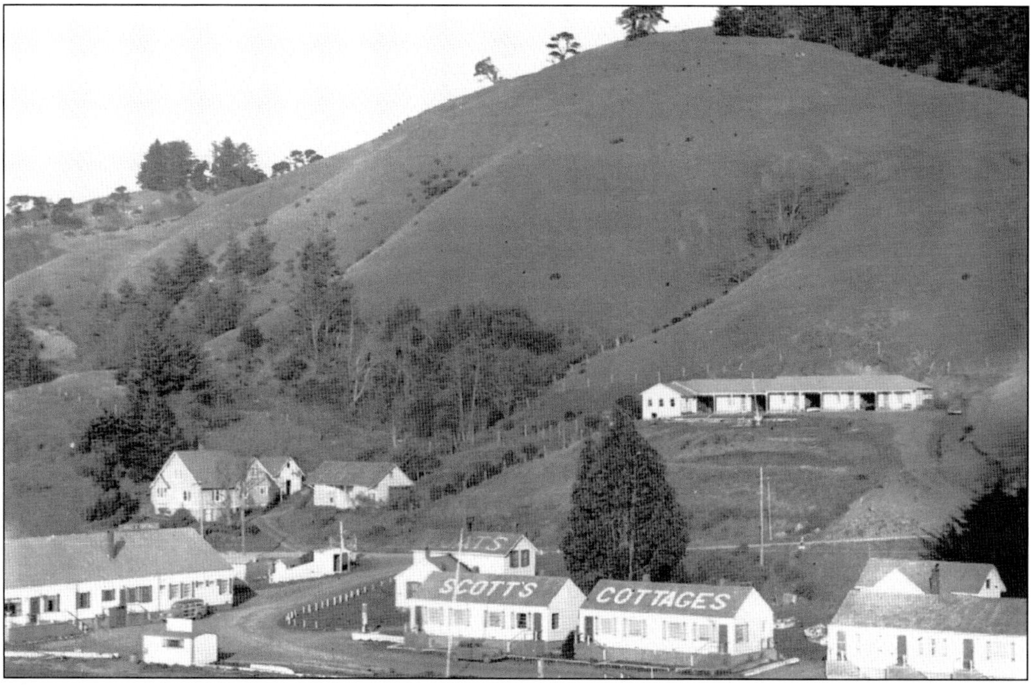

The town of Wedderburn had its entrance to the north side of the bridge from the North Bank Road with traffic arriving on the Roosevelt Highway. The motel on the high side of the bank was Sidles Motel, which was later moved when Highway 101 came through from the east side of the entrance to the bridge. First known as the Red Baron, the old Sidles Motel today sits above the Rogue River on the North Bank Road and is known as the Rogue River Motel; it is privately owned. The Sidles Motel and the Del Rogue restaurant, bar, and cabins were separated by the Bailey Beach Road, now known as the Wedderburn Loop Road. (CHS.)

Two

Attributes of the Rogue River

Gold Beach has the beauty of the ocean, surf animals at low tide, whales, seals, changing sunsets, and the mountains to the east. The Rogue River Bridge separates Gold Beach and Wedderburn. When the bridge was built, it was noted as the most beautiful bridge in Oregon.

The Rogue River has its own beauty, and since the mouth of the river flows into the ocean, it is ever-changing. On the upper Rogue River, before and beyond the town of Agness, the scenery is magnificent, with wildlife such as deer and bears often seen frolicking along the riverbanks. Osprey and eagles fly above, fish leap out of the water, ducks float on the river, and families of otters swim in the little inlet. The natural scenery is a delight for photographers.

The upper Rogue River was home to many Native Americans prior to the arrival of miners. The river, the mountains, and all the natural resources, such as animals and vegetation, were essential to the survival of Native Americans. Due to the damage to the river from the many apparatuses used to mine and the mistreatment of the Indian women by a few of the miners, a war broke out between the Indians and white men.

Today, it is once again a tranquil place to raft, fish, or just enjoy quiet time in the wilderness at one of the lodges that are spaced out along the river.

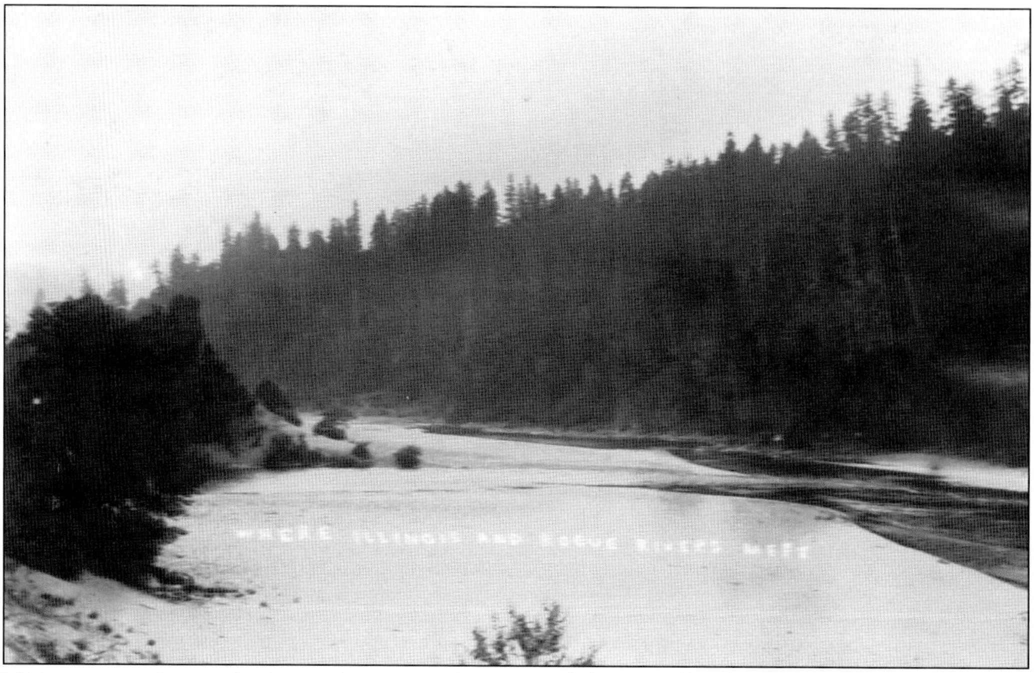

Thirty-two miles up the Rogue River at the town of Agness, the Illinois River and the Rogue River join. The present Rogue River Bridge spans the two rivers and connects the South Bank Road to Agness. The bridge was in the process of being built when the 1964 flood hit; parts of the bridge needed to be repaired, and other sections needed to be rebuilt. (CHS.)

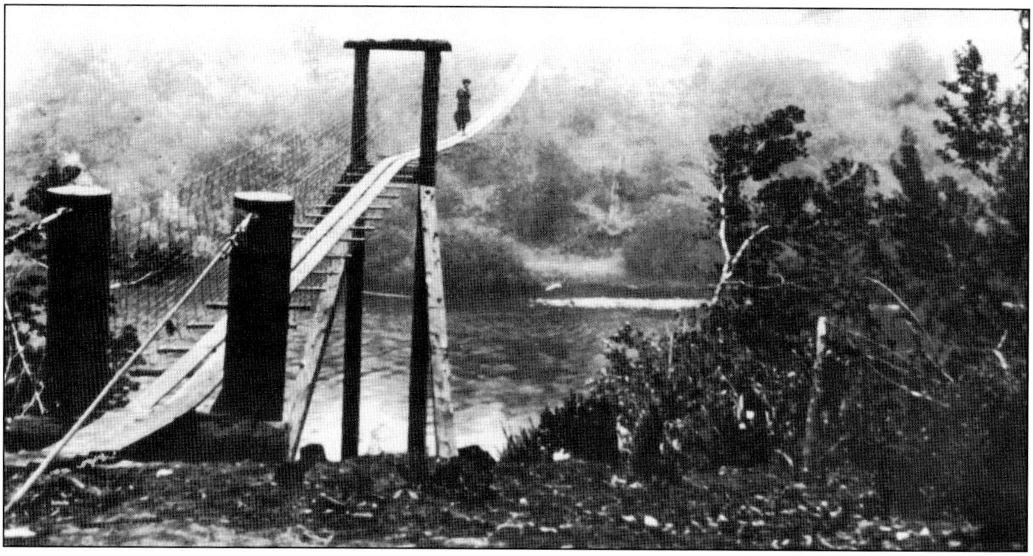

The first Agness footbridge was built at the same place as the present Illinois River Bridge, which spans the junction of the Illinois River and the Rogue River. It was built to allow children to cross the river to go to school and for passage from north to south. It started on the north side at Lucas Lodge, and later, a suspension bridge was built for motorized vehicles. This united the road to Agness on the north side from Gold Beach. The second Cougar Lane store, a bar, a restaurant, a motel, and a campground reside about a half-mile east of the north end of the present-day Illinois River Bridge. Next door is a RV park where people with trailers can camp. (CHS.)

In the early 1900s, Moritz Fritche, a German gentleman, was living up above Marial on the Rogue River. He built his home on the south side of the river, and when he needed supplies, he had to cross the river, as the closest store was in Agness and there was no trail on the south side. He had great ingenuity and strung a cable to the other side of the river and attached two pogo sticks to the cable, making it possible to hop across the cable to his home. Sometimes he was able to catch the mail train from Grants Pass and get his supplies from that town, although it was on the north side of the river, meaning he still had to cross the river. (CHS.)

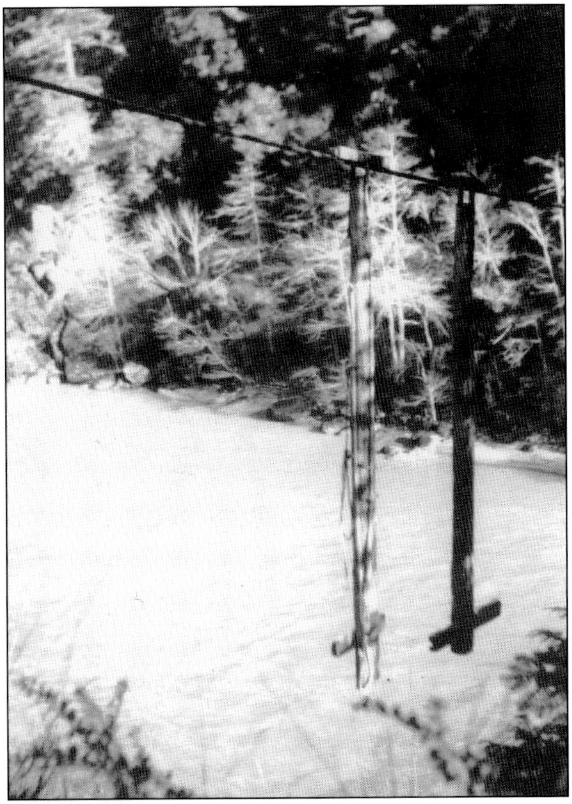

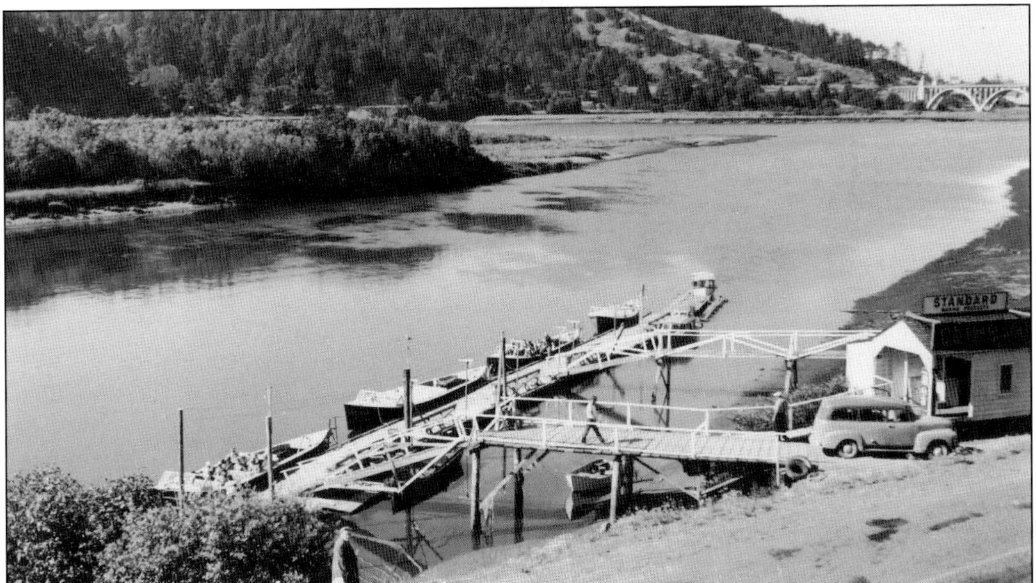

Referred to as "Mail Boat Island," this is the dock for the mail boats, which were the first passenger boats on the Rogue River. When they first were built, it was for the sole purpose of transporting the mail to Agness with stops in between, with the occasional rider to get to Agness or Gold Beach. Only later did it begin to take paying passengers for a day trip. (CHS.)

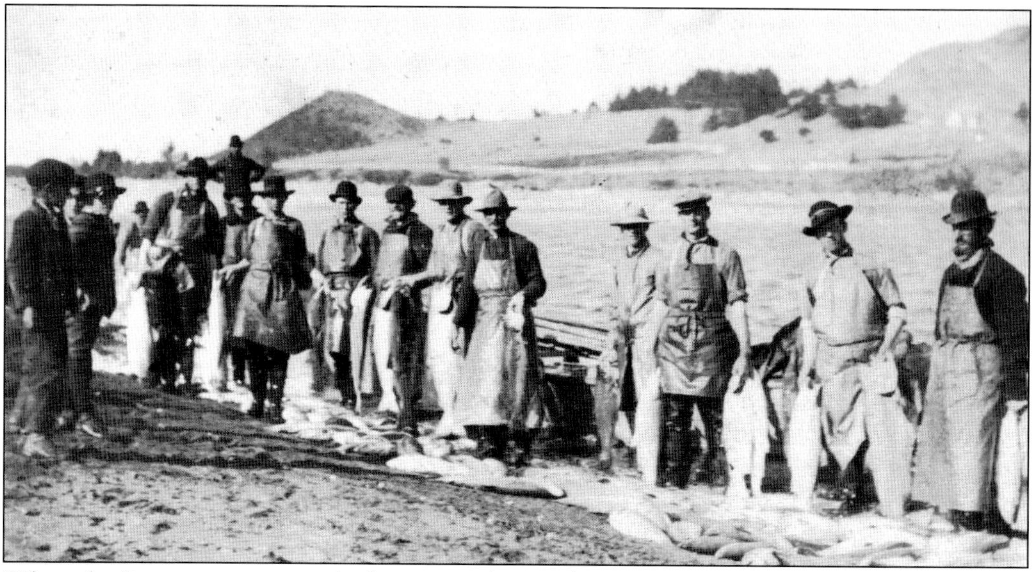

When the first canneries were built, seining (netting) was the easiest way to catch the salmon. There were hundreds of pounds of salmon caught daily, especially at the mouth of the Rogue River. The salmon canneries employed many workers. R.D. Hume also built a can-making factory and a pea-canning factory. He constructed his own salmon hatchery and owned a racetrack on Wedderburn Hill. Hume built a sawmill to accommodate all his holdings. He considered himself a "Pygmy Monopolist." After World War II, netting was outlawed, and the river was open only for sportfishing. (CHS.)

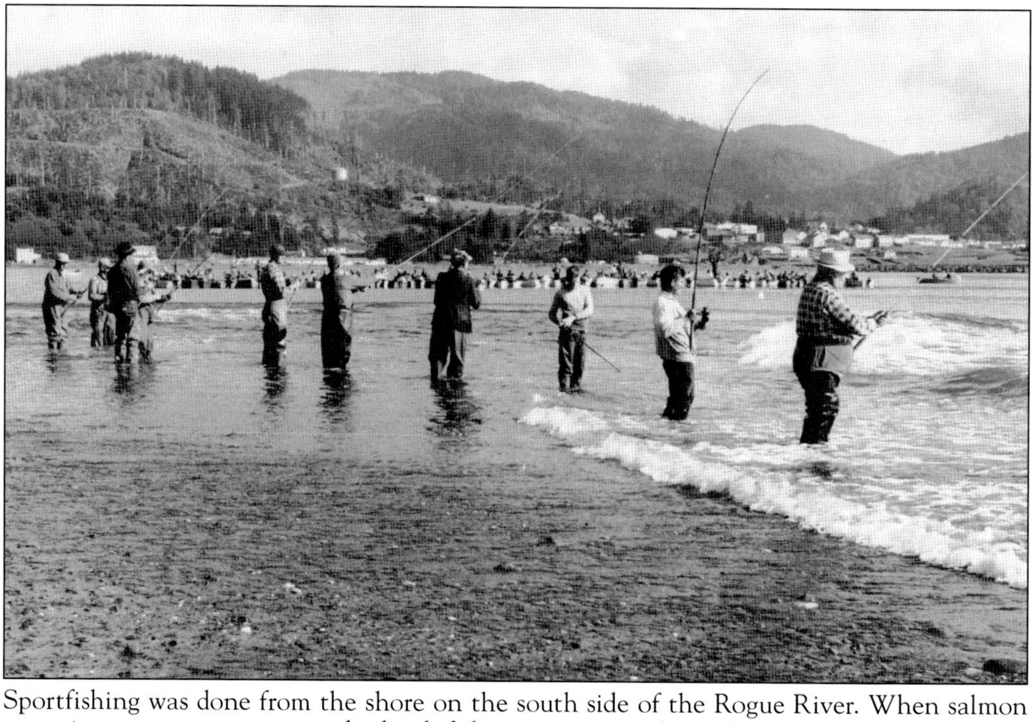

Sportfishing was done from the shore on the south side of the Rogue River. When salmon are going upstream to spawn, the bank fishermen can catch nearly as many as those in the hogline. (CHS.)

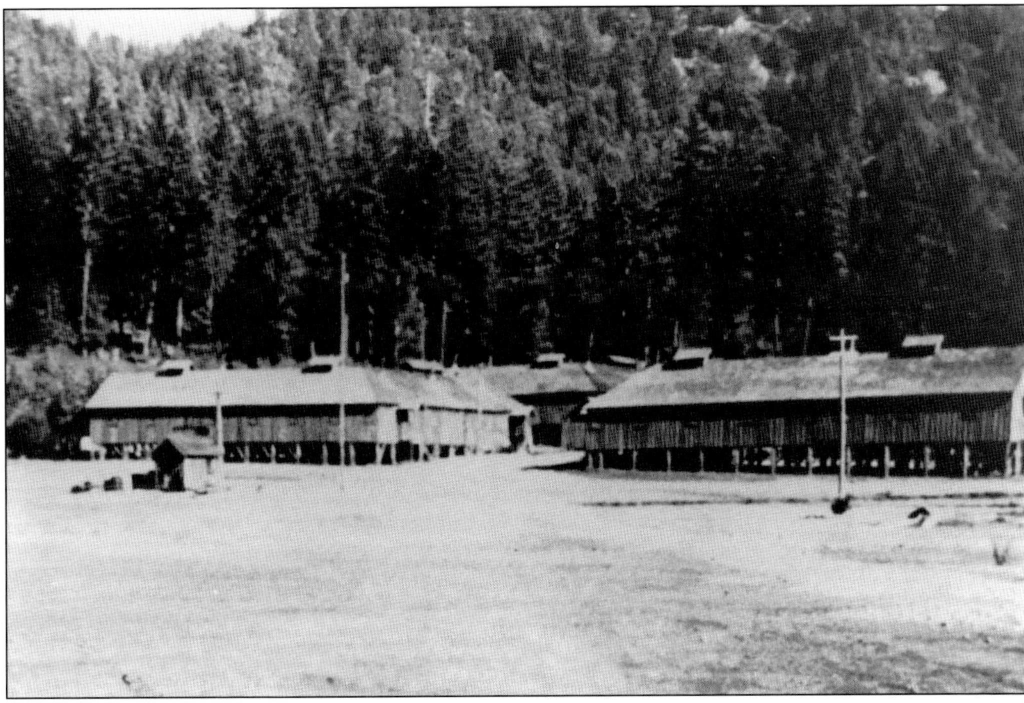

During the Great Depression, many government programs were organized to put the needy to work at small jobs in order to make ends meet. One of these programs was the Civilian Conservation Corps (CCC). One CCC camp in Curry County was located at Agness, and another was at Pistol River. This program arrived in Southern Oregon in 1933, the same year that the program was started nationwide, with men coming from all over the country to work. They built roads, trails, campgrounds, and other public projects. The pay was $30 per month plus room and board. They usually kept $5 and sent the rest home to their families. (CHS.)

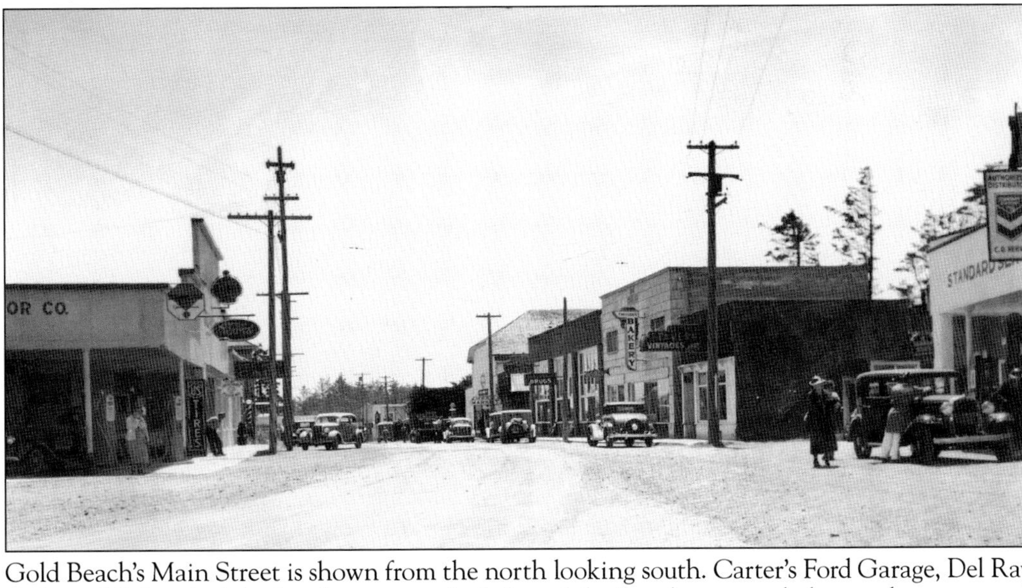

Gold Beach's Main Street is shown from the north looking south. Carter's Ford Garage, Del Ray Café, and Schmidtie's barbershop are on the left, and the Peoples store, a bakery, a drugstore, and a tavern are on the right. This photograph was taken about 1937. (CHS.)

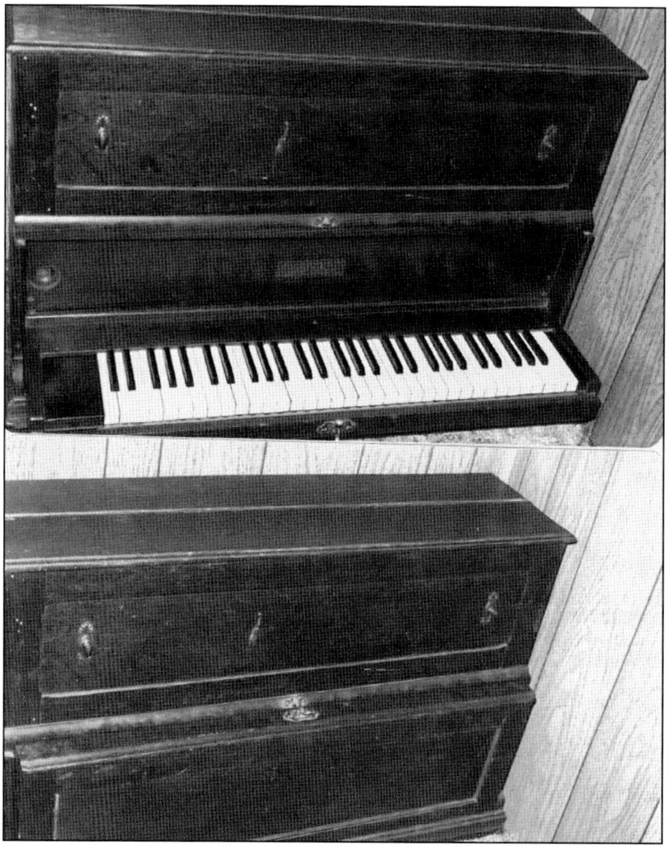

The piano pictured here came around the Horn and was a yacht piano. The keyboard folded and snapped shut, and it was small enough to attach to the running board of an old Model T, so it could travel to different dances or church services. On the front were little holders for candles. This piano is a family treasure that belonged to the author's father, Michael Grogan. (Boice collection.)

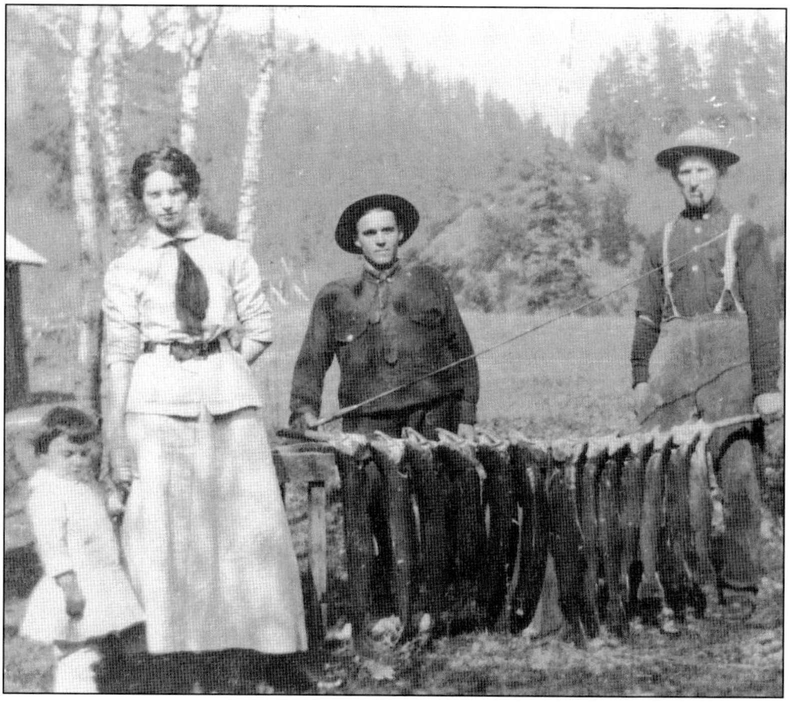

Here is the catch of the day for this family. During hard times, it was not easy to survive. It was wonderful to be able to can or smoke fish for future meals. This, as well as wild meat and vegetables from the garden, was an added staple food for a family living on an upriver farm on Rogue River. Their main means of living was off the land and what it had to offer. (CHS.)

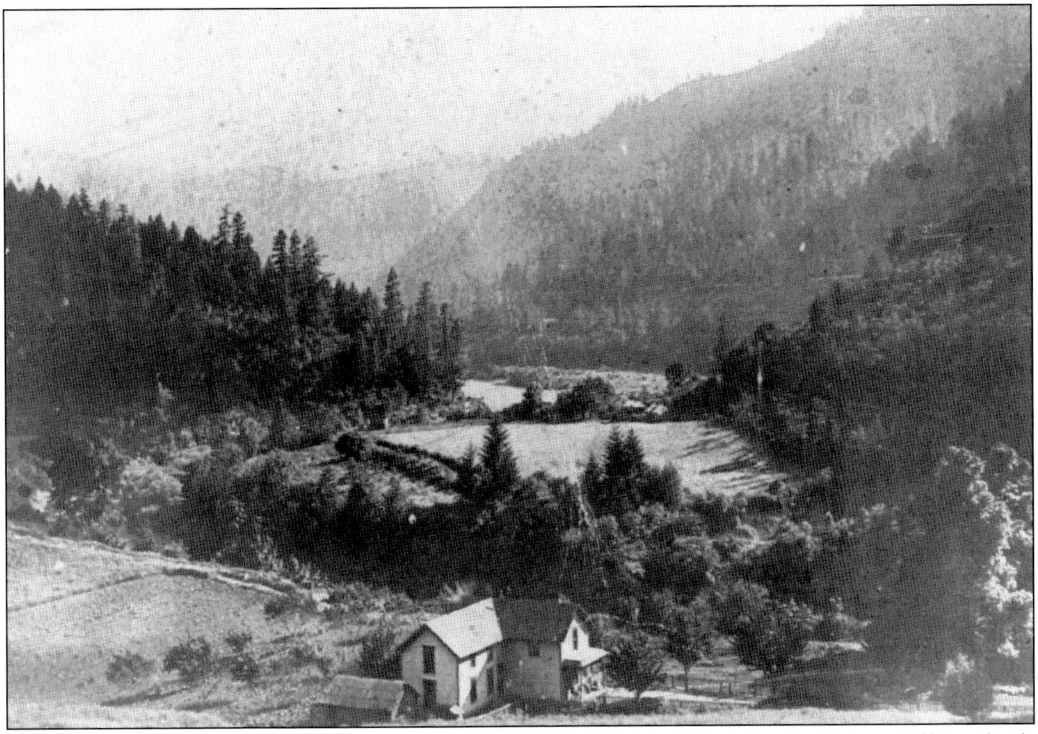

At Marial in the upper Rogue River area, about 55 miles from the mouth, George Billings built this homestead and raised his family. At one time, he was the postmaster of the small Marial Post Office. The upstairs of his barn was used as a place to dance for the neighboring families. People often traveled long distances to partake in a Saturday night dance, which was followed by a Sunday school meeting the next morning and a potluck supper before leaving Monday morning. It is now known as the Anderson Ranch and is owned by the BLM (Bureau of Land Management). (CHS.)

Many years ago, the river was flowing on a different path to the ocean, but after the 1890 flood, the river changed its course, and when this tree was left high and dry, its roots were still close to the water's edge. With the tree's root's reaching for water, over the years, the shape of the tree changed, and this is its current shape resulting from the river change. The tree is located at the base of Clay Hill Lodge and just east of Clay Hill Rapids. (CHS.)

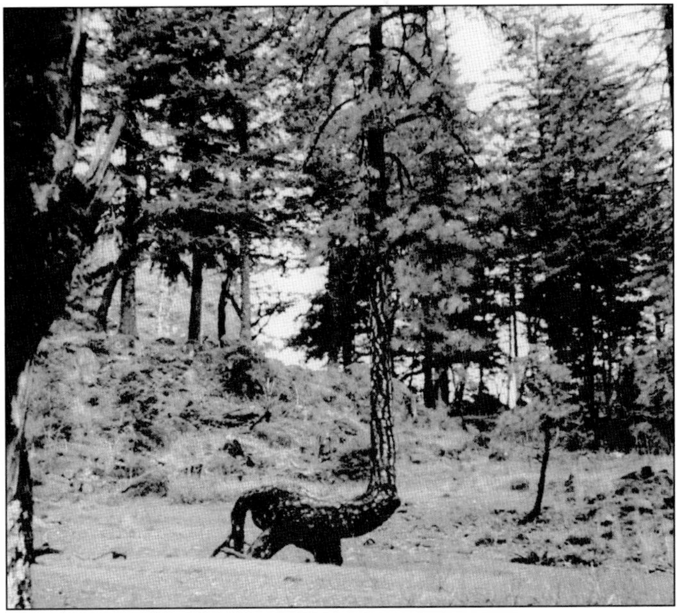

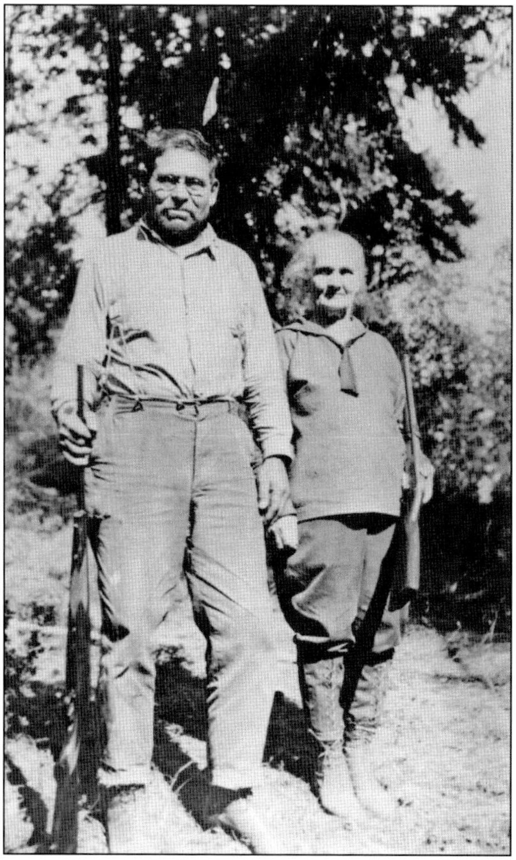

George and Anna Billings had a homestead up above Marial. There was a post office there, and George was the postmaster. In time, he sold his ranch to the Andersons, who later sold it to the BLM; it is still known as the Anderson Ranch. (CHS.)

This is how Main Street looked in 1912. The first building is the 1870 courthouse. Next is the People's store, then the post office, and last is the Bishel Hotel. (CHS.)

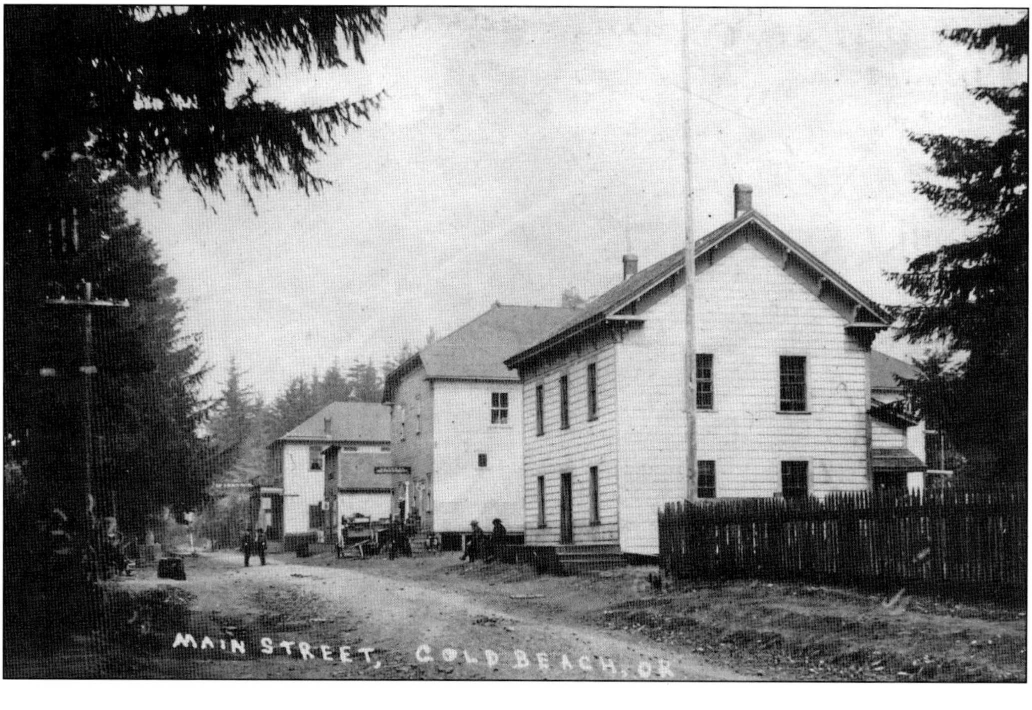

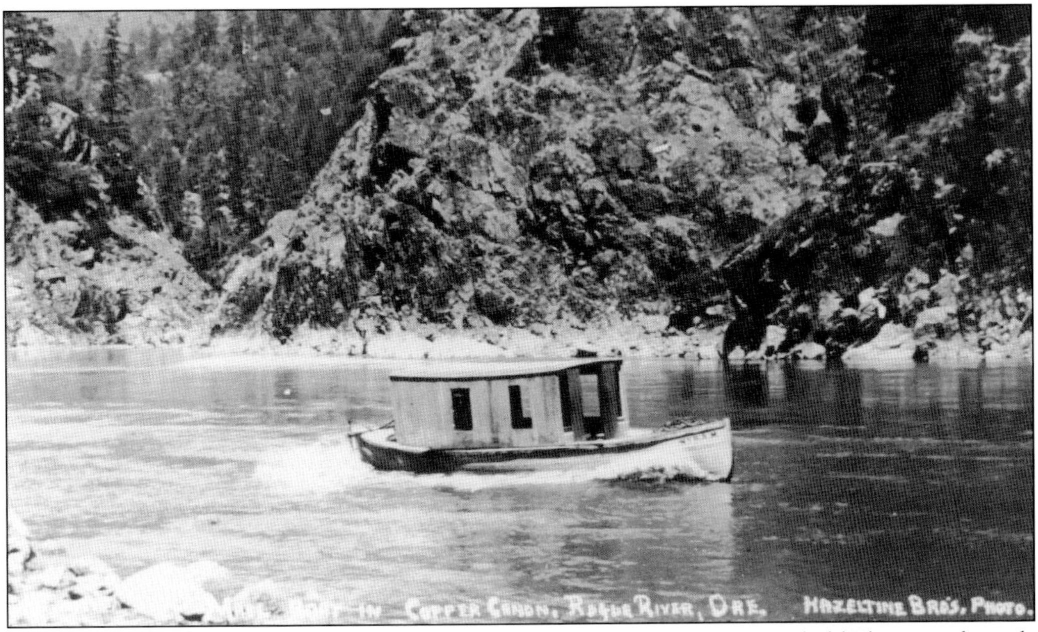

Frank Lowery owned the Lowery Inn on the lower Rogue River. It provided lodging and meals for the many fishermen who floated down the Rogue River. He built the first covered boat on the river and transported the mail to Agness. (CHS.)

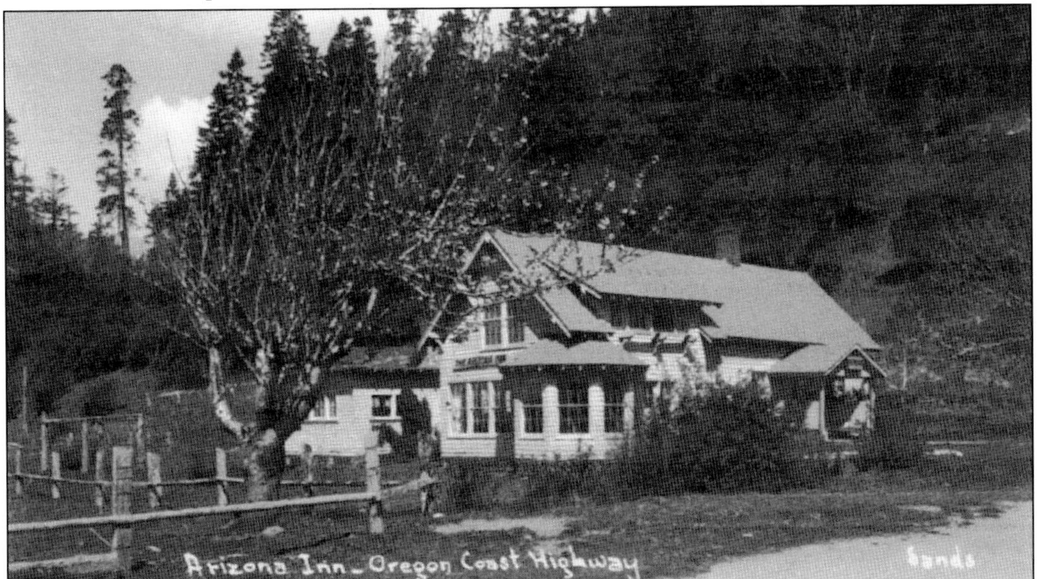

In 1924, Arizona Inn was a stagecoach stop for the loggers, and mill hands were its boarders. The owners were Arthur and Docia (Smith) Sweet of the Sweet family who homesteaded the Elk River Dairy Farm. It is located 15 miles north of Gold Beach, and they hosted those traveling by stagecoaches and later cars. They also set up a dairy, and Arthur milked the herd, separated the milk, and hauled the cream to the cheese factory at Euchre Creek. He raised a garden and cleared land for future pasture. Most of the supplies they needed were found 15 miles away, so they depended on stagecoach deliveries. Today, the old building has been torn down, and a new camp, as well as a small motel, is set up there on both sides of Highway 101. (CHS.)

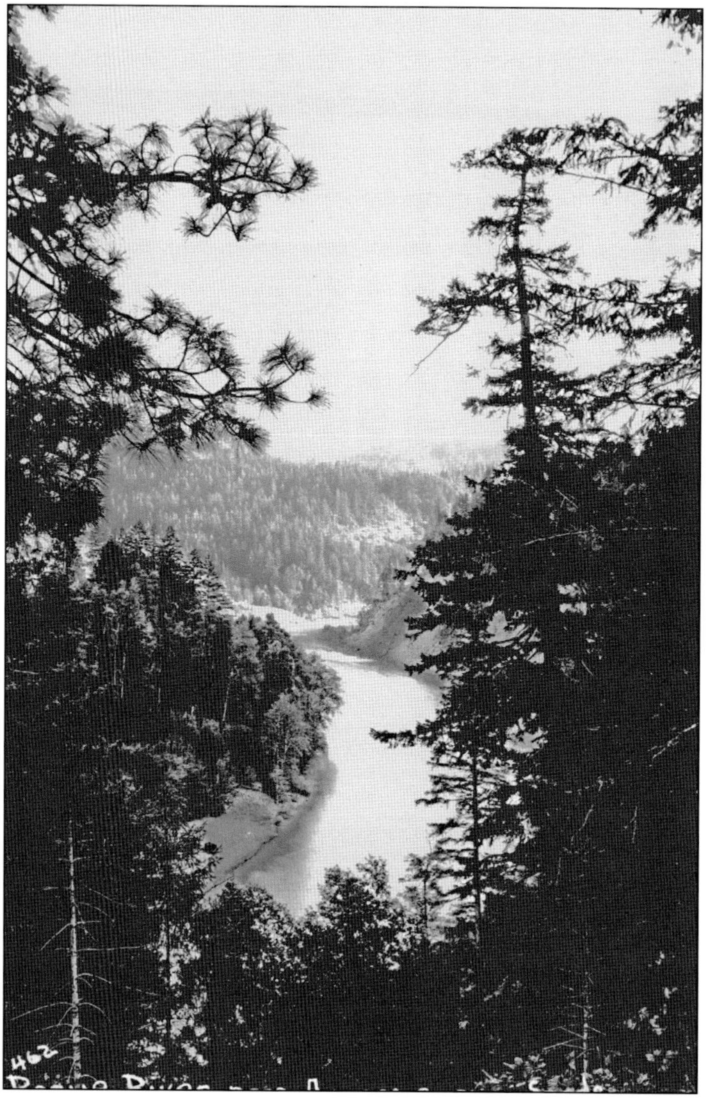

The Rogue River at Huggins Canyon is pictured. This is the deepest part of the river, about 50 miles up. The walls are narrow and very peaceful. This is where sturgeons that are caught by the downriver fishermen live. (CHS.)

Brookings in 1914 was a very small town, and there were just a few families living there. When the C&O Lumber Mill closed down in just one day, Brookings almost became a ghost town. A few farmers stayed on to continue farming, but most of them lived in the Harbor area and up the Chetco River. Today, the town of Brookings is the largest town in Curry County. Both Brookings and Harbor have larger populations than the other three towns. (CHS.)

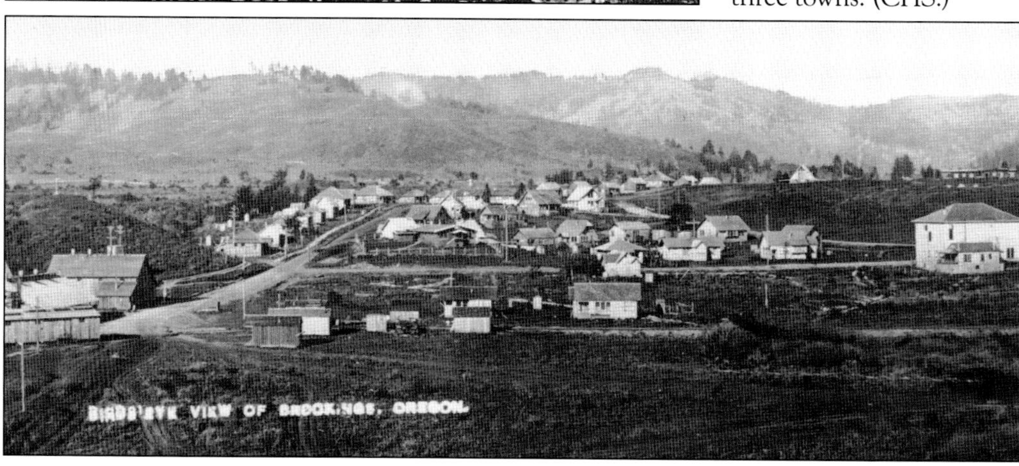

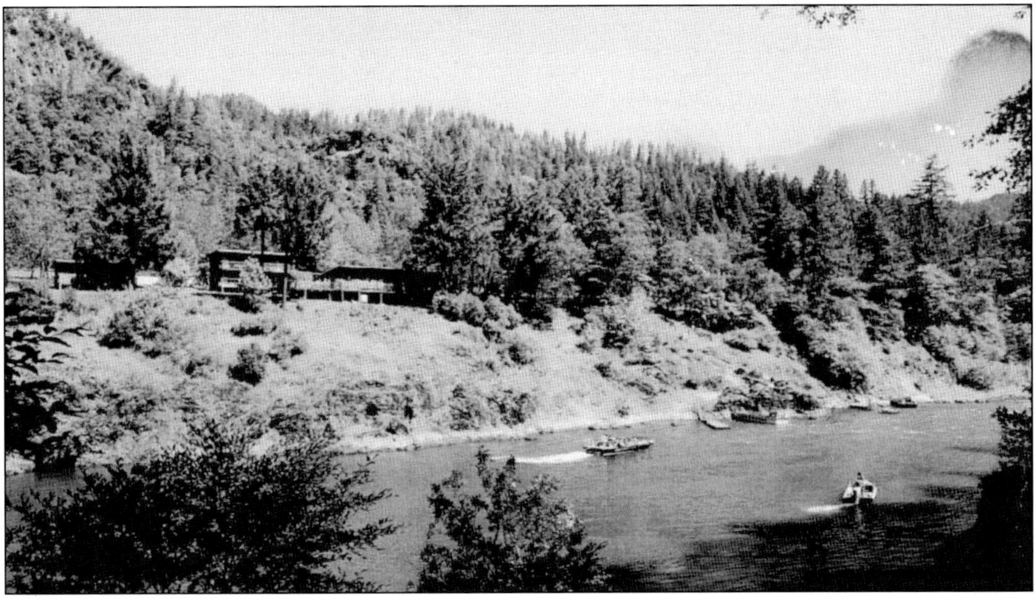

The drivers here are waiting to dock their boats and drop off passengers to either stay overnight or to make the lunch stop. The picture shows the Paradise Lodge sitting high above the waterline. The view upriver and downriver from the deck of the lodge is gorgeous. (CHS.)

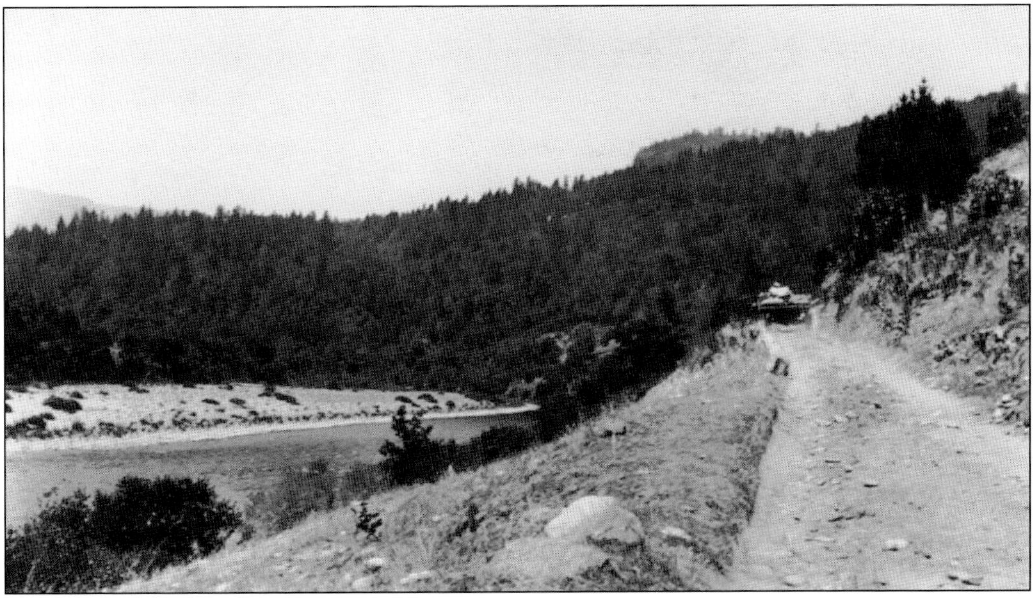

From the docks where boats let off the passengers to have lunch at Lucas Lodge, this is the road that runs parallel with the river on the north side of the Rogue River, and if a passenger could not walk up the hill, he or she would be driven to the lodge. (CHS.)

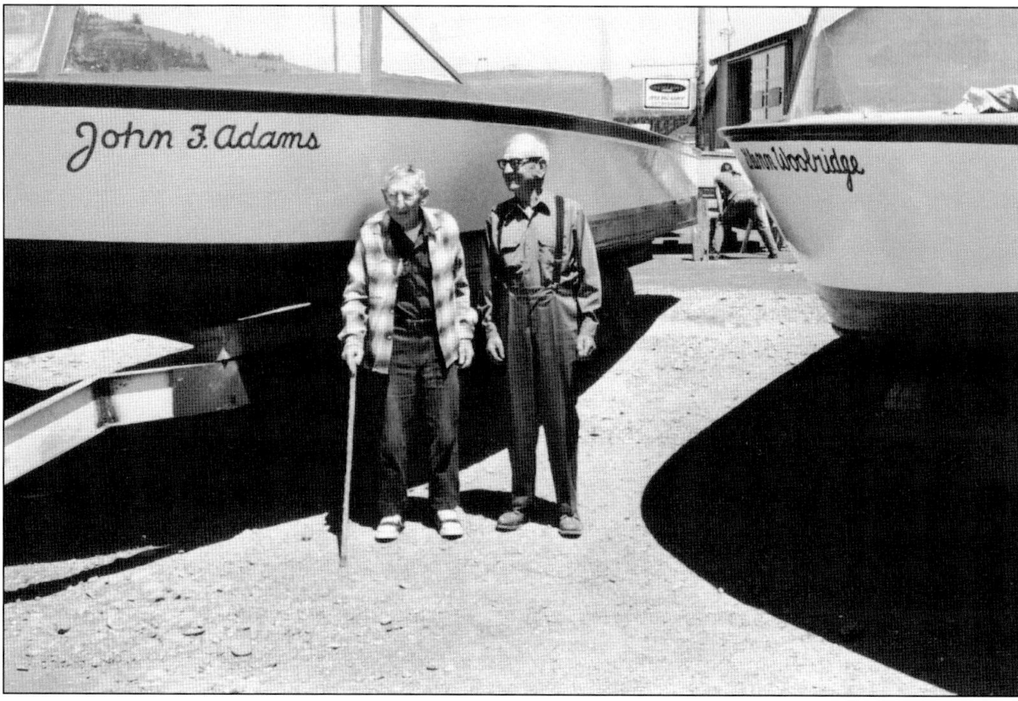

As one of the oldest pioneers of the area, John Adams, with his wife, Sadie, stands under his namesake passenger boat. (CHS.)

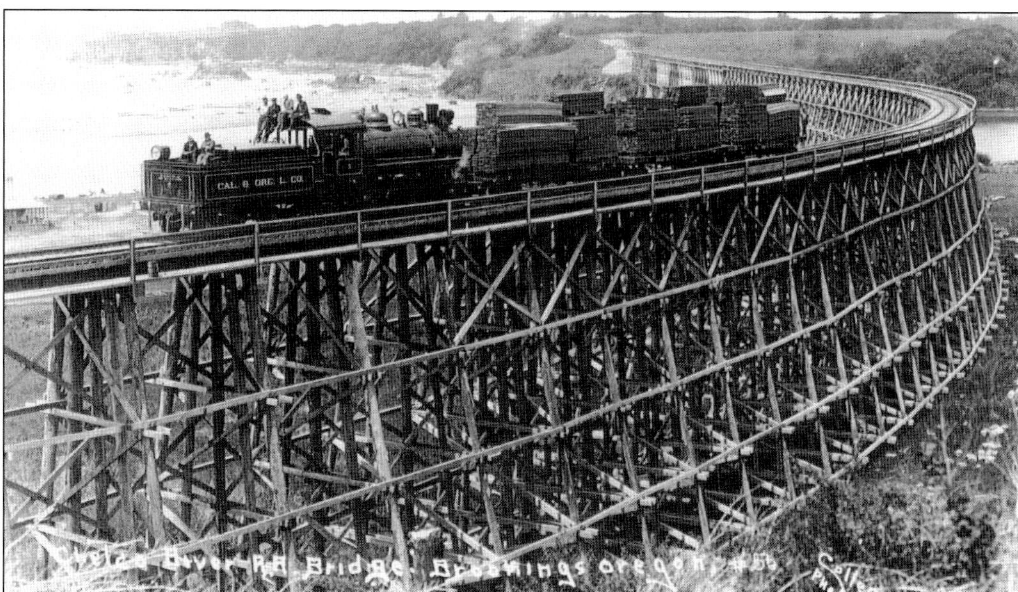

Here, a train with operators riding on the front, as there was no cab, crosses the Brookings-Harbor train trestle. It went as far three miles up the Chetco River and across the state line to Northern California, north of Crescent City. (CHS.)

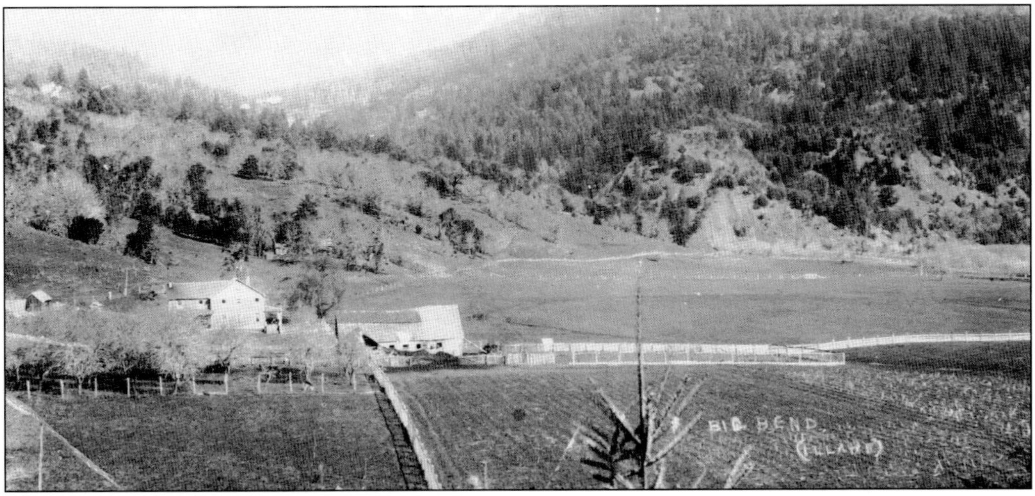

This is Big Bend in the early years when, along with the ranch, there was the White Hotel, pictured below, and school located there. A gasoline-powered motorized cable car crossed the Rogue River to the Fitzstephens ranch at Forster Bar after the swinging bridge was taken out by the flood. In later years, Big Bend had boats to cross. At one time, Big Bend was known as Illahe. (CHS.)

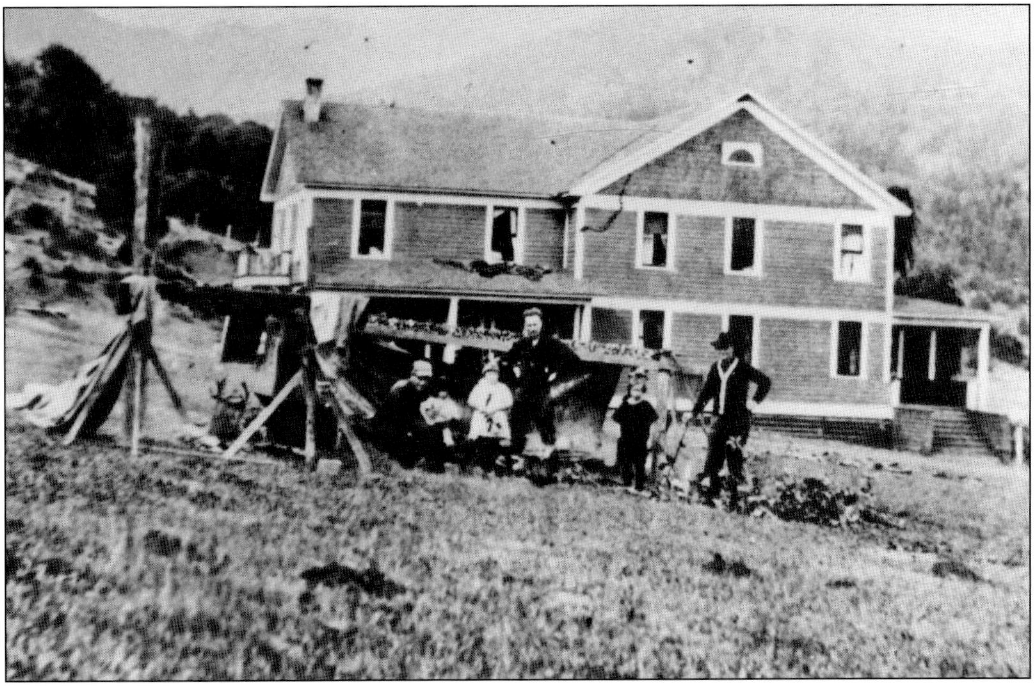

The White Hotel at Big Bend–Illahe was just above Agness. The hotel was located in a small community with only a school and a farm. Being on the north side of the river, community members constructed a swinging bridge to cross the river from the south side. When the bridge was not available, they built a cable with a gasoline-powered cabana to get to the farm. The rest of Illahe was on the south side and reachable by car. (Paradise collection.)

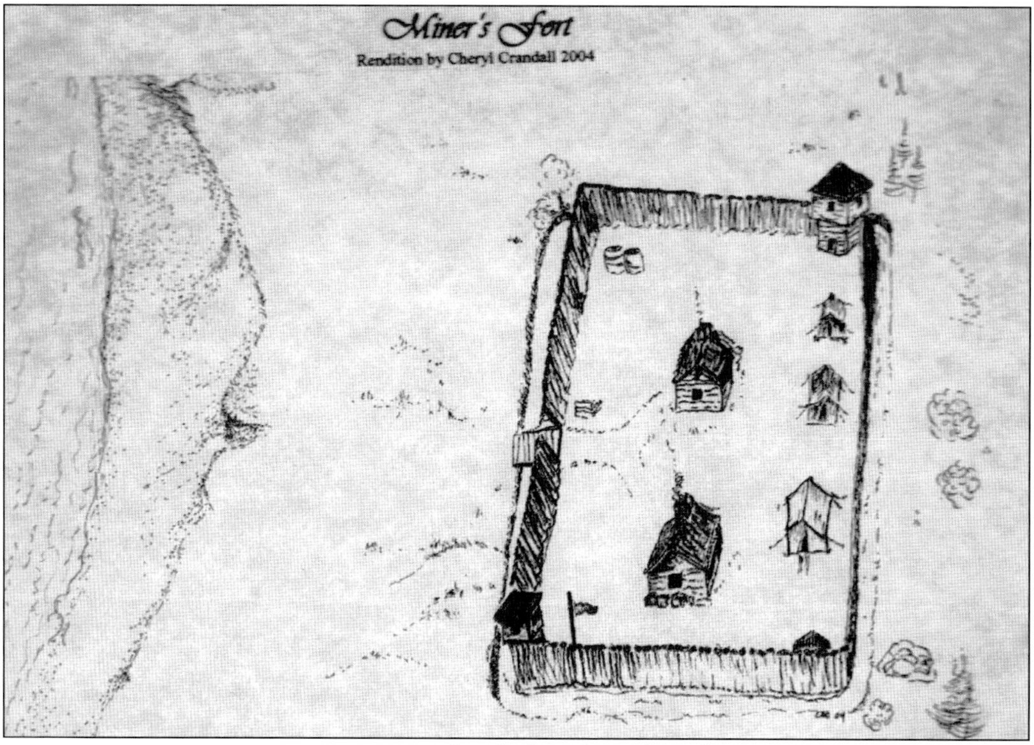

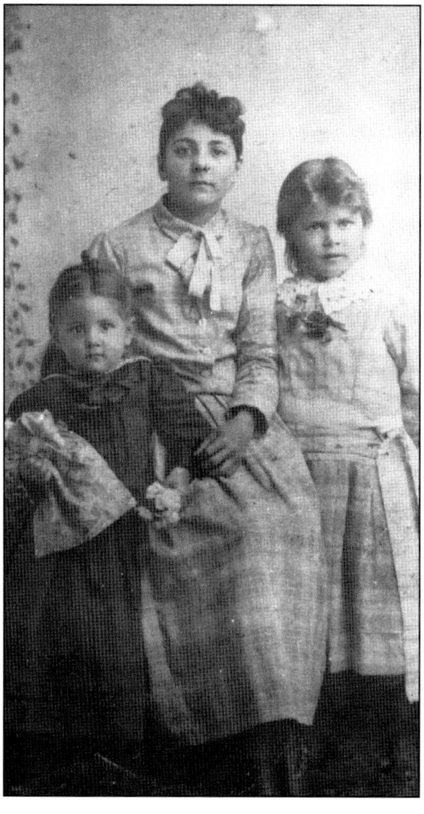

Just before the 1856 Indian war, miners suspected that things were getting more eruptive everyday. A battle was brewing upriver on the Rogue between the white miners and Indians. The miners built a fort for protection against an all-out war. Located on the waterfront, the fort had a moat, a drawbridge, and a couple of cabins plus tents. There was food stored there, and with the moat, those found within the fort were fairly safe. The Indians were unable to penetrate the fort easily. This picture shows an artist's rendition of how it might have looked. When the Native Americans came downriver on the warpath, Sheriff Michael Riley heard the first shots and quickly rushed to town to warn the local people of the danger. They had time to bury some of their keepsakes, take food and clothing across the river, and enter the fort. The Indians found and destroyed valuables, burned the homes of many, and killed those who were unable to escape to the fort. (CHS.)

These three young girls are the granddaughters of Charlotte Tichenor Guerin, the sister of Capt. William Tichenor, who founded Port Orford. Charlotte homesteaded Eckley, previously Newcastle. The oldest is Mary Charlotte Guerin Pomroy, the second girl is Caroline Guerin Boice, and the youngest sister is Julia Guerin Anderson. (CHS.)

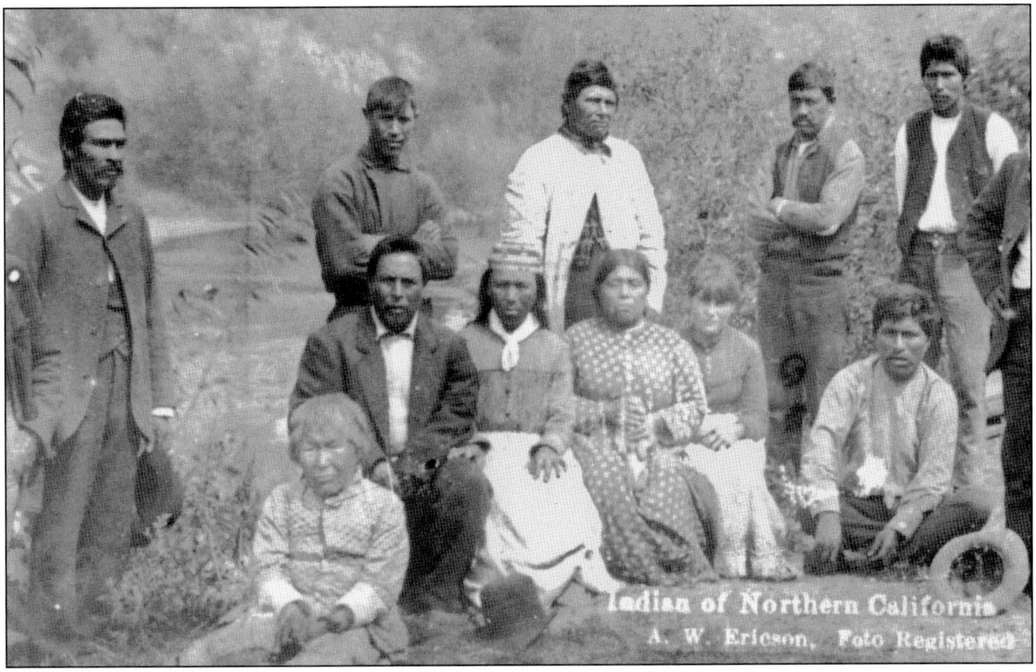

These are group pictures of some Native Americans. Each September, a powwow is held in Agness in honor of the many generations of Indians who lived in this area in the early 1800s and 1900s. This is a festival that is anticipated every year. They dance in full regalia with their drums. (Both, CHS.)

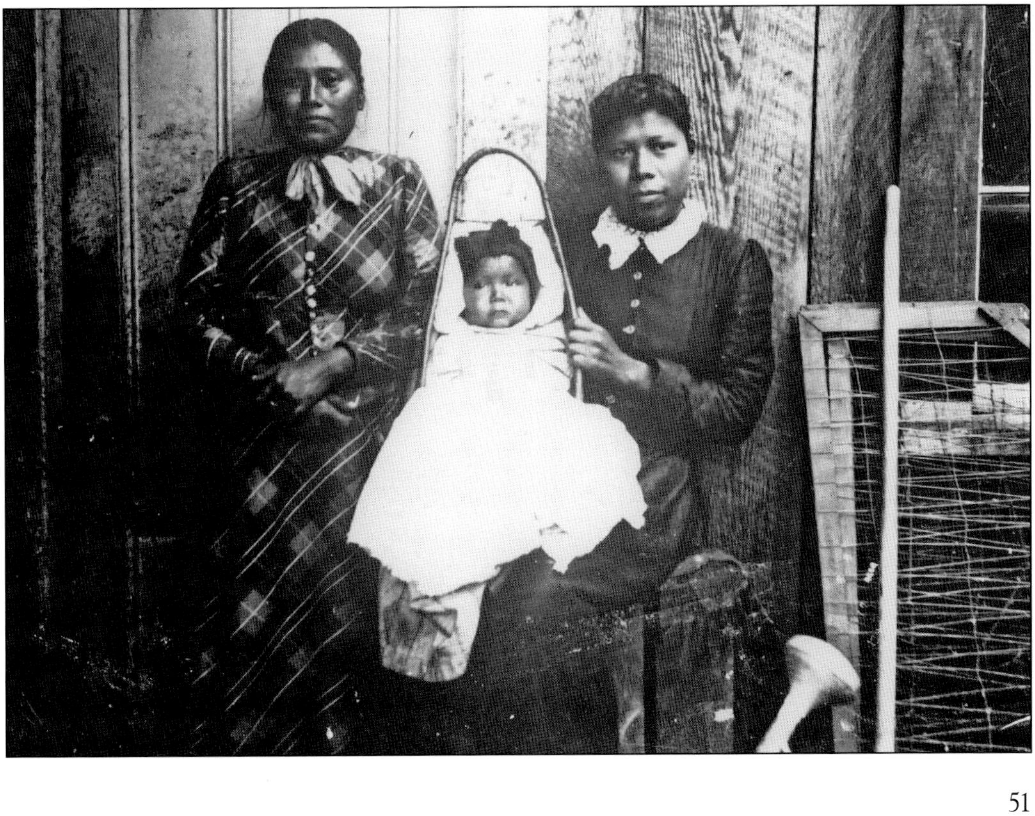

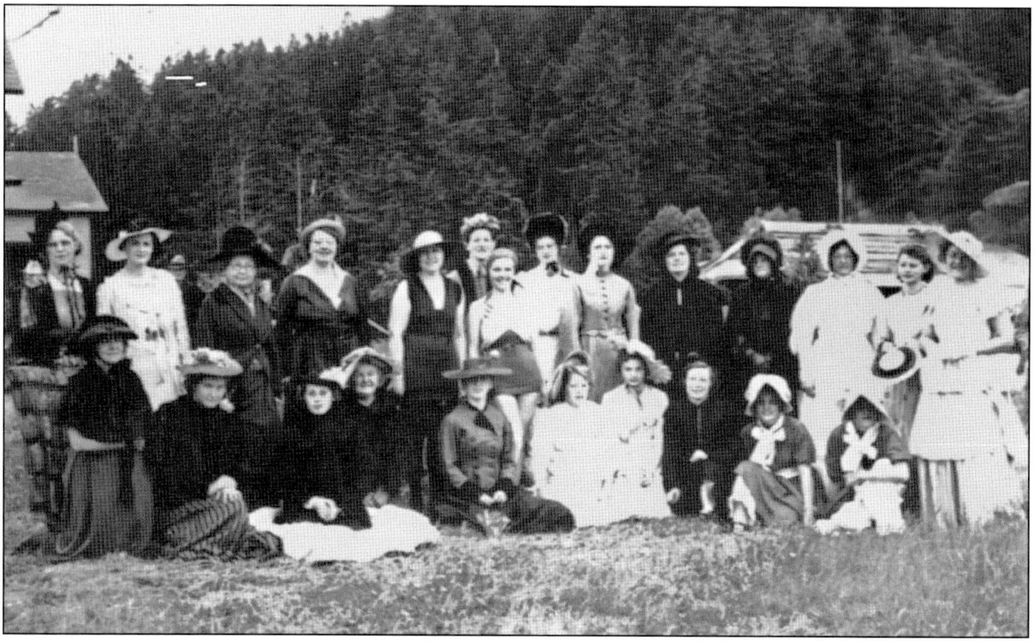

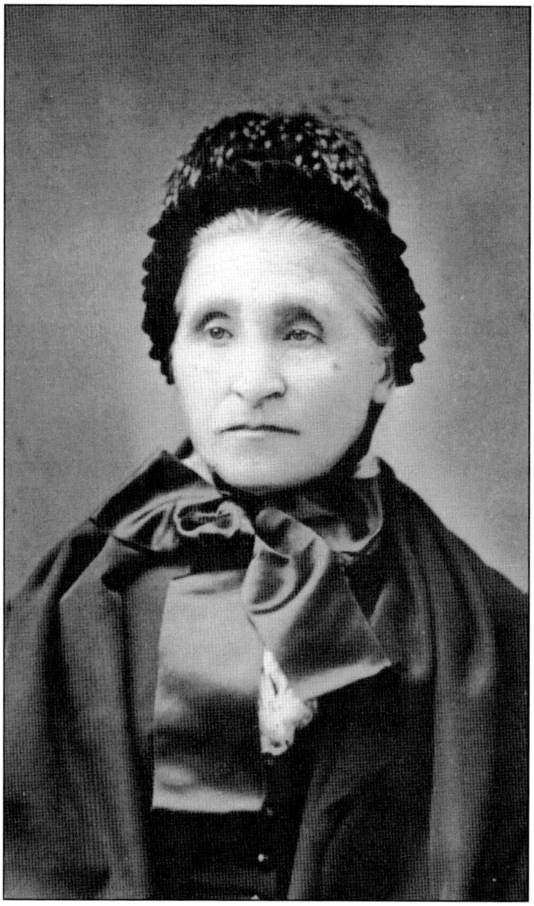

This image shows the Fat Lamb Show in Gold Beach. It was a yearly celebration prior to the building of the fairgrounds and buildings. Much more was added to the fair, like a parade, animal displays, 4-H horseracing, and other fun happenings. This picture shows an audience of ladies dressed in their finery. In later years, to the delight of the children and teenagers, a carnival was added. (CHS.)

This picture is of Christina Geisel. With her family, she lived just south of Nesika Beach at the park dedicated to them, called the Geisel Monument. They owned a store there and were attacked at the beginning of the 1856 Indian war. Christina's husband and sons were killed, and Christina, her one-year-old daughter, and her new baby daughter were kidnapped and taken to their capturers' village. They were forced by the Indian women to work and were mistreated. When the people hiding in the fort heard of their kidnapping, they pooled some of their supplies to buy them from the Indians; Christina and her daughters were then finally taken to the fort. Later on, thinking Christina had money, two young men killed her and set her house on fire. (CHS.)

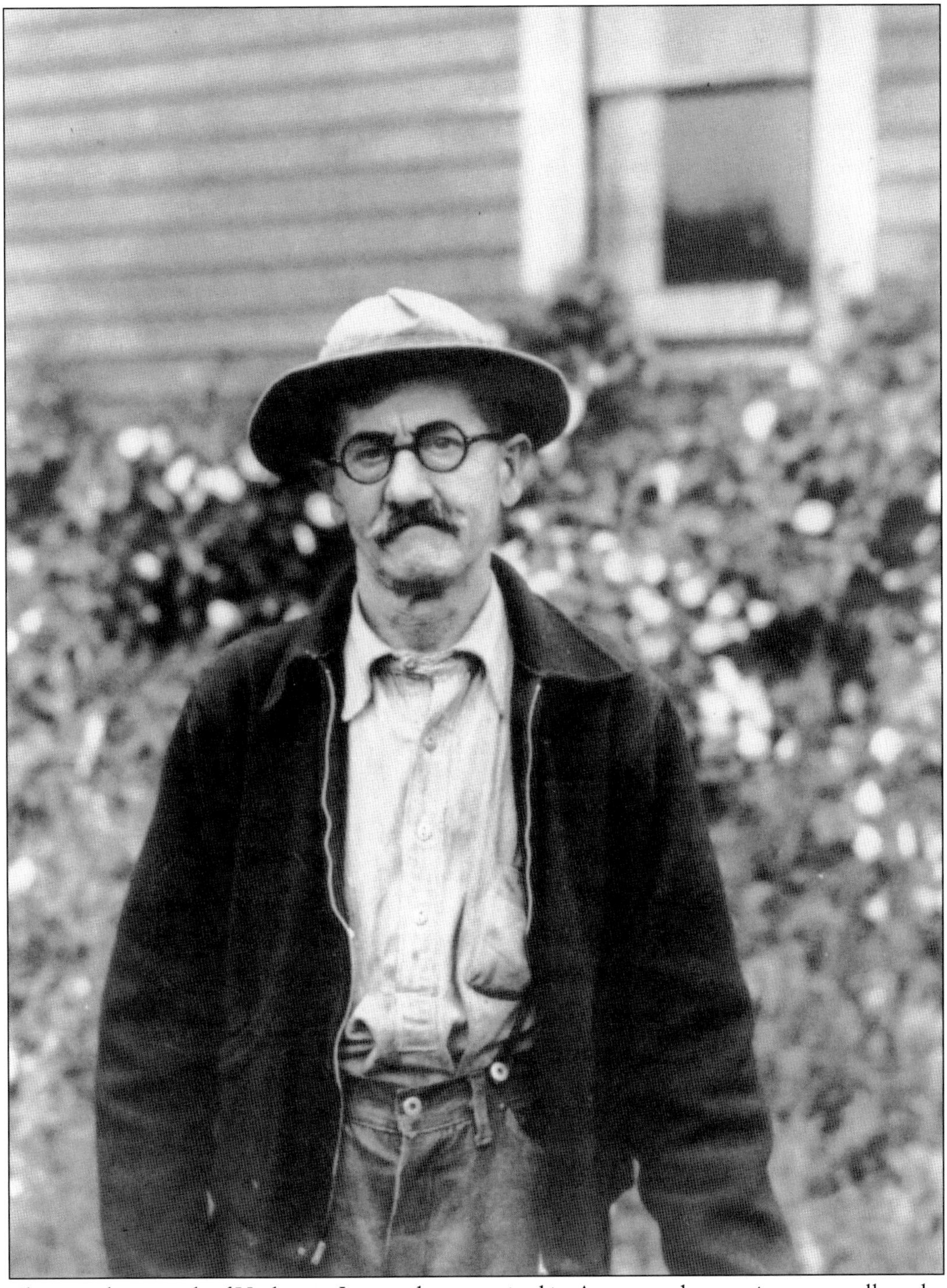

This is a photograph of Hathaway Jones, who was raised in Agness and was quite a storyteller—he proudly proclaimed that he was the biggest liar on the West Coast. He had many hours on the trail delivering mail to make up all of his stories. There have been books written about Hathaway, and each year, the Curry Historical Society presents the Tall Tales Contest with three age groups and prize money for the top three in each group. (CHS.)

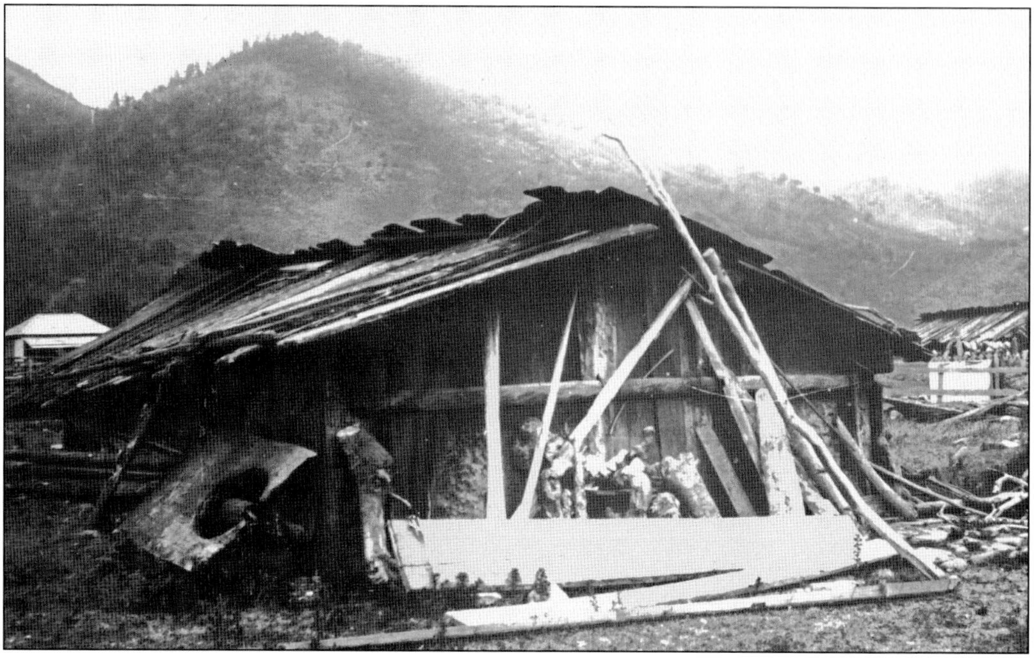

Native Americans used their ingenuity long before the white man came into their territory, and although some used animal skins to make their teepees, many others used the forest to make their homes from handmade boards. They would dig a deep trench, set the base down into it, and build onto the base, piling dirt around the sides to keep out the cold and to keep it cool in the summer, much like old-fashioned cellars. They placed a hole in the top to take care of the smoke. They built benches around the sides for sitting and for storing blankets and other necessities. (CHS.)

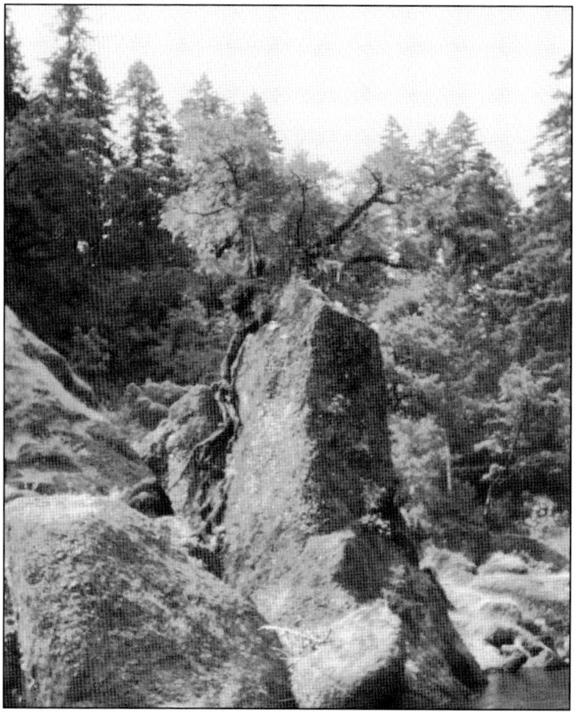

Up the Rogue River past the Clay Hill Lodge, there is a large rock on the south side of the river, where a tree is growing up the side of the rock with its bare roots spiraling down to the waterline. It is a remarkable attraction. It has been growing there for many years. (CHS.)

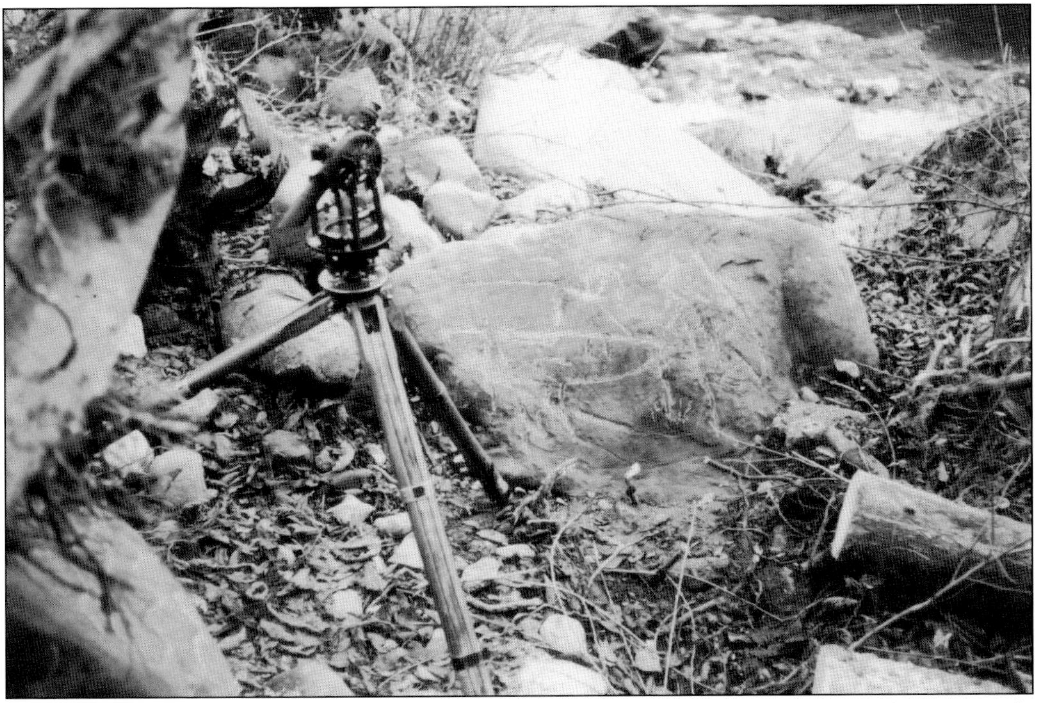

This is a petroglyph, a rock engraving, and it is one of many that were discovered at Two-Mile Rapids, just below the Old Diggins Mine. This is where the river was diverted to allow for the use of heavier machines for mining. Some of these petroglyphs were on display at the Agness museum, which has since then been closed. (CHS.)

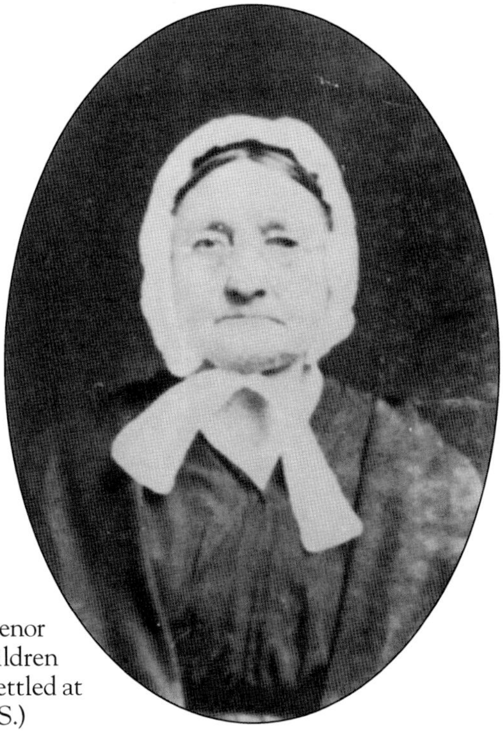

Abigail Tichenor, the mother of Capt. William Tichenor and Charlotte Tichenor Guerin, followed her children to Curry County from Newark, New Jersey. She settled at Eckley, Oregon, first known as New Castle. (CHS.)

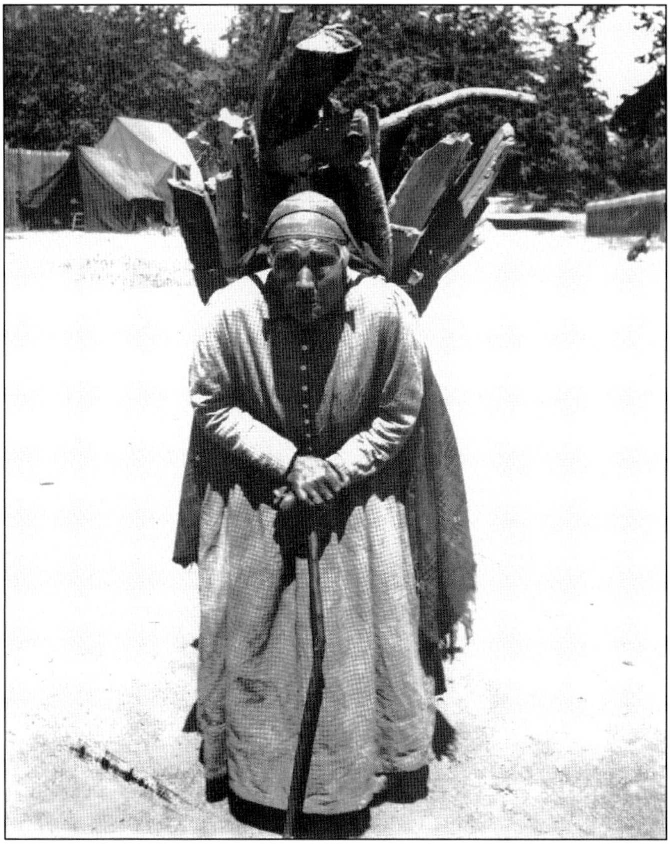

Here are two Native American women, one old and one young. The left photograph shows how Indian women used a pack board to carry their supplies or young children. Native Americans used this technique long before the invention of backpacks. In some ways, they were ahead of the pioneers. Eventually, the white people used some of their ideas. (Both, CHS.)

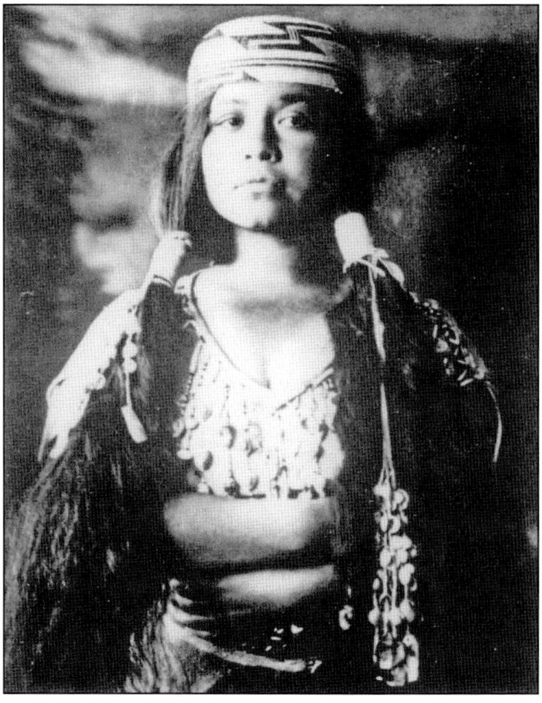

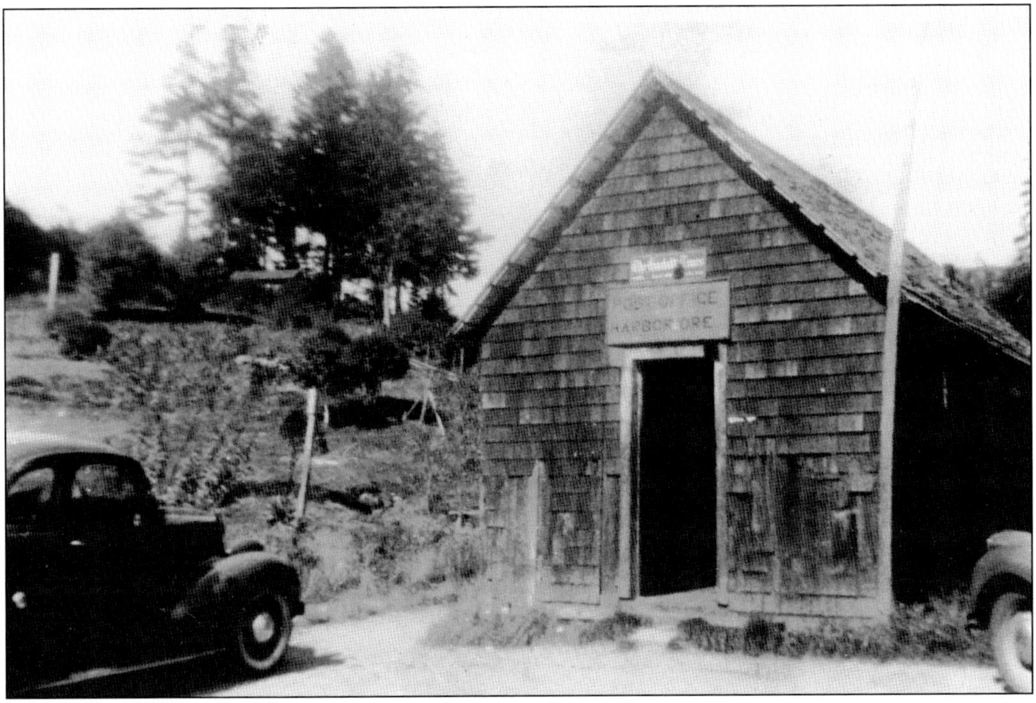

A school at Potato Illahe was built in the Big Bend–Illahe area and was located where John Adams owned his ranch. (CHS.)

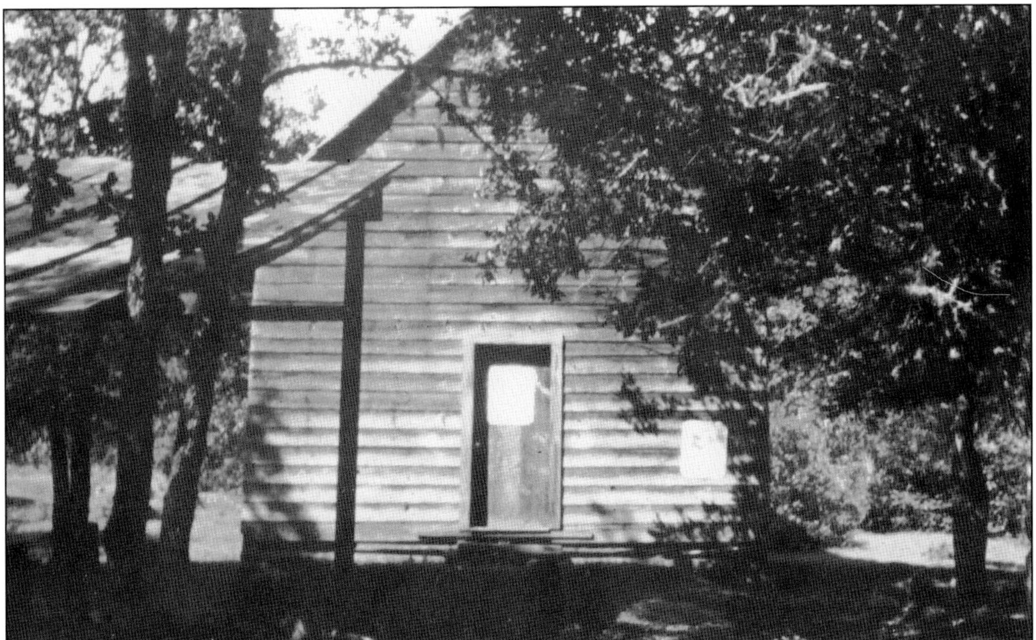

Located between Gold Beach and Agness at Quosantna, this was an early elementary school for those who lived at Dunkleberger Bar or close by. Today, it is a state park for camping and has a boat ramp. It is a good spot for picnics. (CHS.)

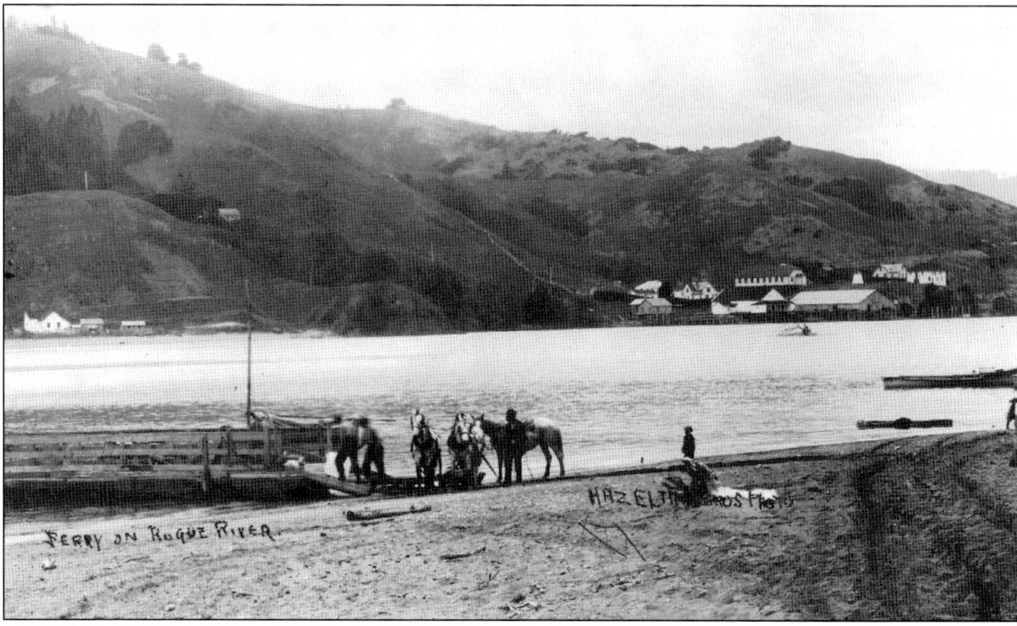

This shows a few men and a horse getting ready to board the ferry, which is leaving from the south side of the river around 1925. (CHS.)

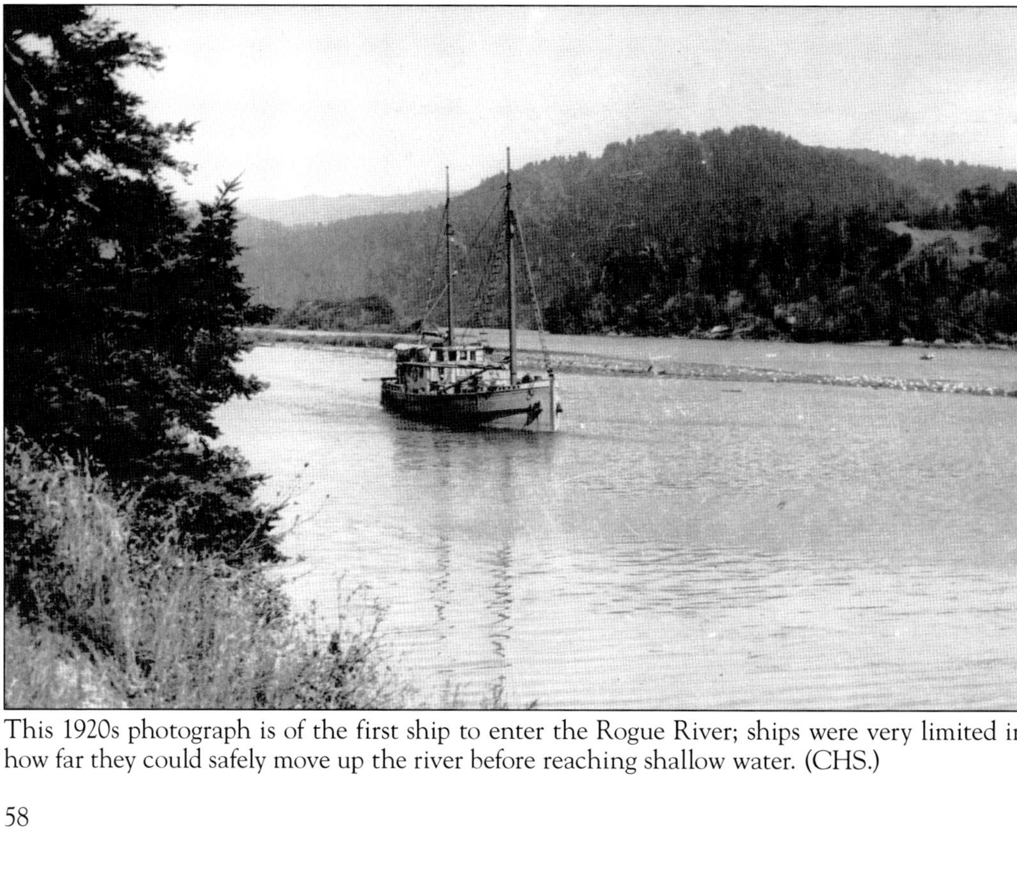

This 1920s photograph is of the first ship to enter the Rogue River; ships were very limited in how far they could safely move up the river before reaching shallow water. (CHS.)

Three

The Pygmy Monopolist

Robert Dennison Hume was the founder of Wedderburn. After his cannery on the south side was mysteriously burned, Hume floated his other buildings across the river and set them up on the north side of the Rogue River. In 1895, he platted a town and soon became the owner of a salmon cannery, a can-making factory, a warehouse, a hotel, a pea-canning factory, a saloon, two newspapers, a store, a racetrack, and some racehorses. He also owned all the tidelands along the lower Rogue River, with thousands of acres for crops and grazing. He operated a successful fish hatchery. He also built a sawmill on Lobster Creek and constructed small coastal ships. He had rental houses on both sides of the river. When he erected his Wedderburn trading store with a post office, he also started a branch store in Agness.

When he bought his first racehorses, he named his racetrack the Marchmount Jockey Club. People came from all over to the races, and many brought horses for their own racing opportunities. Between races, they had baseball games and spent time just visiting.

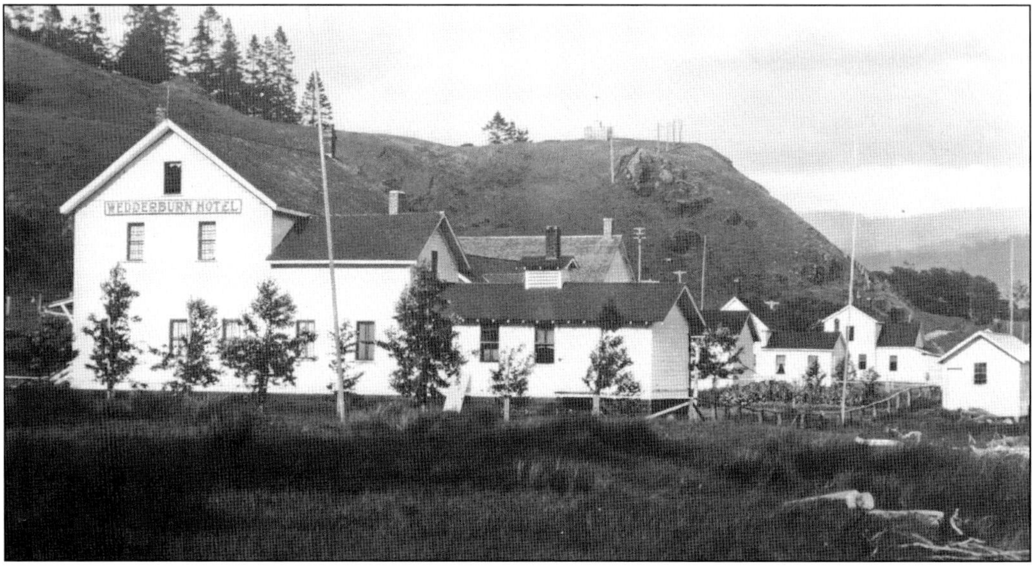

R.D. Hume first built a small hotel, called the Wedderburn Hotel, and over time added to it, with more rooms in the middle and on the east end of the main building and also other smaller buildings surrounding. It soon became a large hotel. With the new additions, it was christened Bay View Hotel. Guests could sit on the porch, watch the ever-changing ocean, and tell their favorite stories. There was a murder there over a woman that involved a miner and a sewing machine salesman. They both shot at each other, but the salesman was not hit, so he was not charged for the other man's murder. It was ruled self defense. (CHS.)

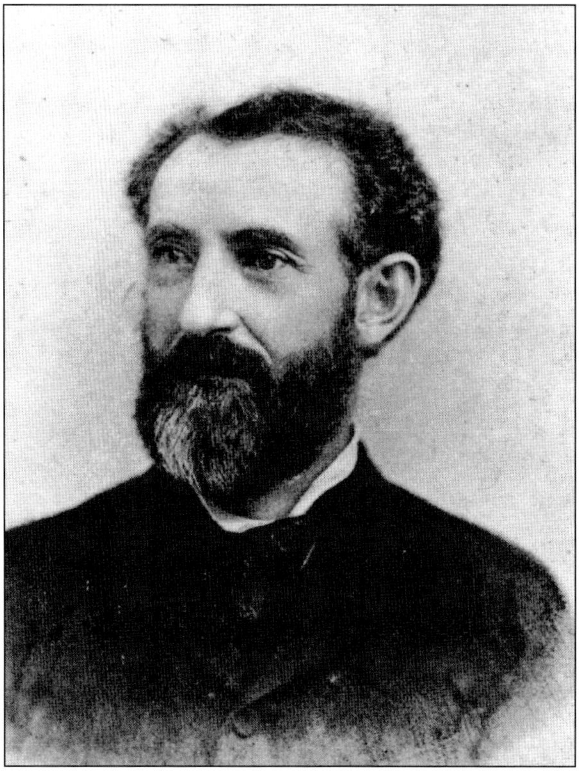

R.D. Hume, the founder of Wedderburn, Oregon, called himself a "Pygmy Monopolist." He built the first salmon cannery and owned two hotels, two newspapers, a pea-canning factory, a racetrack, a can-making factory, and a warehouse. He built the first fish hatchery and owned all the tidelands along the lower Rogue River for farming and supplying his pea factory. Later, he built the first sawmill on the Rogue River. He had the first tug built in Coos Bay, naming it the *Mary D. Hume* after his wife. Hauling his supplies, the tug was able to enter the mouth of the river. (CHS.)

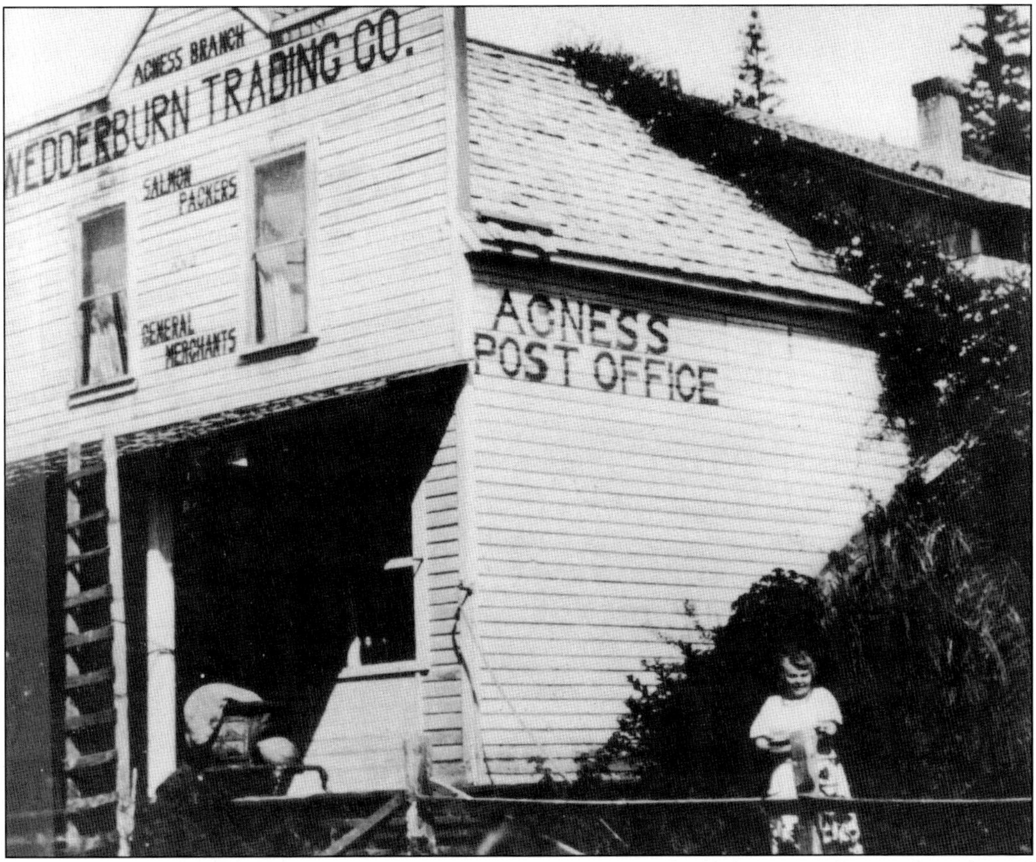

The Wedderburn Trading Co. built the first store in Agness. It held the post office and was leased and managed by Mabel (Hamm) Lucas. She built the first hotel, and it is still Lucas Lodge. At a later date, the store was sold to Bernard and Clarice Jackson. They made some renovations and named it Cougar Lane. They lived there for many years before moving to the north side of Agness, building a second Cougar Lane store there. They also built cabins, a restaurant, and a RV park. While on the south side of Agness, the mail from the east was brought by the mule train from Josephine County and from the west by the mail boat. (CHS.)

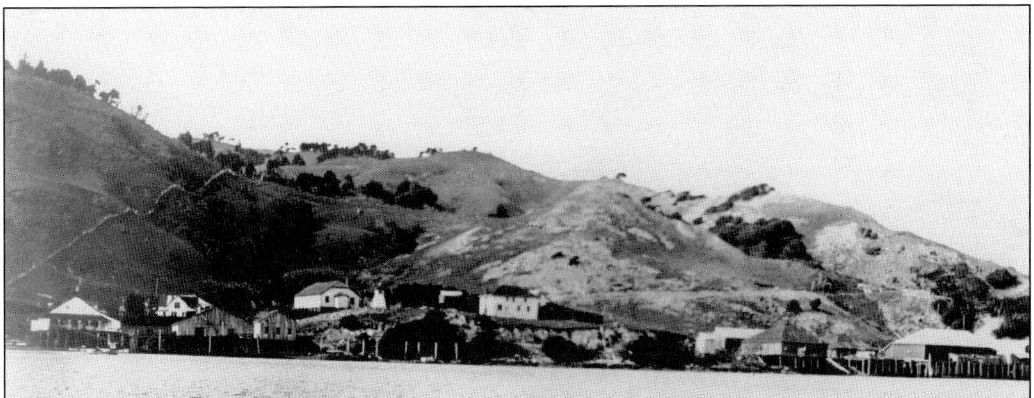

This is how Wedderburn looked when R.D. Hume first founded it in the late 1800s. Over the years, it grew with the aid of the Hume and all his businesses. (CHS.)

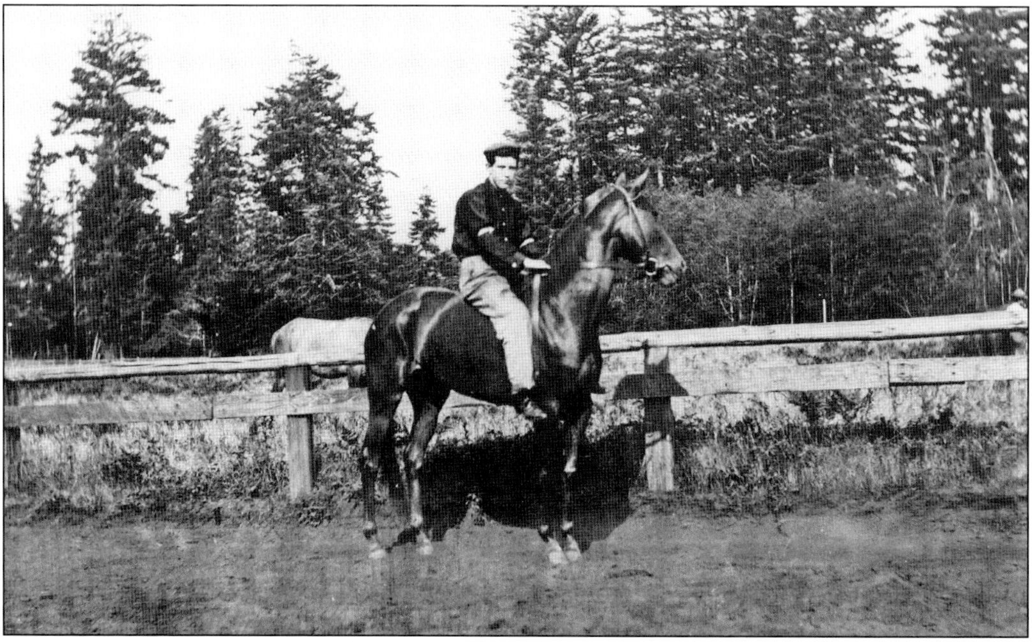

Here is one of R.D. Hume's racehorses at his racetrack on Wedderburn Hill. The stands were often filled with guests from other towns. Many of the spectators brought their horses for the races. There was plenty of betting and drinking for the spectators. (CHS.)

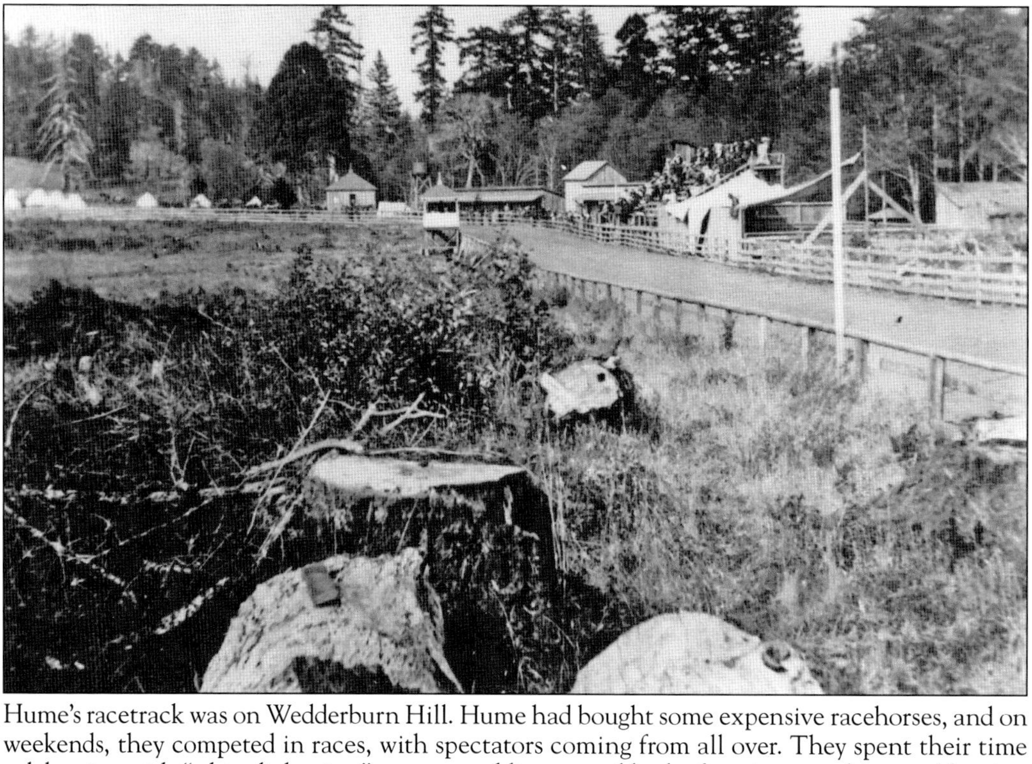

Hume's racetrack was on Wedderburn Hill. Hume had bought some expensive racehorses, and on weekends, they competed in races, with spectators coming from all over. They spent their time celebrating with "white lightning," or prepared liquor, and had a fun time watching and betting on the winners. Other horses were also brought for the major races. (CHS.)

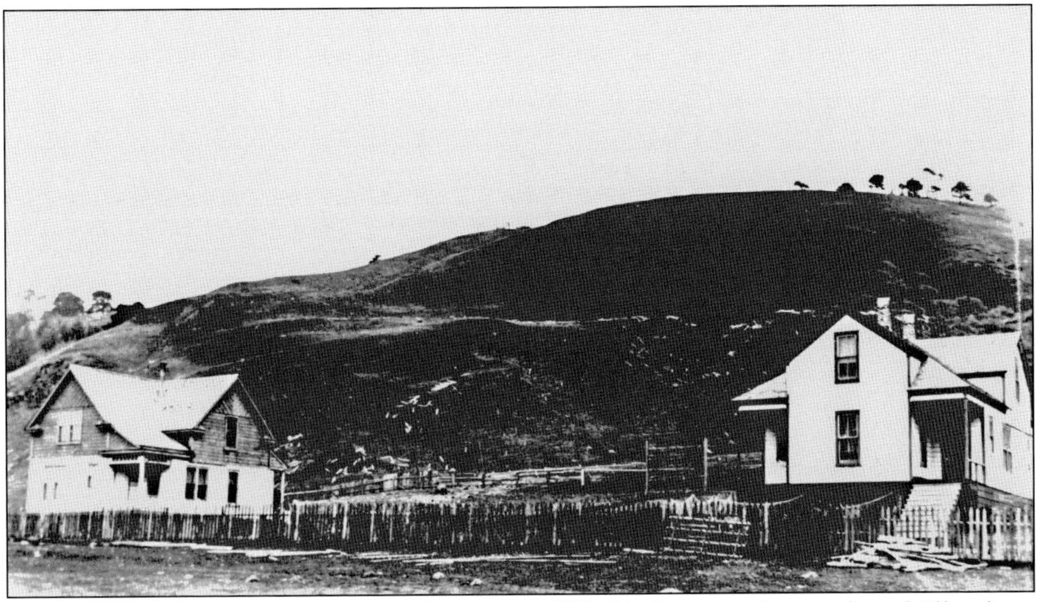

In 1895, at the mouth Rogue River, the towns of Wedderburn on the north and Ellensburg (Gold Beach) on the south were divided. When his cannery burned to the ground mysteriously, Robert D. Hume floated these two unburned buildings across the river and founded the town of Wedderburn. He erected many other buildings and owned the whole north side of the Rogue River. He became a man of means. (CHS.)

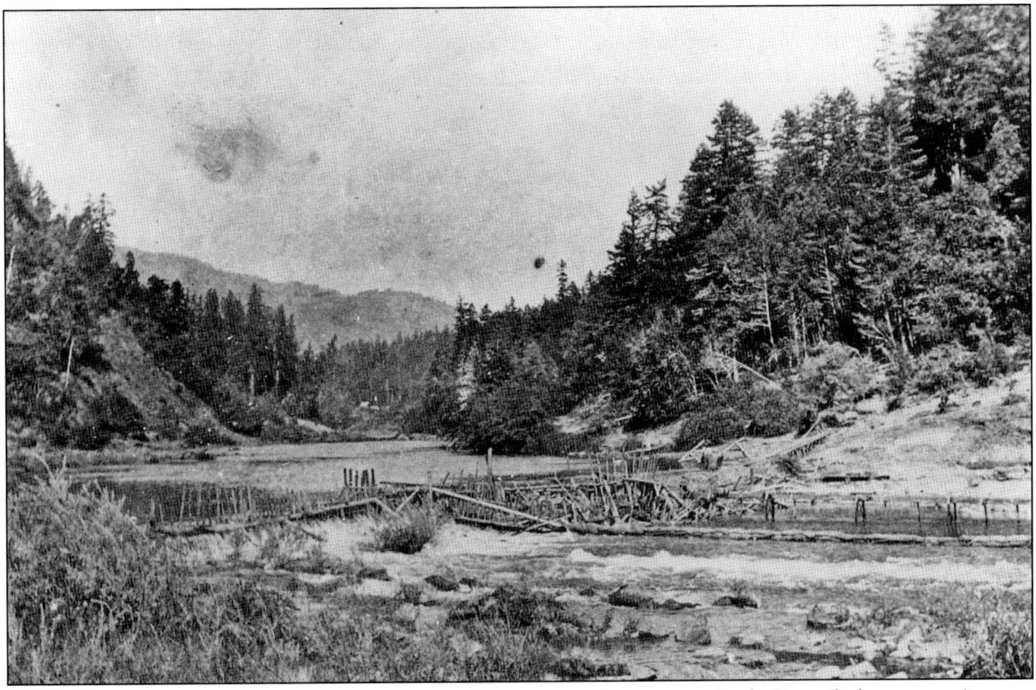

Old Diggins Mine is on the Rogue River and is just above Two-Mile Rapids between Agness and Foster Bar and just below Illahe and Big Bend. The course of the river at this place was changed to allow for the use of heavier machines for mining that particular spot on the Rogue River. (CHS.)

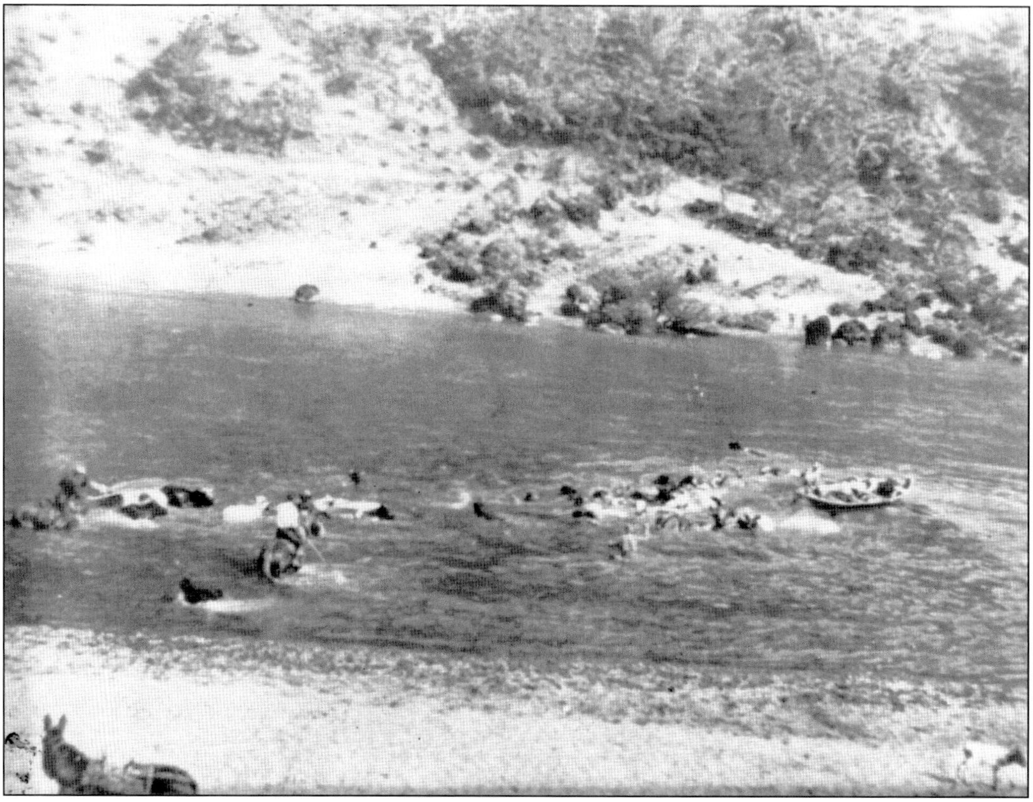

Jack Adams, Bob Miller, John Cooley, and Don and Larry Lucas are herding their cattle across the Rogue River below Shasta Costa Creek on the way to their summer range on Burnt Ridge and Fish Hook. (Jack Adams collection.)

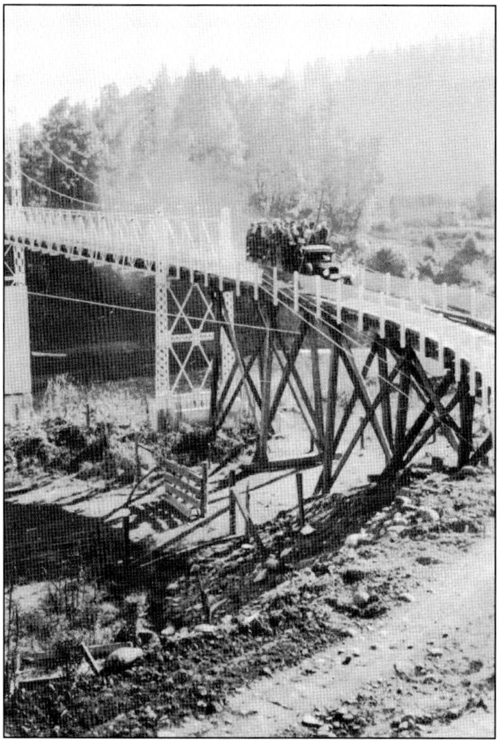

The first Rogue River Suspension Bridge was a swinging bridge made just for foot traffic. This photograph is of the second suspension bridge, constructed to accommodate motorized vehicles. It was stable enough to hold trucks. The 1964 flood took out the bridge. (CHS.)

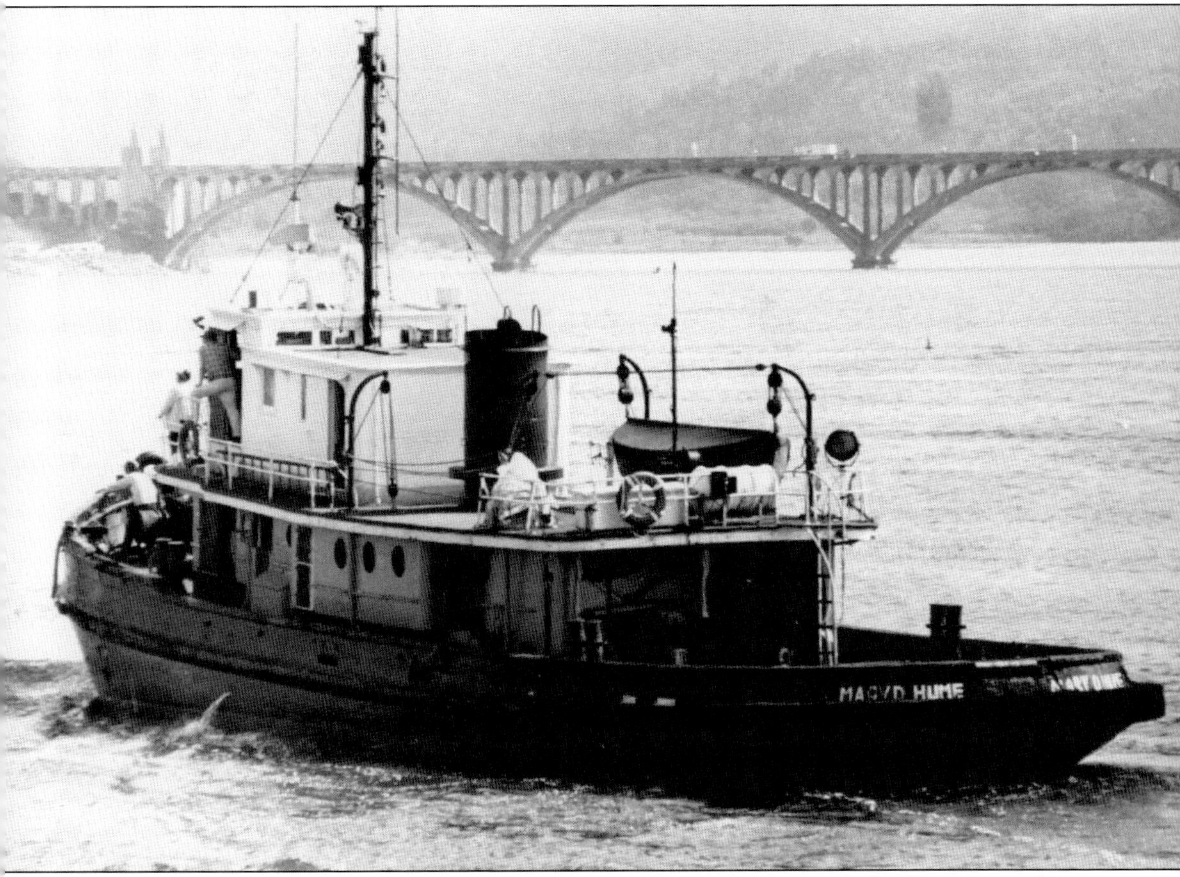

The *Mary D. Hume* was a tug built for R.D. Hume in Coos Bay. It exported all of his commodities to San Francisco, which included products from his salmon factory, his pea factory, and fish from his hatchery. The tug was tested to be able to stand the frozen Beaufort Sea. It set many records in the six and a half years it stayed in the Arctic Circle. The Curry Historical Society finally brought it back to Gold Beach, but soon a fancy lawyer took it over from the CHS and left it to fall apart just east of the mouth of the Rogue River. (CHS.)

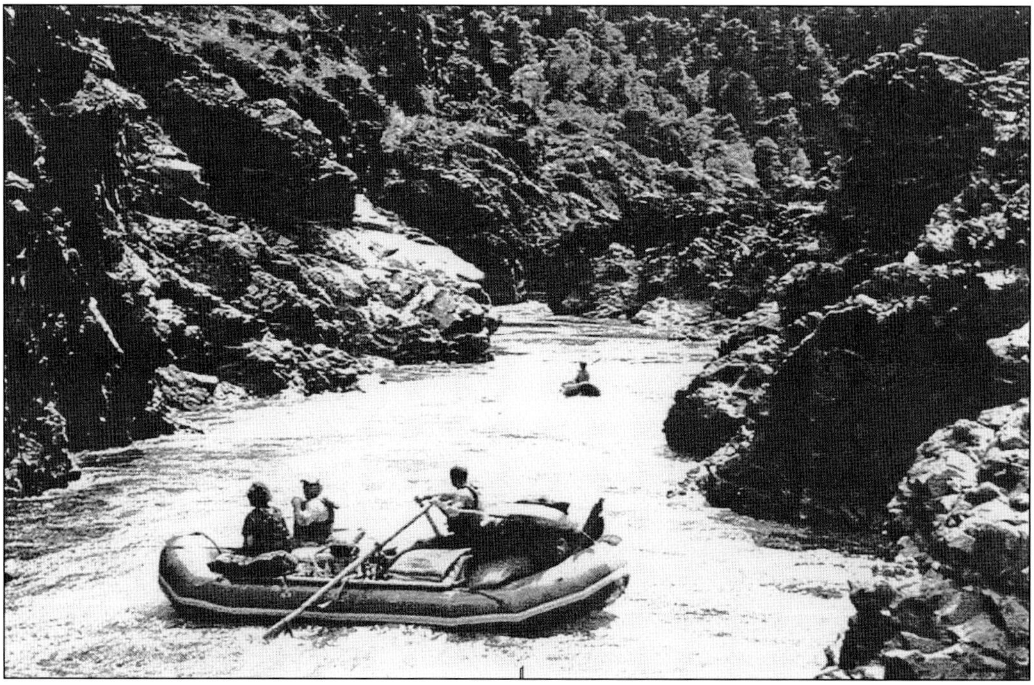

Most raft trips are guided, but sometimes a family will apply for a permit and do their own paddling and camp along the way. Occasionally, the guided trips offer the opportunity to camp, but most stay at the various lodges, which include Black Bar, Marial, Paradise, Half Moon, Clay Hill, and Illahe. Rafts are taken out of the river at Foster Bar and transported over the mountain by vehicles. (CHS.)

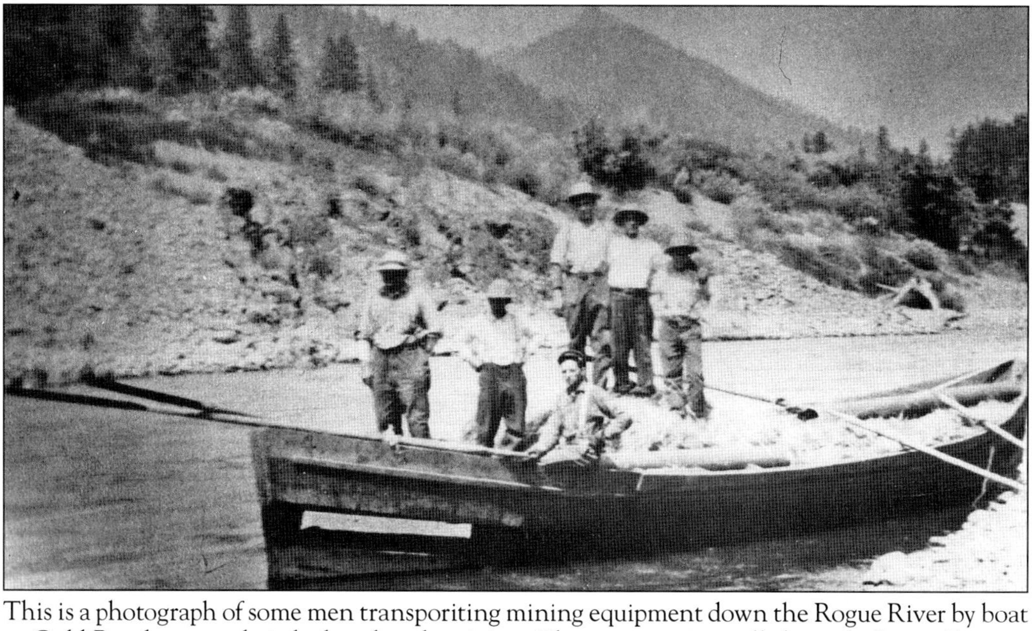

This is a photograph of some men transporiting mining equipment down the Rogue River by boat to Gold Beach to try their luck at beach mining. There were mines all through Curry County, and these men did not want to chance missing that big strike. The glitter of gold was still in their eyes. (CHS.)

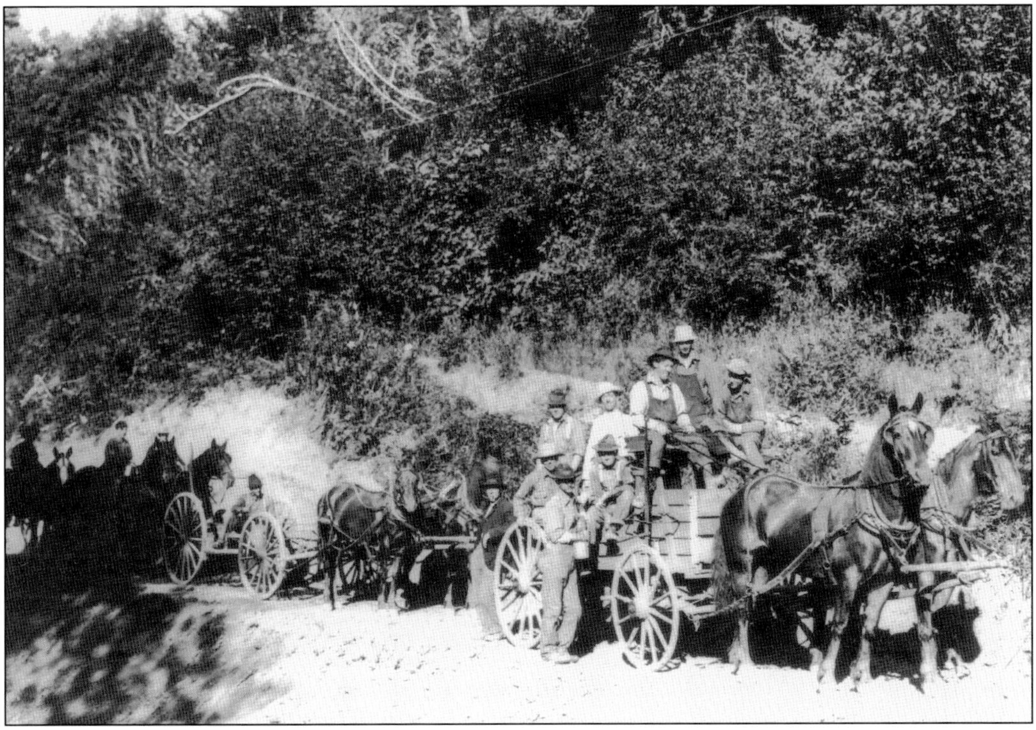

A farmer, with his helpers, is hauling his hay to his barn; this was the same wagon used to haul logs for building his house and any other buildings needed on his property. In those days, neighbors helped neighbors in constructing their homes. When there was a loss of any buildings, there were many neighbors always willing to help. (CHS.)

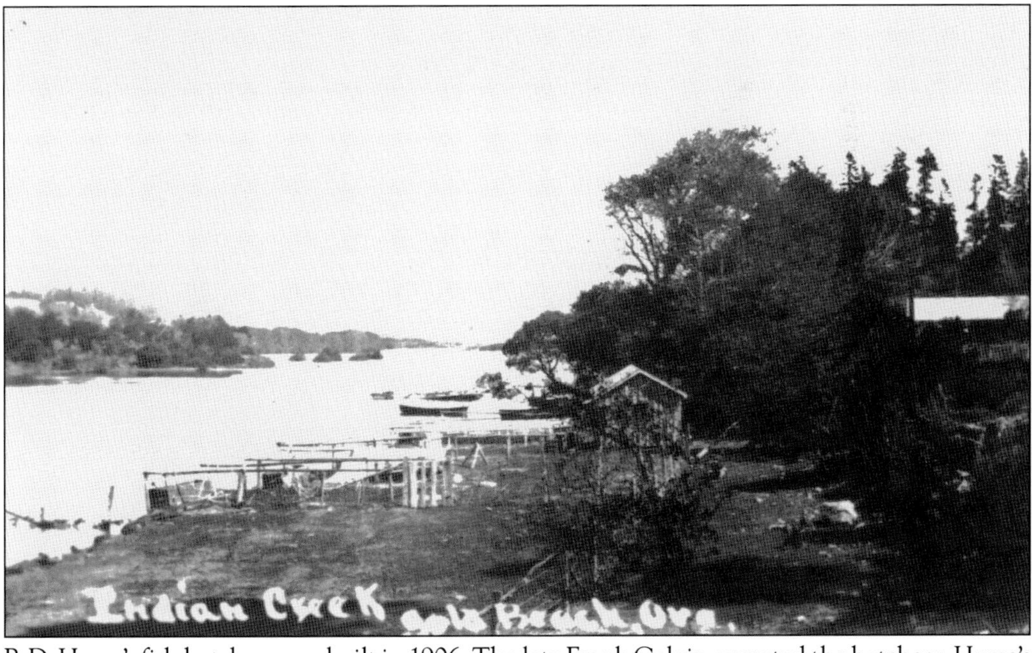

R.D. Hume's fish hatchery was built in 1906. The late Frank Colvin operated the hatchery. Hume's was the first built and is still located at Indian Creek today. (Edsel Colvin.)

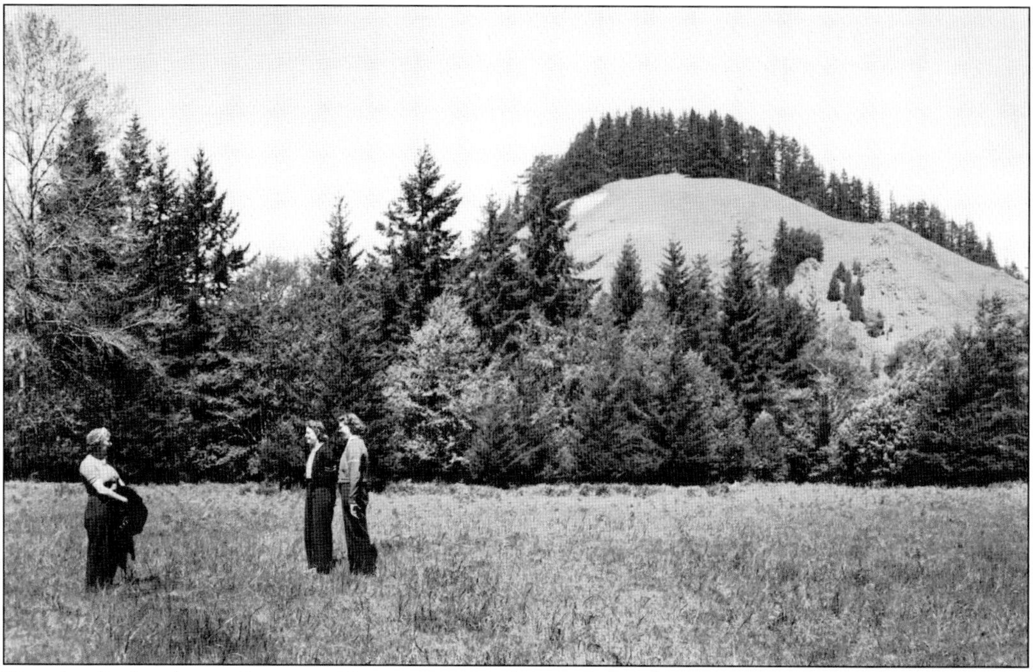

Huntley Park is located seven miles upriver on the south bank of the Rogue River. It is set up for overnight campers, with an open area for day guests to picnic. It is a good place for swimming or just taking in the sunshine and watching the boats going by. (CHS.)

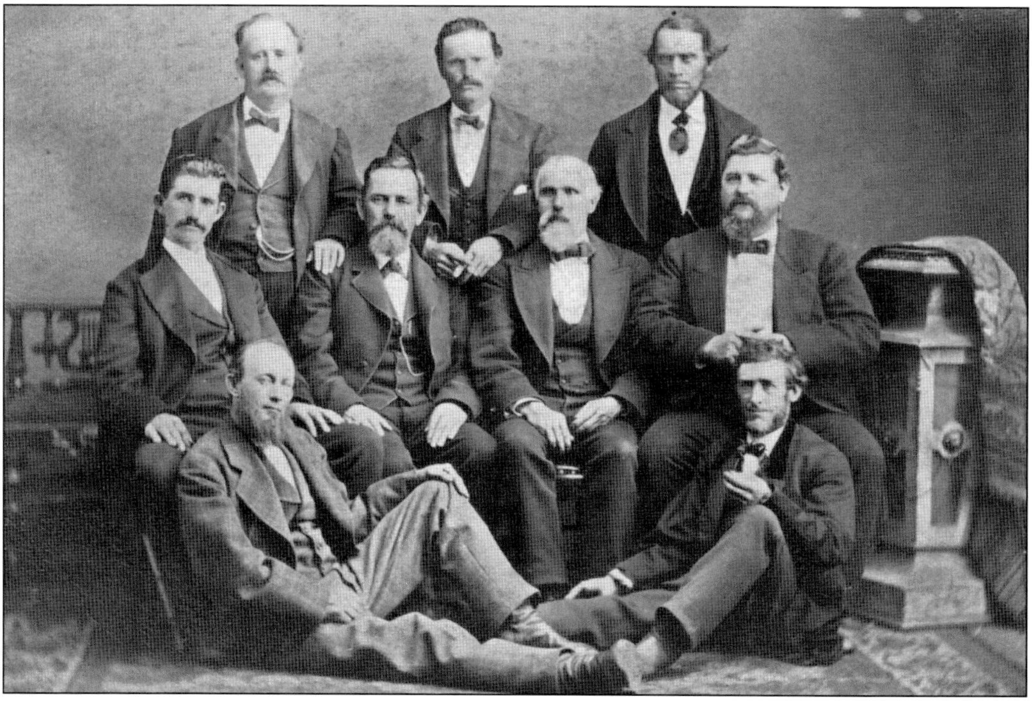

These nine men organized what they named the Webfoot Club in San Francisco. They are, from left to right, (first row) Asia Crook and Frank Frame; (second row) William Bailey, Asher Moore, Michael Riley, and Delos Woodruff; (third row) Seth Blake, Jesse Carey, and A.J. Edison. (CHS.)

Four

Industries in Southern Curry County

There have been many industries, like mining, over the years in Gold Beach that brought the many families to this part of the coast. The mountains, the beaches, and the Rogue River were the call to the miners. Wherever they looked was the pull of the miners—the chance to get rich. Sadly, it soon played out, and next were logging, milling, and fishing, both commercial and sport. Gold Beach was growing, and as it was still isolated until the 1950s, it was self-sustained. Soon, the government closed down logging and made netting salmon illegal, causing the large canneries to close. However, fishing was still open to the sportsmen, and the last industry of passenger boating was opened, which is now the main industry of Gold Beach. In Langlois are the cranberry bogs, with lily fields to the south; carving myrtlewood and redwood were the other industries.

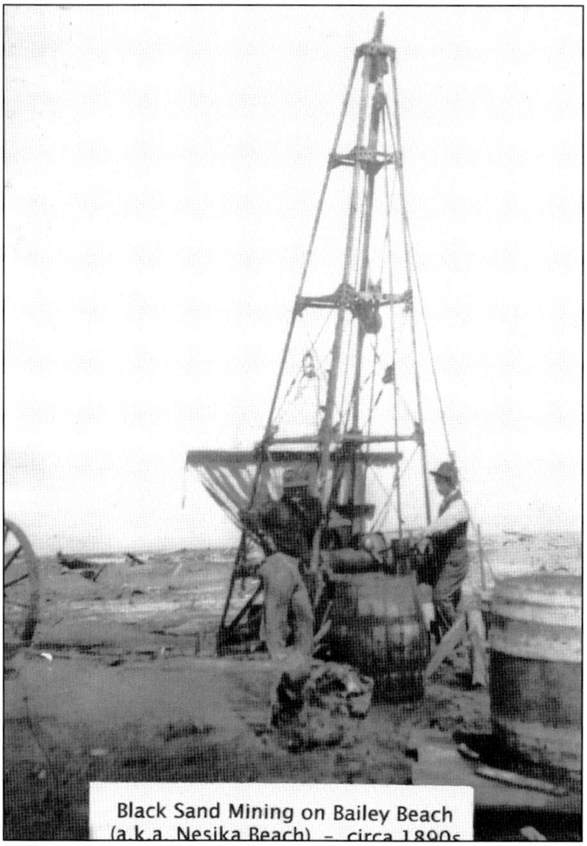

The machines shown on this page, which resemble each other, were used for entirely different actions. At Bailey Beach, the machine shown here was used to mine gold from the black sand. There were many different ways miners used to extract the gold; the other ways included panning, flumes, pressure hoses, sluice boxes, trestles and stamp mills, plus other varied types of machinery. (CHS.)

This picture is of the only oil derrick in southwest Oregon. It was located on Langlois Hill. A company in Portland owned it, and it is not certain whether or not the company ever found oil. The company discouraged anyone from coming on the property. It was in use for about a year and a half and ended up drilling in two close locations. The first drilling proved that the equipment was too light, so the company had to bring in heavier equipment for the second drilling. There is very little information on this particular industry. (CHS.)

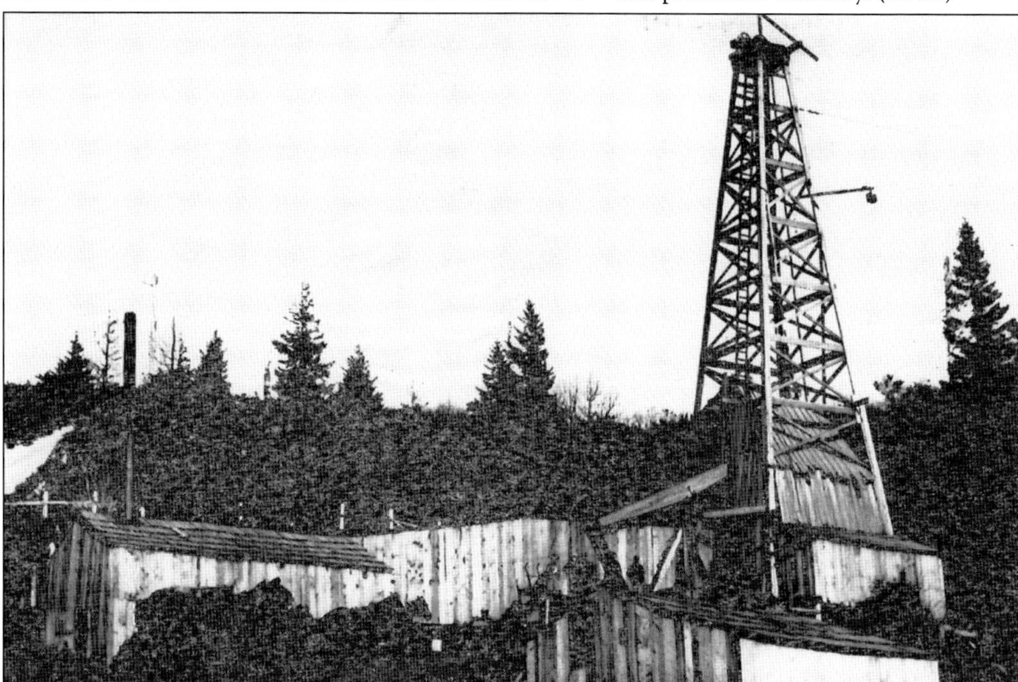

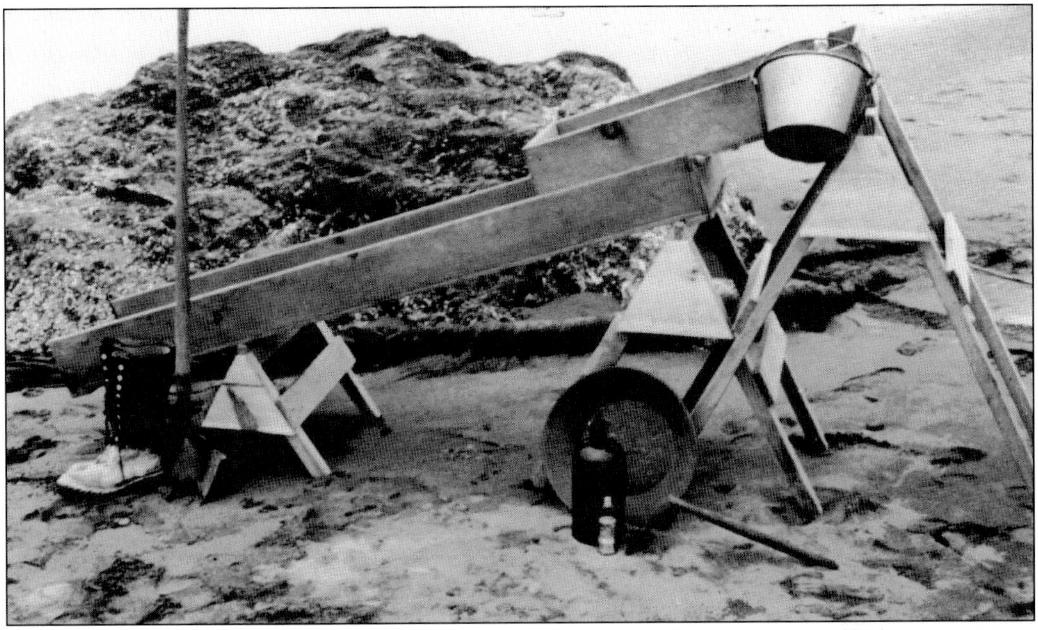

This is a piece of mining equipment that was used by miners for extracting gold from the black sand of the beach. It is called a sluice box and was more commonly used for black-sand mining than in the bigger areas or mines. Miners made fair wages but had to rely on working at just the right time, especially with the tides. Many times, they had to do their mining by lantern light at night with a low tide. (CHS.)

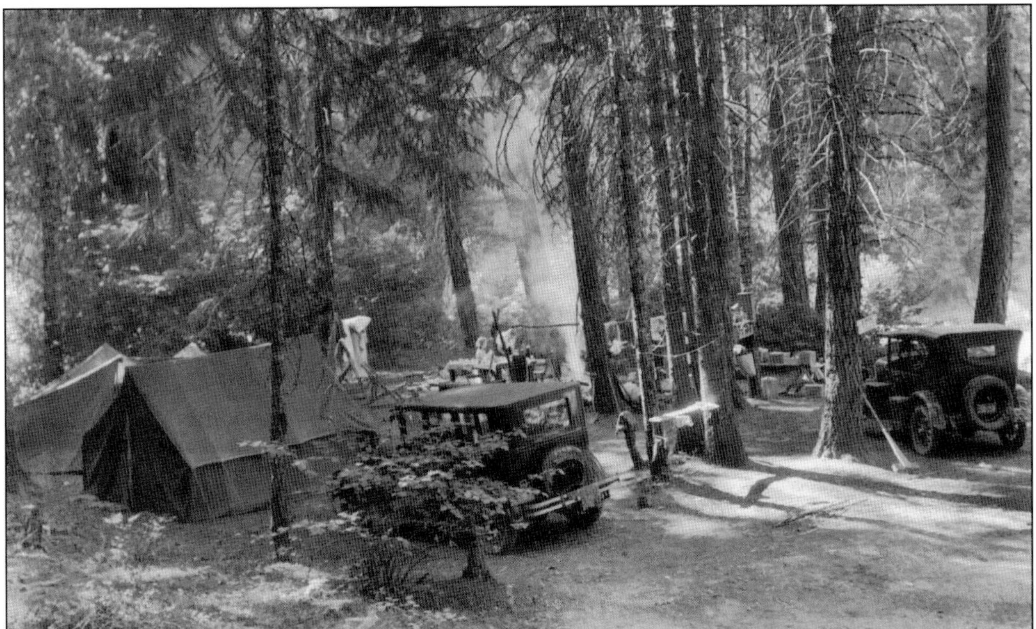

Gilbert Gable, one of the earlier residents of Port Orford, was an affluent businessman of that era. He was the owner of the Inman Mine camp on the Sixes River and was also one of the organizers in the planning of the state of Jefferson. He lived in Port Orford and was a chief executive officer of several business enterprises. (CHS.)

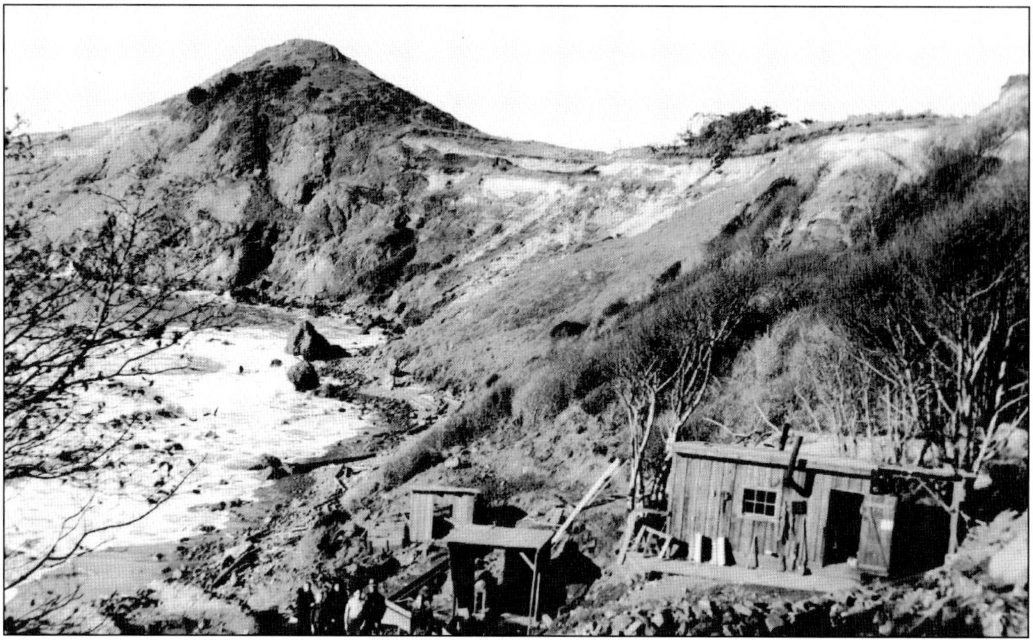

During the gold rush, a mine was built on Hubbard Mound for mining the black sand and was named the Madden Mine. It is about seven miles north of Gold Beach on the Old Coast Highway. Today, it is a good spot to walk out and enjoy the sight of the Pacific Ocean. Many beautiful homes were built out by the mound, sitting above the beach with a view of the ocean and the sunsets from their homes. Like snowflakes, no two amazing sunsets are alike. (CHS.)

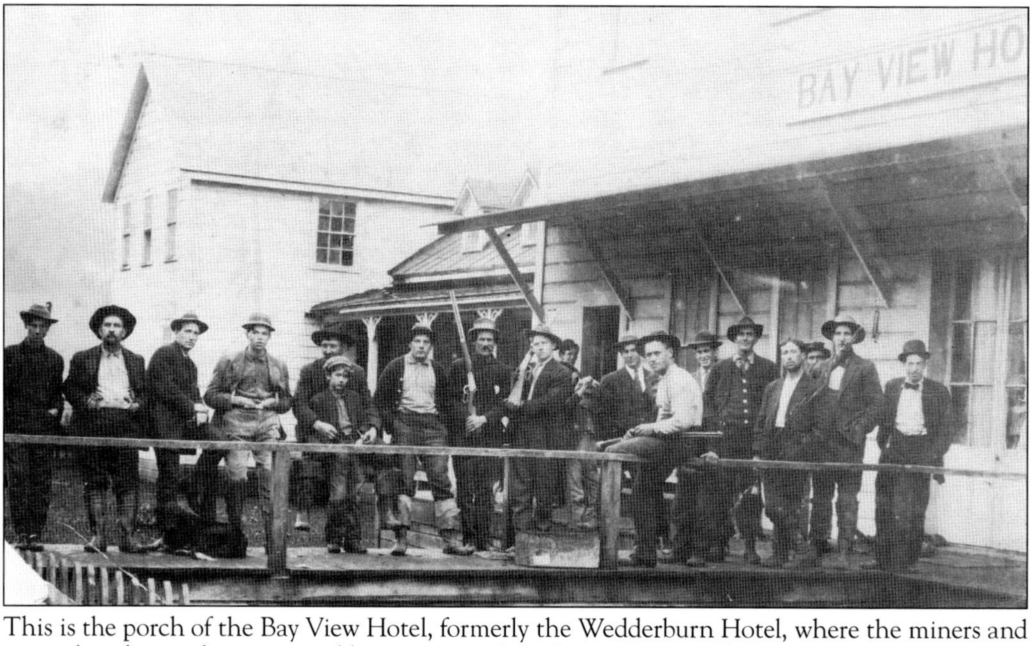

This is the porch of the Bay View Hotel, formerly the Wedderburn Hotel, where the miners and guests loved to sit for a visit and have a view of the Rogue River and the Pacific Ocean. It was a way to pass the time after mining or fishing all day. It was often time to smoke a good cigar and have a few drinks. (CHS.)

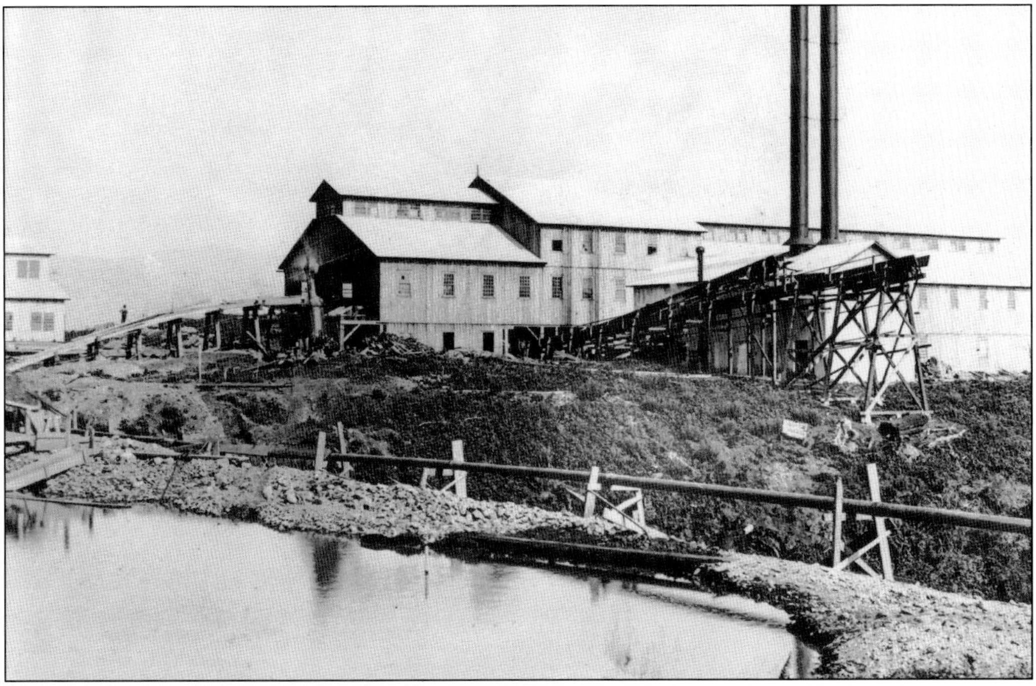

This building was located at the Brookings C&O Lumber Co. It was the mill where logs were cut and dropped into the holding pond. The logs were loaded on the train across the Chetco River to take them to the ships ready for passage to San Francisco. The train's route went to Northern California and up the Chetco River for three miles. (CHS.)

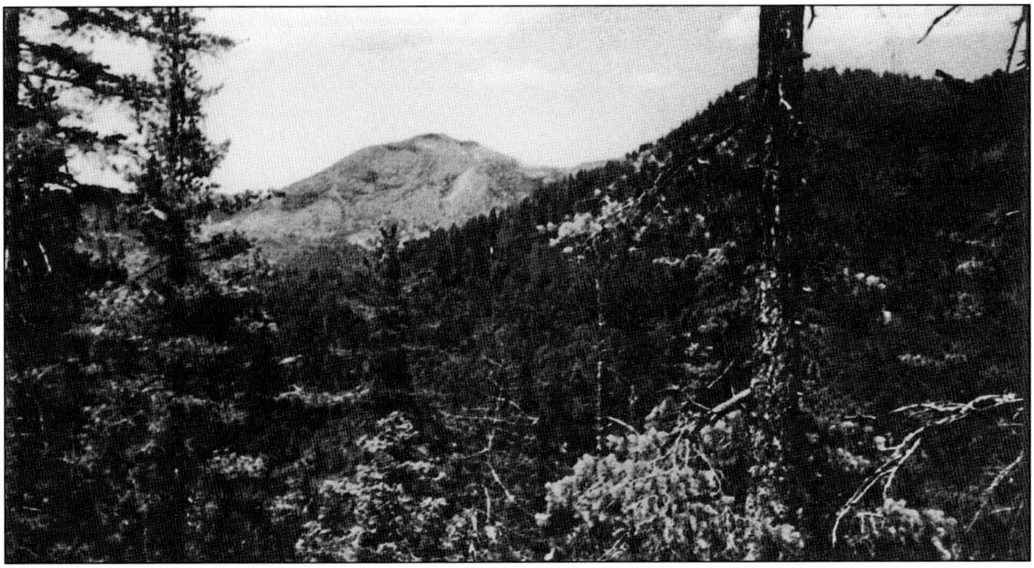

This is photograph of the Kalmiopsis Wilderness. Its location is between Brookings and Gold Beach in the eastern part of Josephine County. During summer, more experienced hikers are able to try to reach its summit at Pearsall Peak. It also connects with the Illinois River. It covers 180,095 acres of true wilderness. Elevation ranges from 500 to 5,098 feet (Pearsall Peak). Its deep, rough canyons; sharp rocks; ridges; and clear mountain streams and rivers add to its character; all of it is located in Oregon. (CHS.)

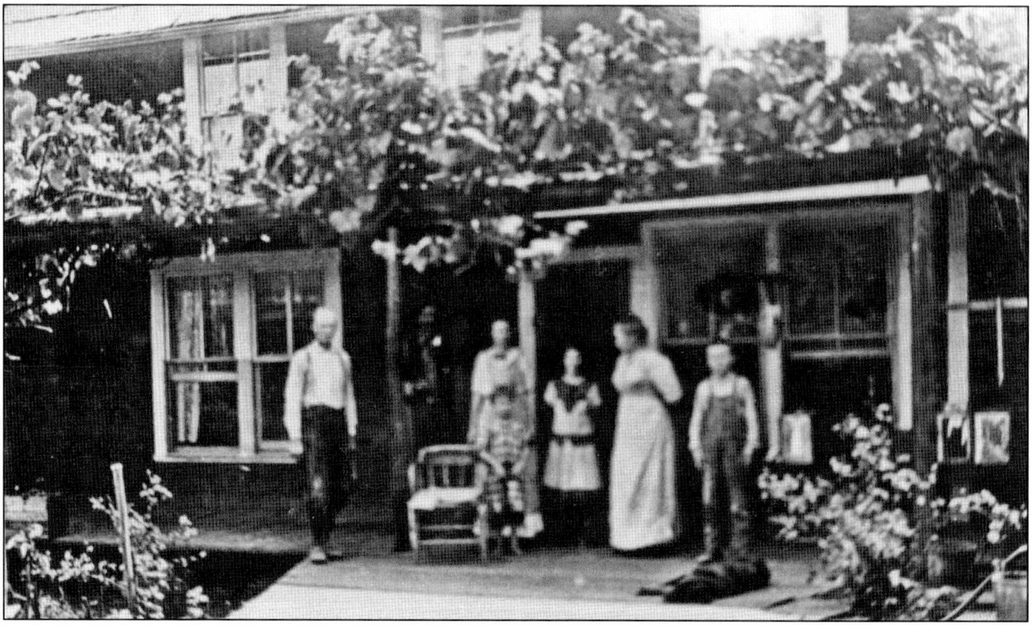

Here is the Agness Hotel with J.D. Cooley as proprietor. In the early 1900s, the first hotel in Agness was on the south side of the river, where it was noted as Old Agness. A second hotel that is now known as the Lucas Lodge later replaced it. It is a stopping place for lunch for the passengers on the shorter trips offered by Jerry's Rogue Jets and Mail Boats. It was famous for its corn on the cob. It is a homey lodge with a few rooms for overnight. (CHS.)

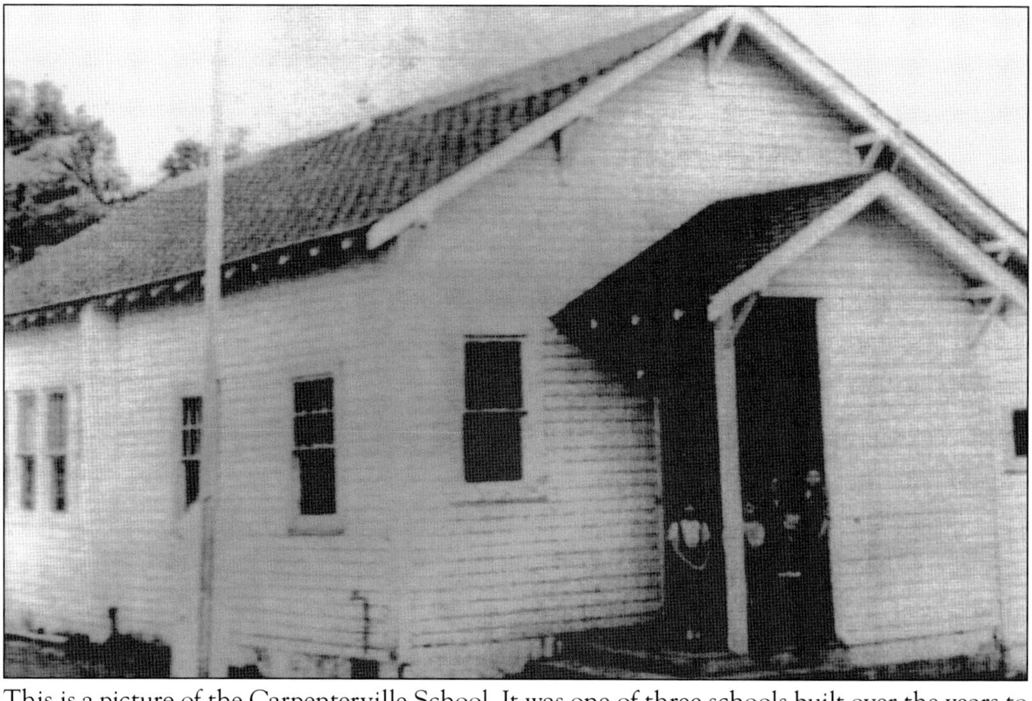

This is a picture of the Carpenterville School. It was one of three schools built over the years to accommodate the children living in Carpenterville. This included the Carpenters, the Ralphs, the Meades, and other families over the years. (CHS.)

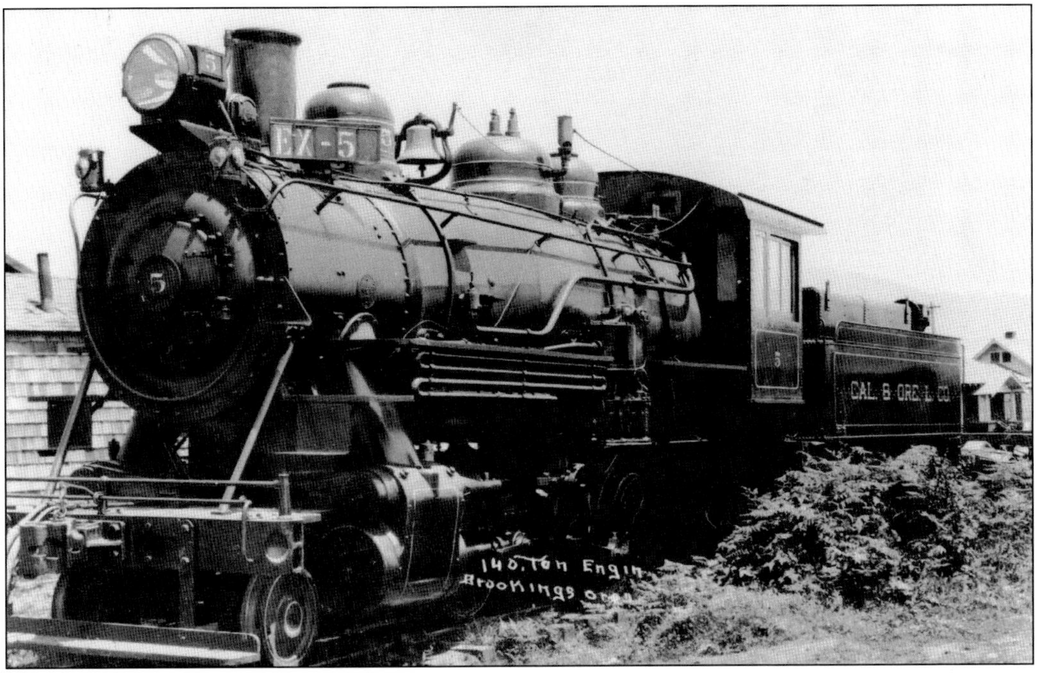

The chief train engine on the Chetco Railroad Bridge is ready to transport the logs for the C&O Lumber Co. in 1914. The lead engine was flat, and the men sat on top of the frame. Later they brought in the larger closed engine to pull the two cars. (CHS.)

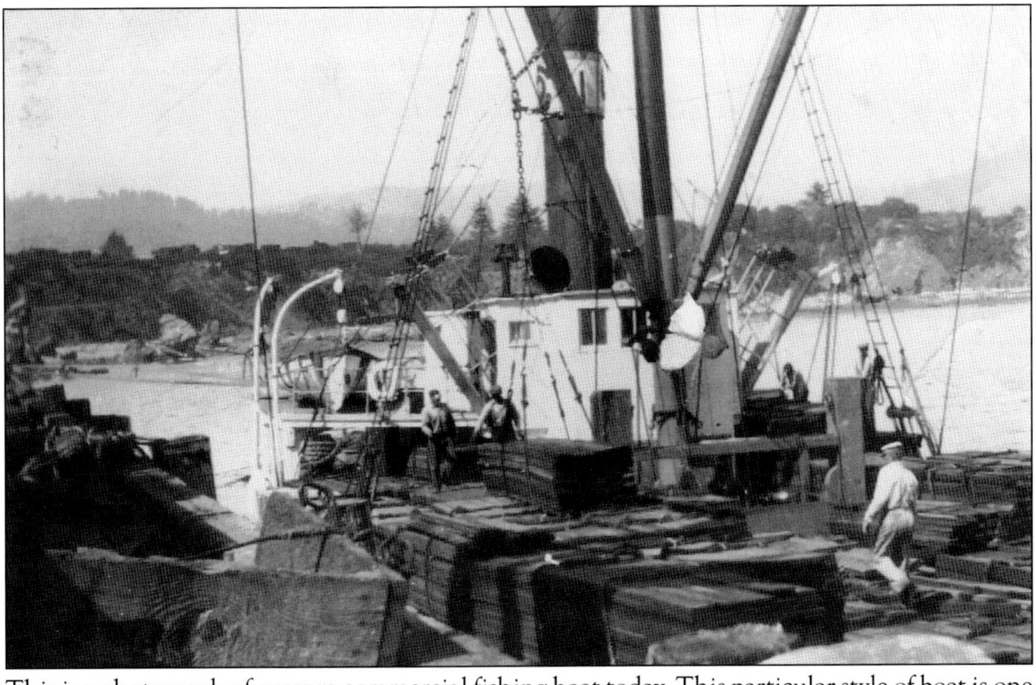

This is a photograph of average commercial fishing boat today. This particular style of boat is one that goes out to sea to fish not only for salmon but also for bottom fish, red and black snappers, and tuna. In the first part of the year, these boats set out crab pots close to the surf, supplying the towns with more seafood. (CHS.)

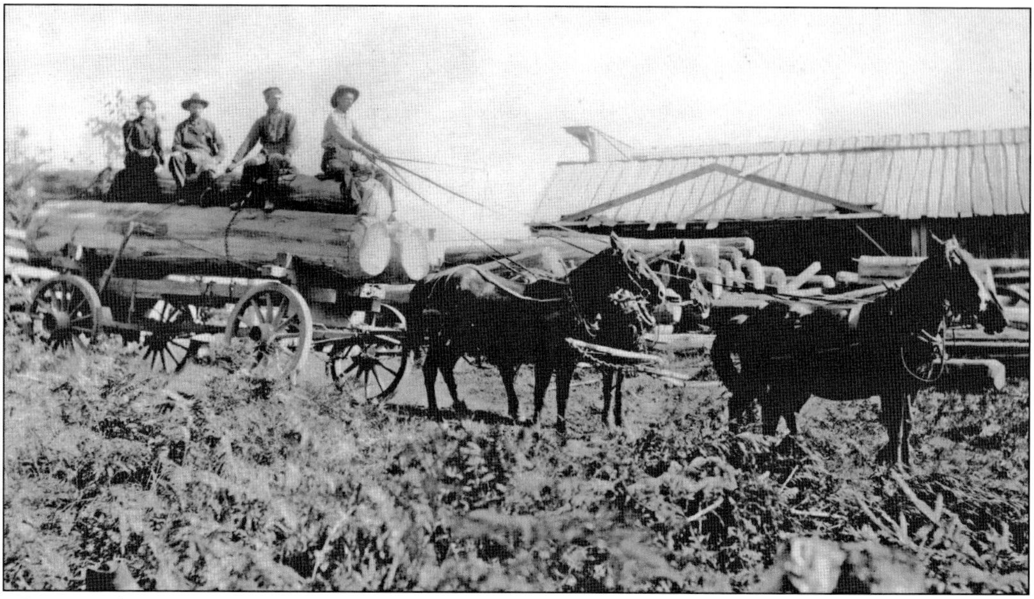

This was the way logs were hauled in earlier times before the use of logging trucks. This is a farmer transporting logs that were probably going to be used for the construction of his home or a neighbor's. (CHS.)

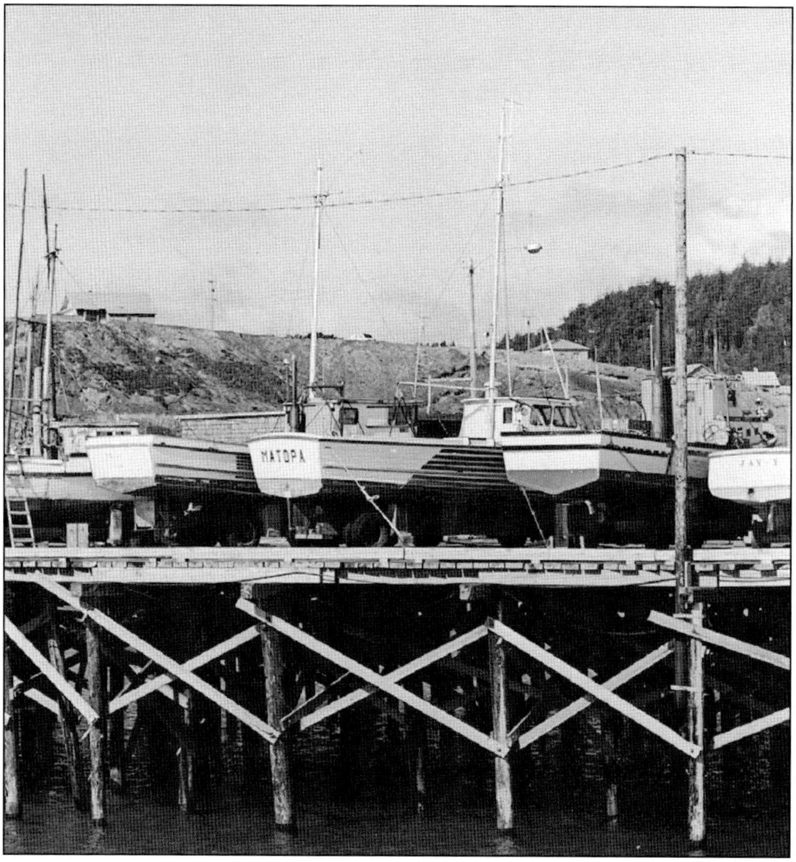

The port of Brookings is a large harbor, and in September 2011, it was touched by a small tsunami; it did some damage to the port. Several boats were damaged, and some were destroyed. Citizens of Gold Beach were fortunate that there was no damage to their port. (CHS.)

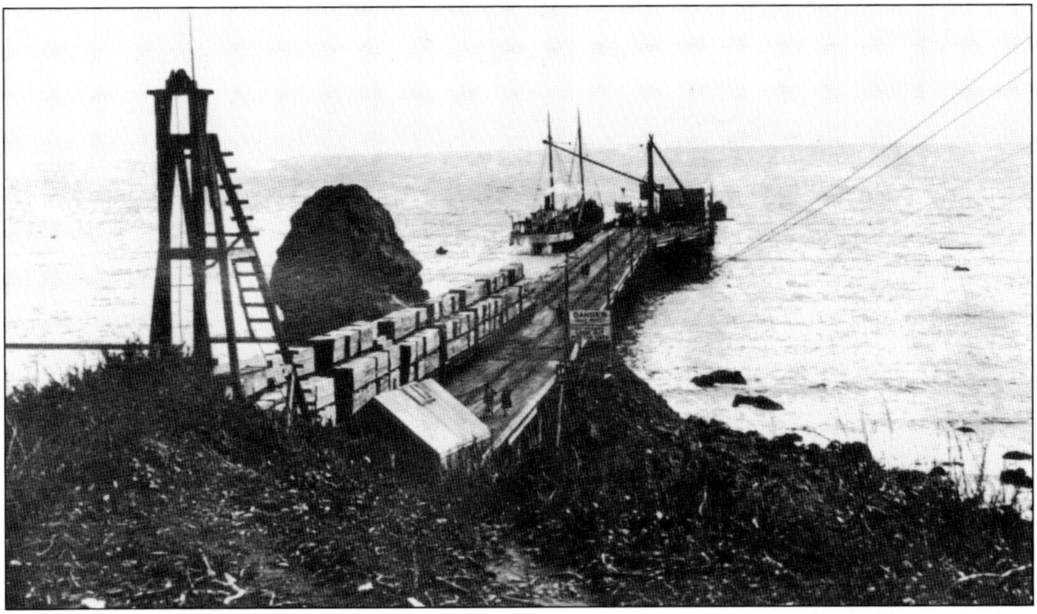

When the C&O Lumber Co. was in full swing in the running of the mill, blocks, tackles, and cables helped to load the lumber onto waiting ships that were to travel to San Francisco. (CHS.)

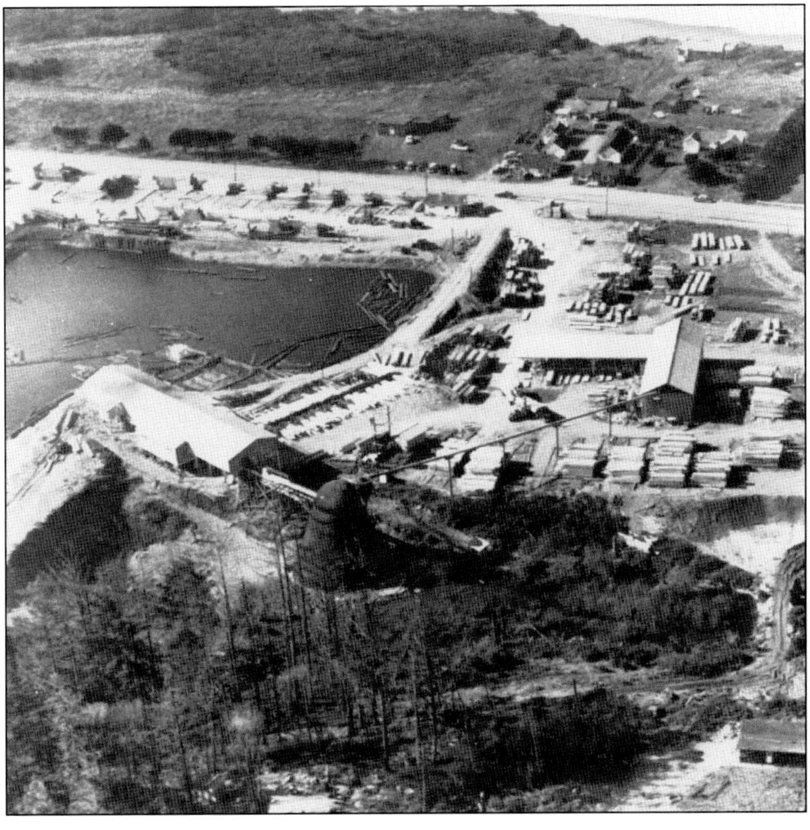

Herb Crook and Oliver Betts built a large mill at Nesika Beach in the 1950s. It was used by many of the small Gypo Logging companies. This was prior to the building of US plywood mill on Jerrys Flat Road on the north bank of the Rogue River. At the same time, Milt Morsing built a large Red and White Store at Nesika Beach. It was a great store but closed when the mill closed. (CHS.)

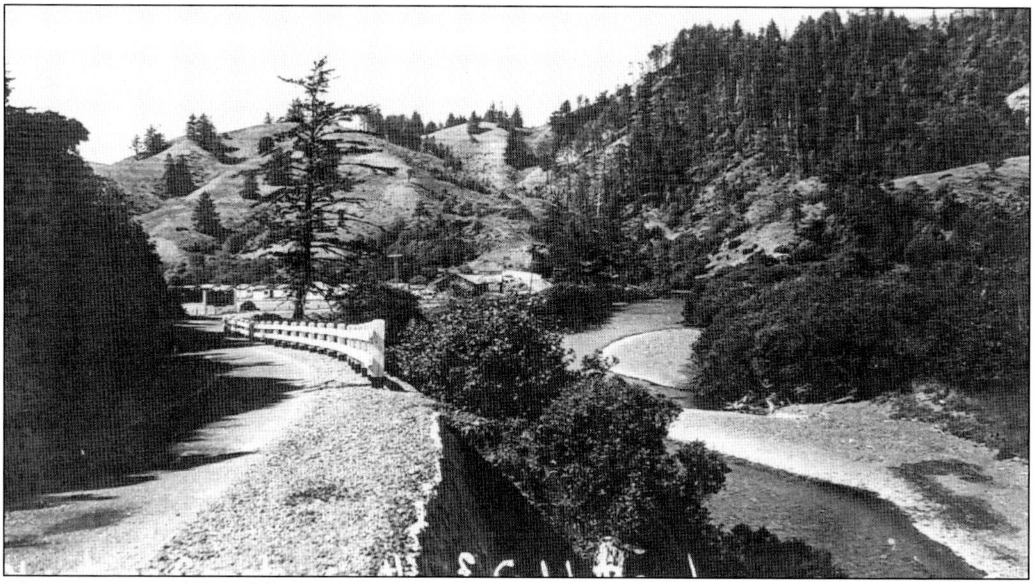

This picture is of the old Roosevelt Highway running through Hunters Creek, located south of Gold Beach, which is now known as Hunters Creek Loop. The new Highway 101 bypassed this area. It now hosts Gold Beach Lumberyard, Sorenson's Automotive, a small store, Engdahl's automotive body repair, Freeman Marine Equipment, and Sunrise Distributers. There is a small community of families living along the creek. (CHS.)

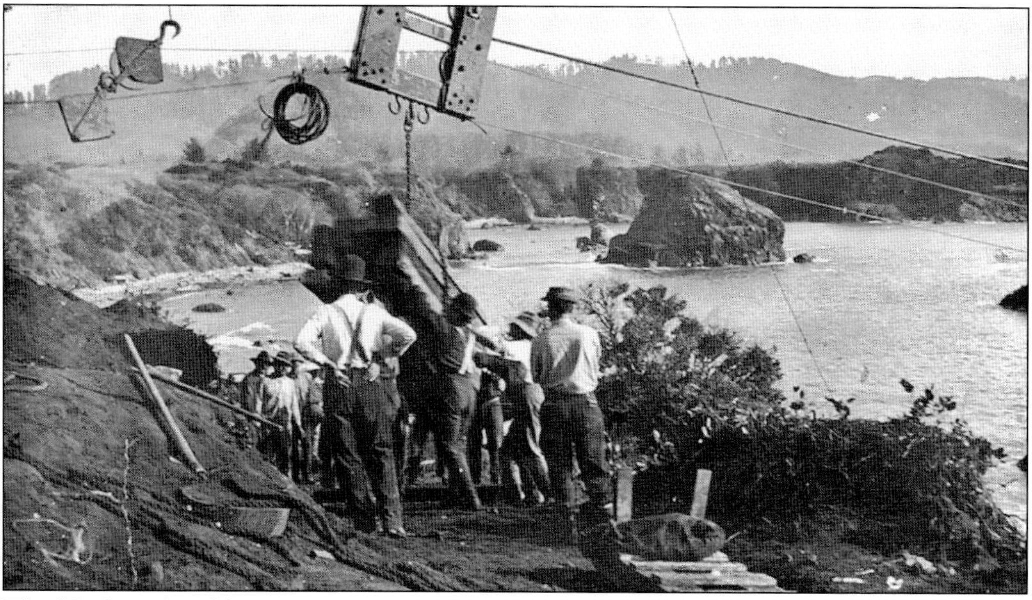

The block-and-tackle setup was necessary to load the logs and lumber onto ships. It was built at the water's edge so it could be transferred to where it was needed. This setup was in Brookings. (CHS.)

Along with the myrtlewood being special in Curry County, so are the redwoods, which grow in the southern part of the county in the Brookings-Harbor area and in Northern California. Also, Easter lilies are found on the southern coast. At one time, lily fields were grown in Gold Beach, but now the base for harvesting lilies is in Harbor. (CHS.)

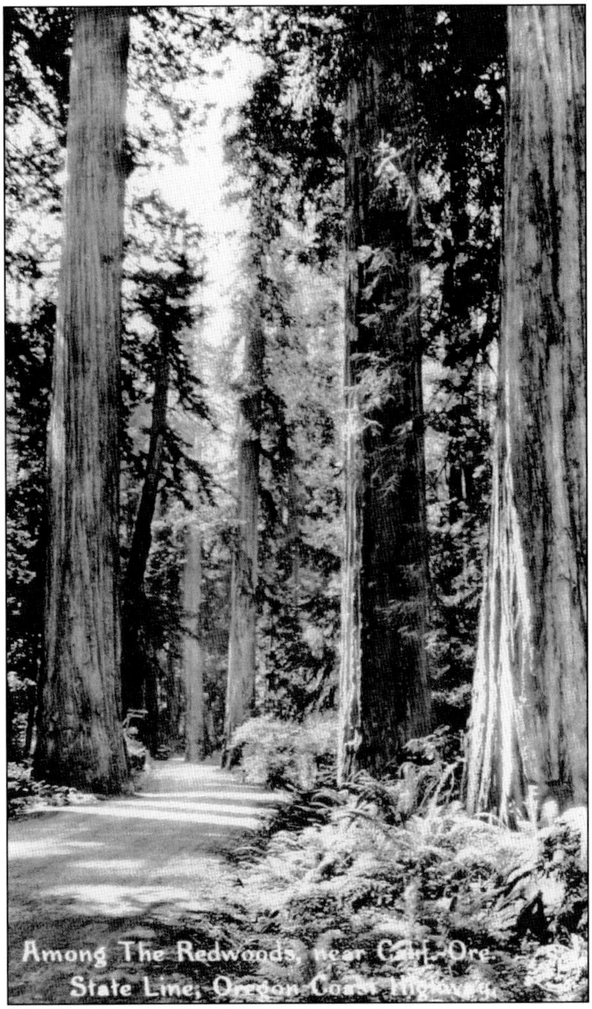

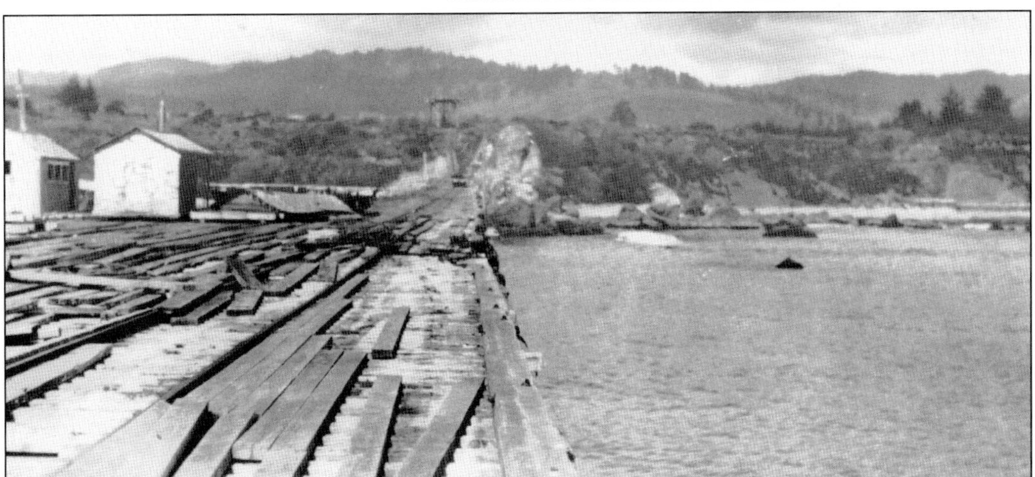

This was the platform that products waited on to be loaded onto ships. (CHS.)

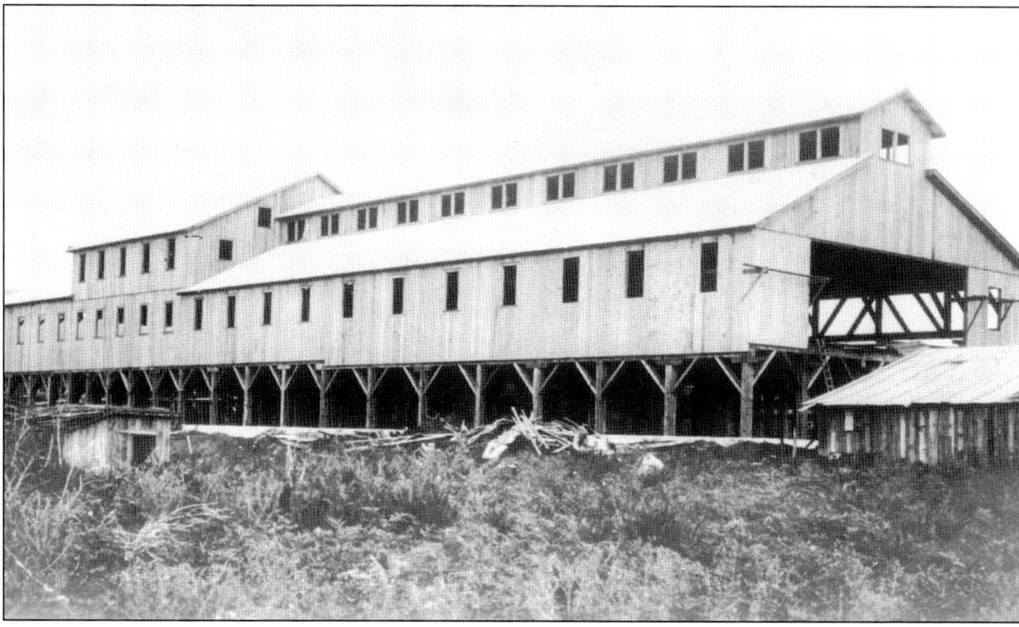

Up Elk River, Henry Adolphson built a plywood mill in the early 1930s, and this was the beginning of trucks hauling logs instead of horses and oxen. (CHS.)

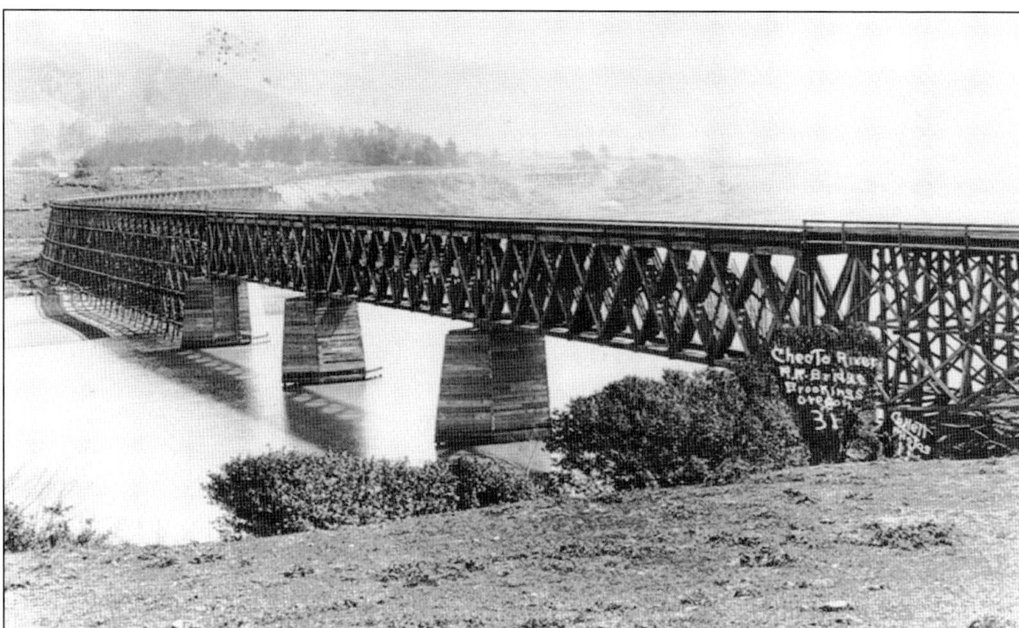

The Brookings train trestle was built by the C&O Lumber Co. in 1914, and when it closed down and left the area, the tracks remained for several years before being taken down. A new auto bridge was built across the Chetco River. The track crossed the Chetco River, ran three miles up the South Chetco River, and crossed the state line into Smith River, California. One day, the whistle blew and the doors of C&O Lumber Co. were closed, never to open again. (CHS.)

Brushes Creek lies along Highway 101, and when Gov. Earl Snell saw the quiet stream at the base of the mountain, he decided not to bypass the area. It flows into the Pacific Ocean and was named Savage Creek at one time. It flows by the entrance of Humbug State Park and farther north through the day camp/picnic area that was built by Oregon State Parks. It was later named after Gilbert Brush, who discovered the creek while exploring the new territory. Sadly, he was partially scalped by the Coquille Indian tribe, but he managed to survive. (CHS.)

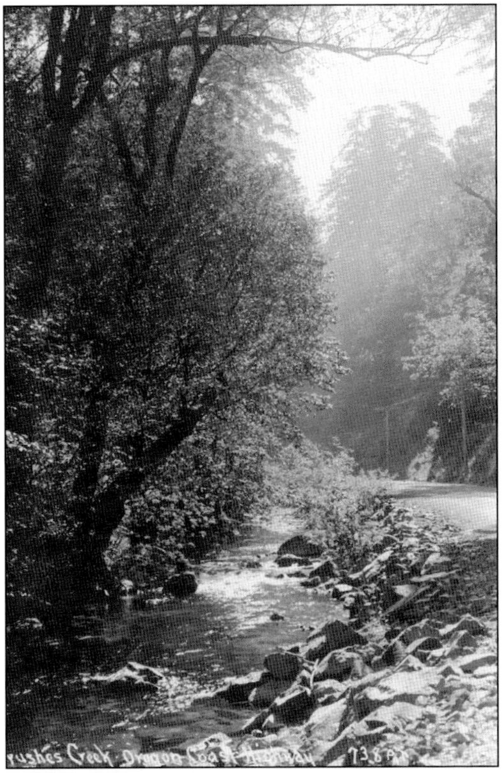

The redwood stump in this photograph was large enough to allow 12 men to stand on it. The redwoods are not only in Northern California but also along the southern Oregon coast. They are now protected, and logging is no longer an option. (CHS.)

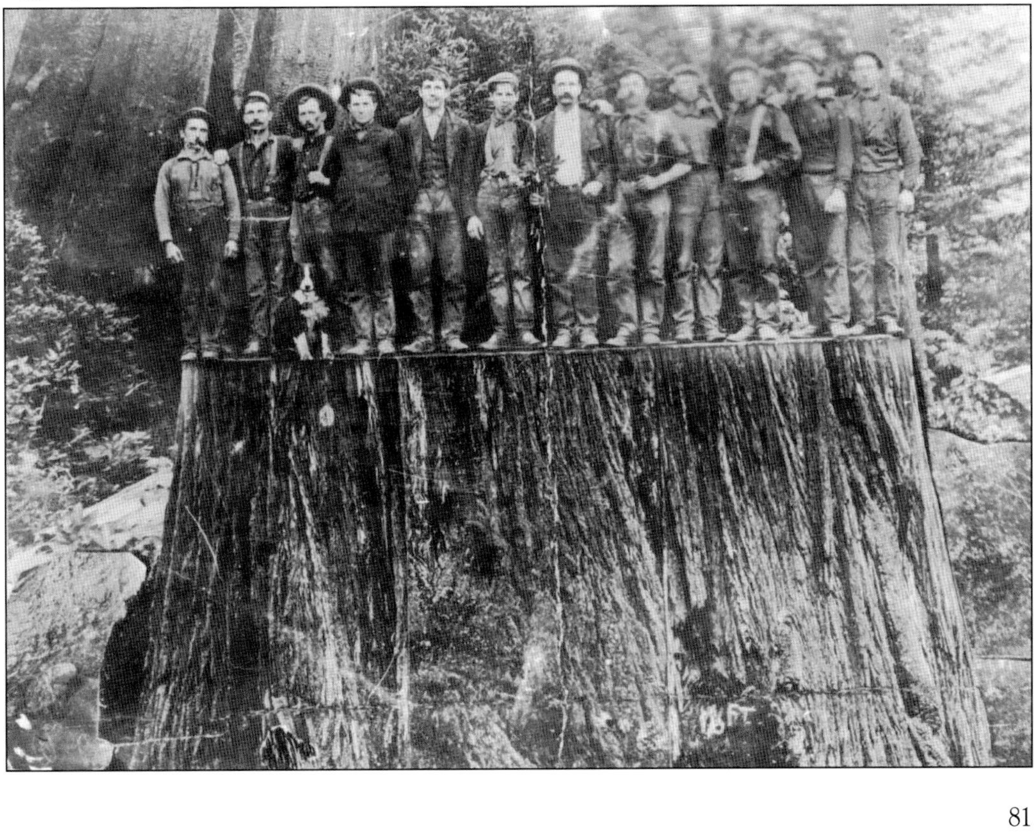

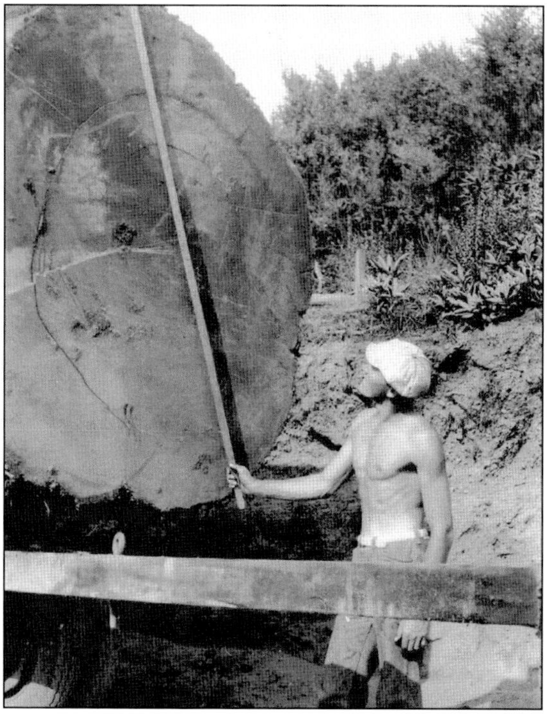

This young man is measuring this large log, which is already loaded, to make sure it is not too high for the weigh station. By the 1970s, there were certain government regulations concerning the height and weight of loads that had to be followed. (CHS.)

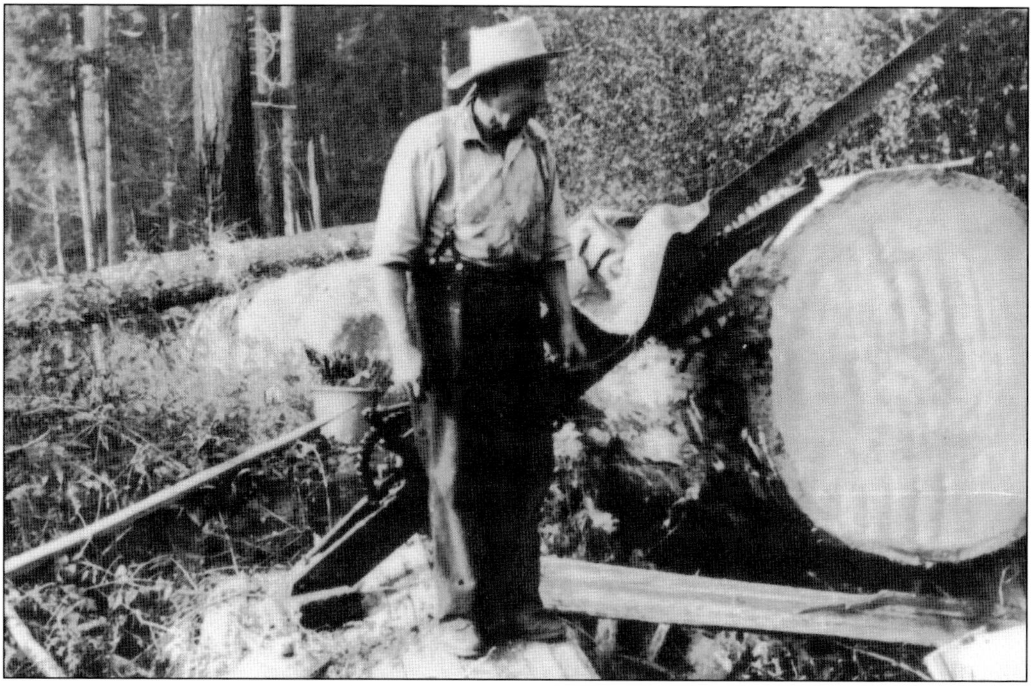

Otto Ismert is seen working his drag saw. The drag saw came into use in the late 1930s. It had a small motor at the base of two wooden planks with a pulley attached to the bottom of a regular crosscut saw. The little gas engine would turn the pulley, and it would cut right through the large logs. And it would not take long to cut large blocks off, making it easier to chop logs for firewood. (CHS.)

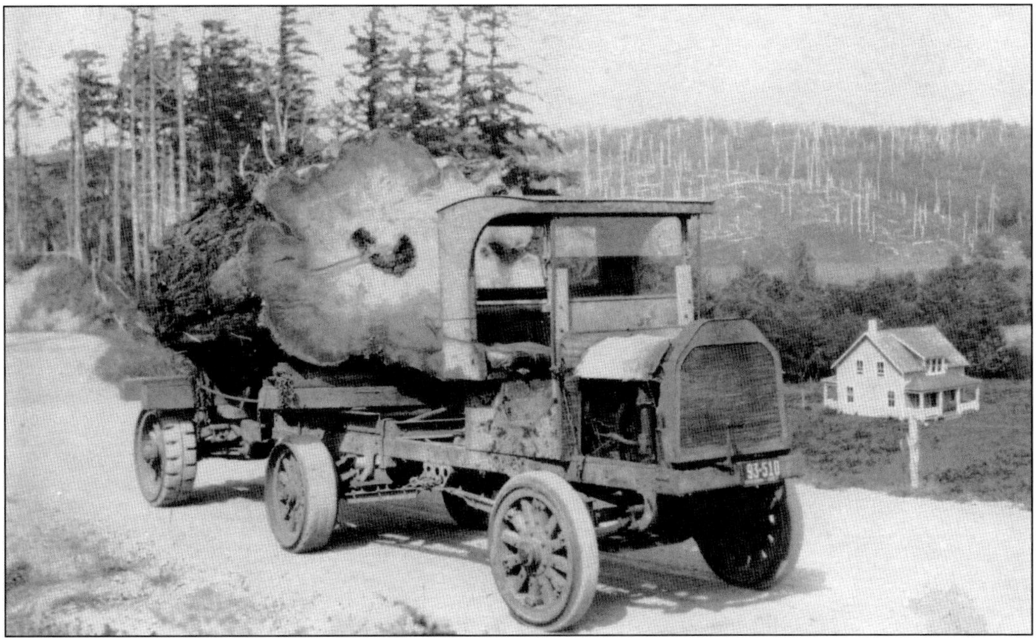

These photographs show two different logging trucks from two different eras. The one shown above is from the early 1920s, and the one below is from the late 1930s. Logging was a large industry before the change in the regulations by the government. The Rogue River had been designated as one of eight national rivers to be under the direction of the US Forest Service and the Bureau of Land Management. This caused the closure of most of the mills, and today, there is only one mill left in Curry County, which can be found in Brookings. (Both, CHS.)

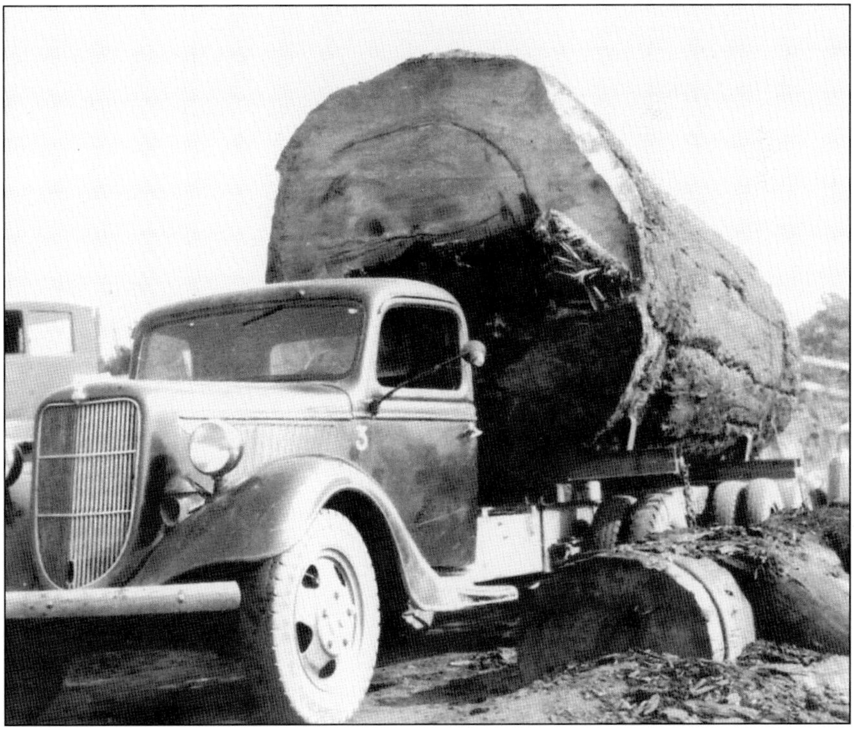

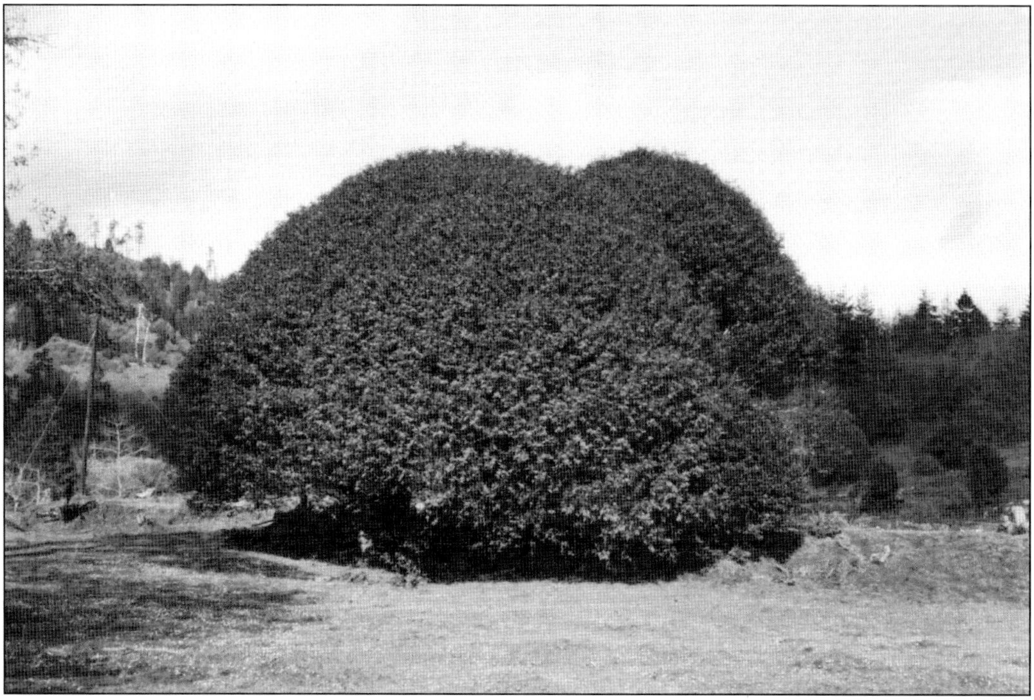

In Curry County, there grows a tree known as the myrtlewood. There are only two places this tree grows, here and the Holy Land. It is a beautiful wood, and when aged and polished, many myrtlewood shops make lovely gifts from this special wood. (CHS.)

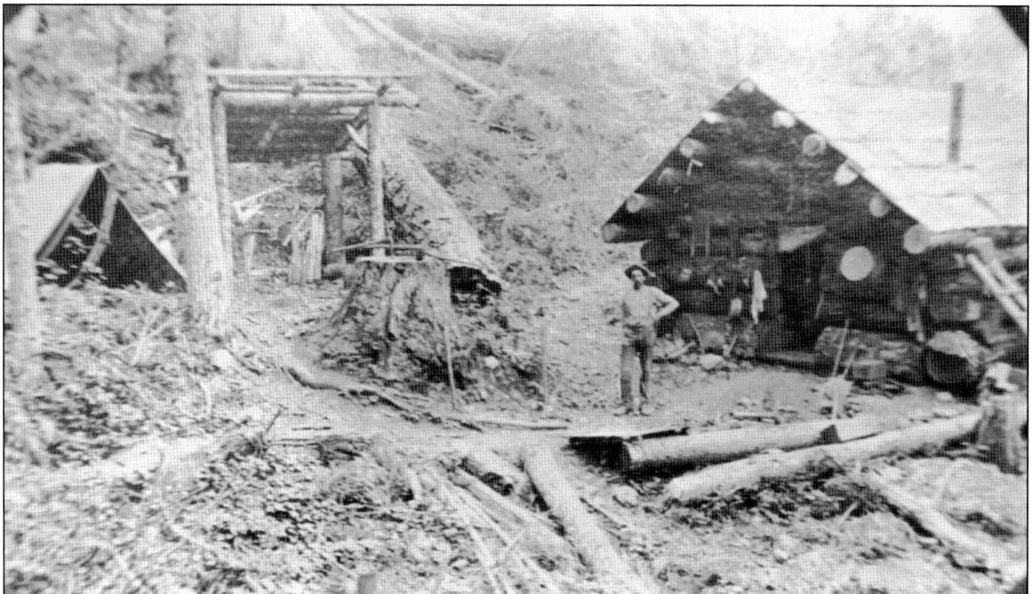

On China Mountain, behind Port Orford, was where many gold mine claims were in the early 1900s. Many miners worked their claims, and this is a mining tunnel owned by the miners. A meteorite was found in this area in the 1800s. A gentleman wrote in his diary of his find and sent a sample of the meteorite to the capital, but the actual meteorite has never been found since that time. Also, it is rumored that Bigfoot has been sighted here. (CHS.)

Five

Roads, Highways, and Bridges of Curry County

Curry County is a special place that has much to offer to locals, visitors, and those passing through. Gold Beach sits above the waterline of the ocean and the Rogue River. For many years, Curry County was isolated due to the lack of roads between counties. The first road was a wagon road made from backbreaking labor, mules, horses, picks, and shovels. It was a one-lane road. If two wagons met, they had to dismantle one wagon, let the other go through, and then restore the dismantled wagon and go on their way. Most of this road followed the original Indian trail, which crossed the beach at times. The animals had a hard time pulling wagons across the wet sand, and occasionally, animals were lost in the heavy surf.

In 1920, construction was begun on the Roosevelt Highway, and it was finished in 1937. Besides the highway, many bridges had to be built, which took many years to complete. The highway was from Coos Bay to the state line. In the 1950s, Highway 101 was completed, and it runs the full length of the Oregon Coast today. This granted travelers and sightseers access to the many vistas.

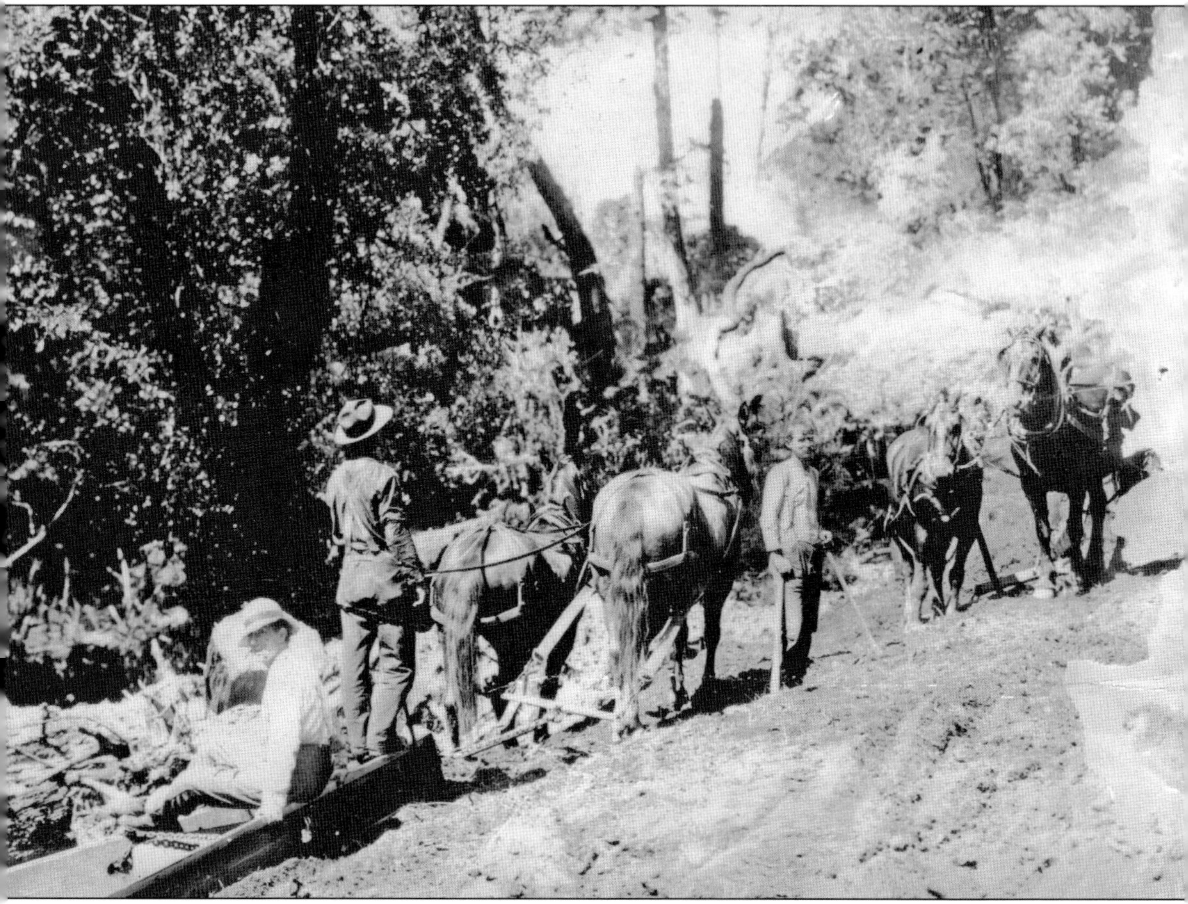

In the mid-1800s, the first road was built by the labor of the men, mules, and horses. It often followed the path of the trail that the Indians used along the beach, cutting through trees and brush when necessary. It was a one-lane road, and if two wagons met on the narrow lane, one wagon had to be dismantled and set aside to let the oncoming wagon pass through, and then the two wagon owners would repair the dismantled wagon and let it go on its way. Occasionally, there were inns where travelers could stop and refresh themselves and their horses with water. Sometimes when the ocean surf was high, it was very dangerous to pass through. This road was used prior to the construction of Roosevelt Highway. (CHS.)

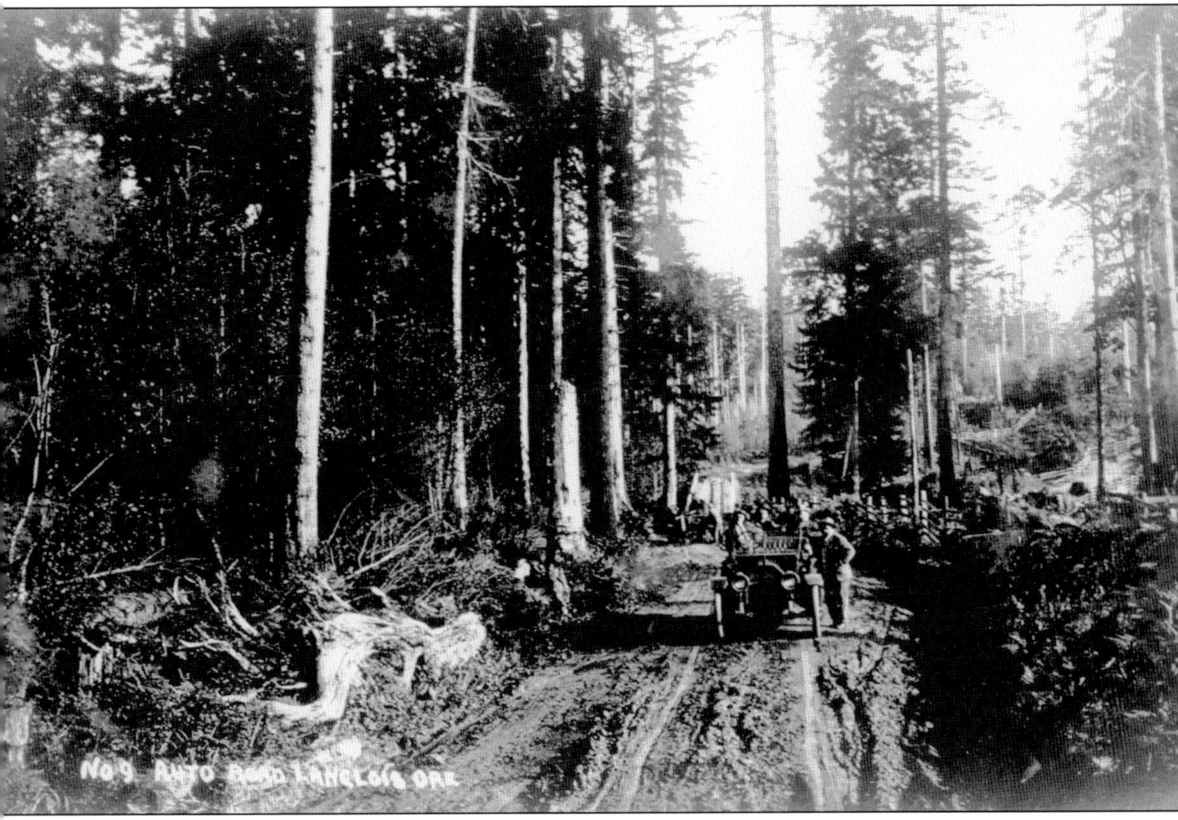

This is an early view of the new Roosevelt Highway. Having started in 1921, it took 16 years to complete, finishing in 1937. It ran the full length of the Oregon coast. There were many bridges that needed to be constructed, and one of the biggest was the Isaac Lee Patterson Bridge across the Rogue River. It was completed and opened to traffic on May 28, 1932, and was 1,932 feet long. It was known as one of the most beautiful bridges built. (CHS.)

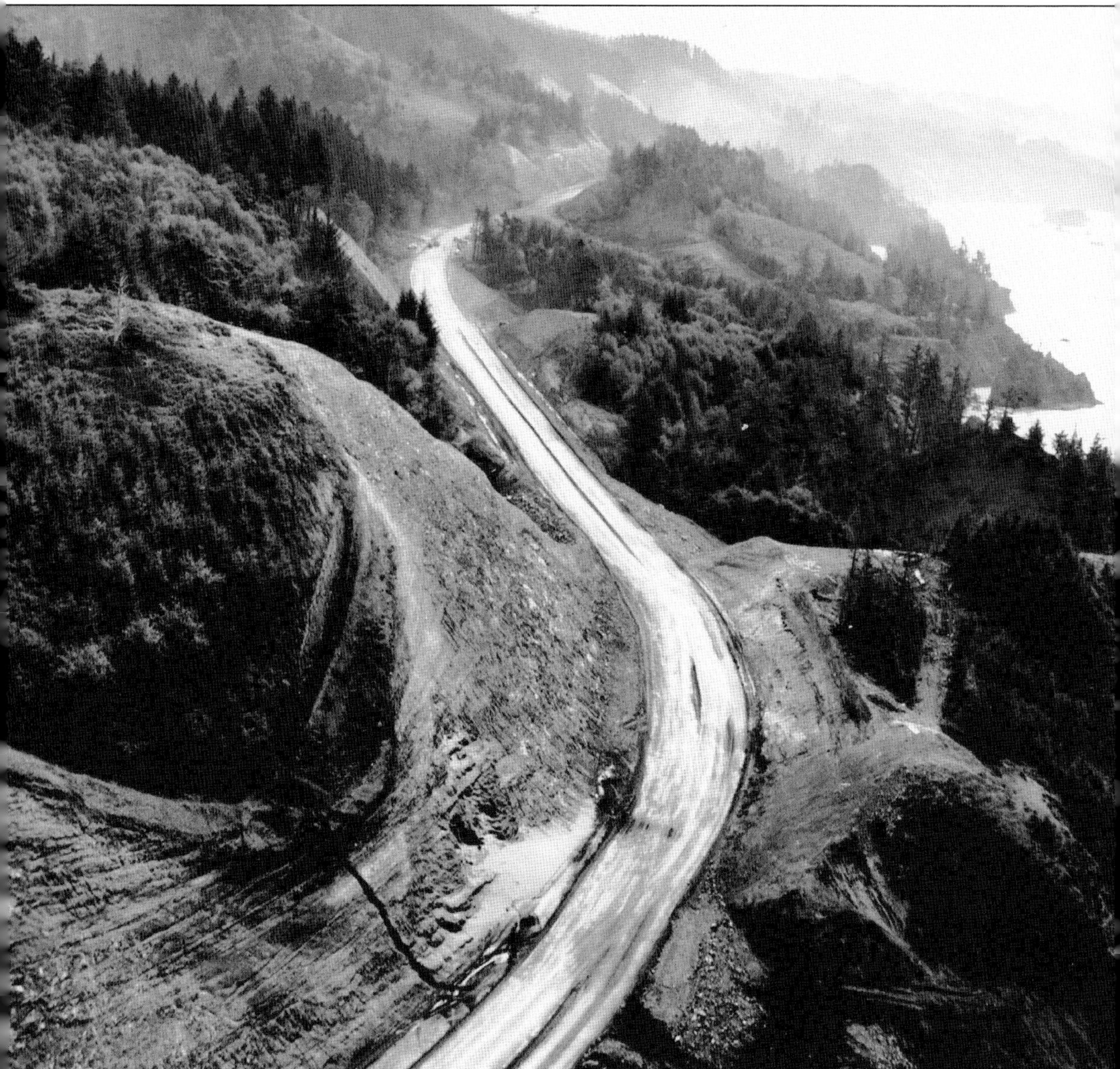

Here is the beginning of Highway 101, south of Brushes Creek and before Rocky Point. It follows the Pacific Ocean. The horizon is visible for several miles heading north toward Port Orford. It is a beautiful drive with turnouts for viewing. (CHS.)

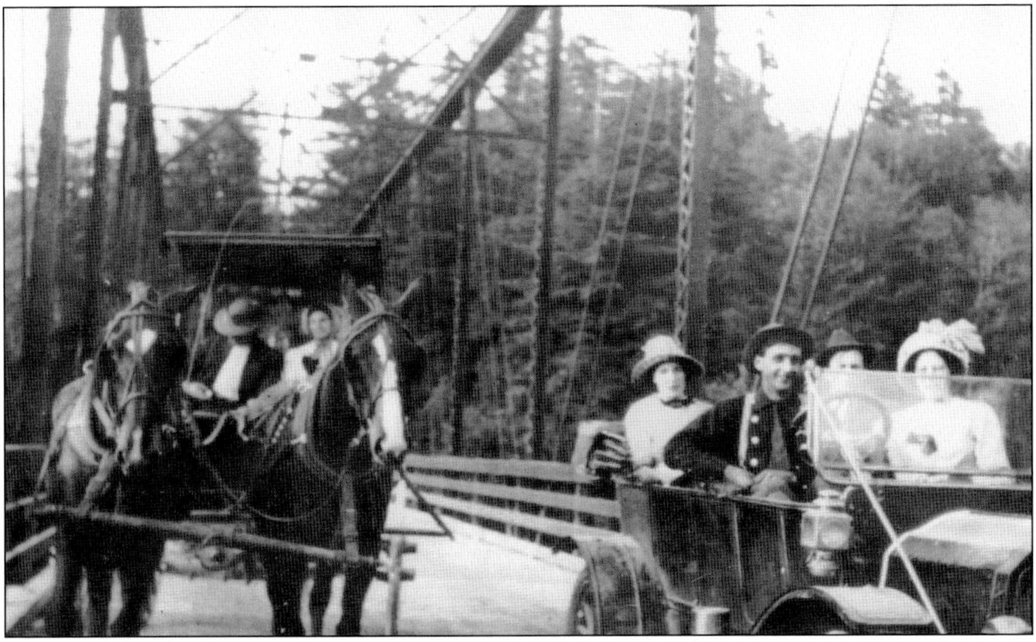

This photograph shows how traveling increased in the nation during the early 1930s. Here, an auto and a horse and buggy are advancing forward on the Chetco River Bridge. Everyone appears to be having a good time. (CHS.)

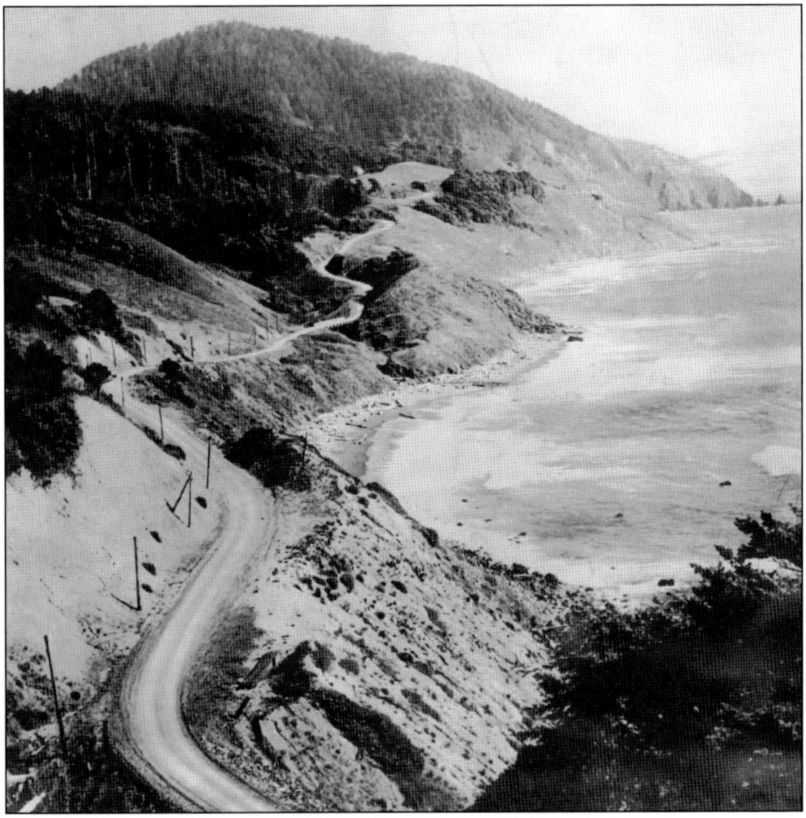

This picture of Highway 101 shows the section that is nestled between Brushes Creek at Humbug Mountain and Rocky Point just five miles south of Port Orford. It runs parallel to the ocean. (CHS.)

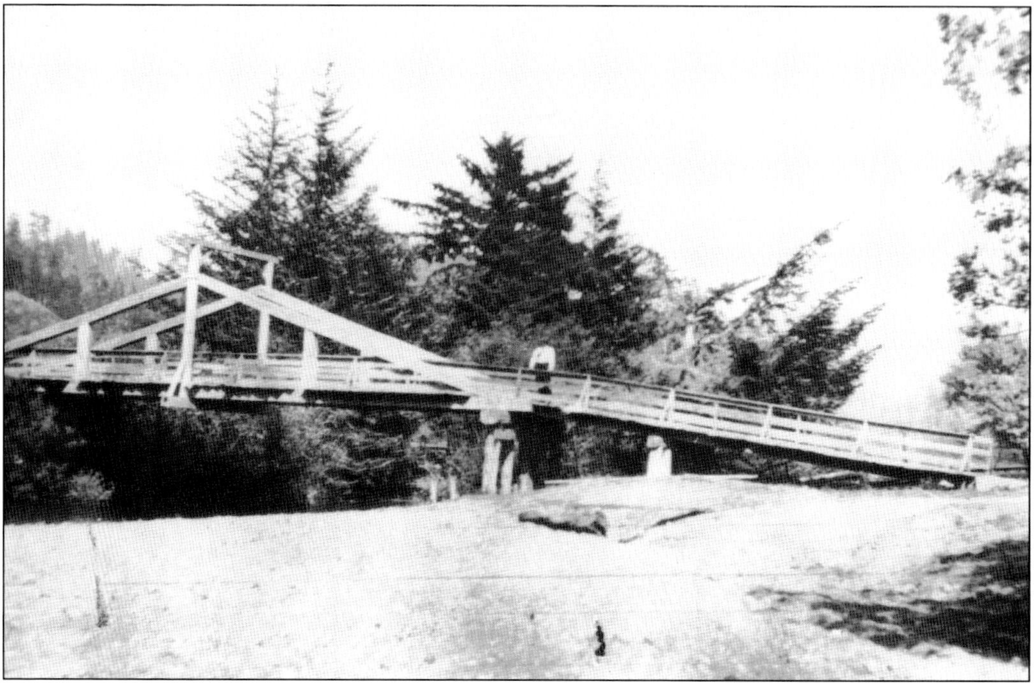

This is the first Flores Creek Bridge in the early 1900s. There were many dairy and berry farms, a cheese factory, and farms near Langlois and on up the creek. Several families farmed there and raised hogs, cattle, gardens, fruit orchards. The forests were logged for their homes. These were their sources to survive. The bridge was built and maintained by the owners of the farms. (CHS.)

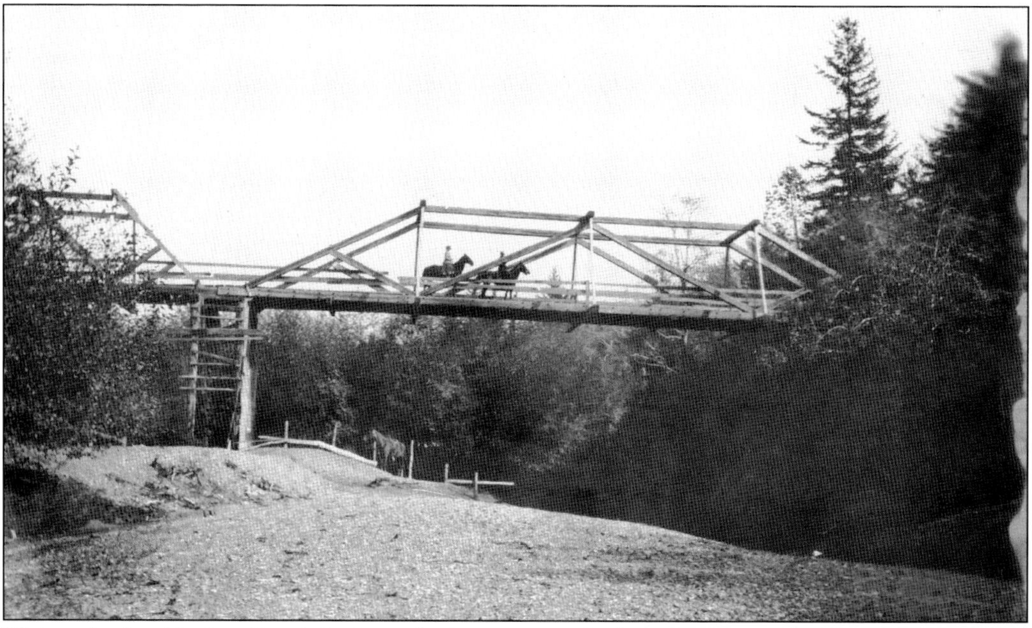

This is the first Euchre Creek Bridge, which was crossed when driving on the Roosevelt Highway on China Mountain. When Highway 101 was built, a new bridge was constructed. The new highway followed the shoreline of the ocean. All who drive 101 will enjoy its continuous view from Port Orford to Brookings. (CHS.)

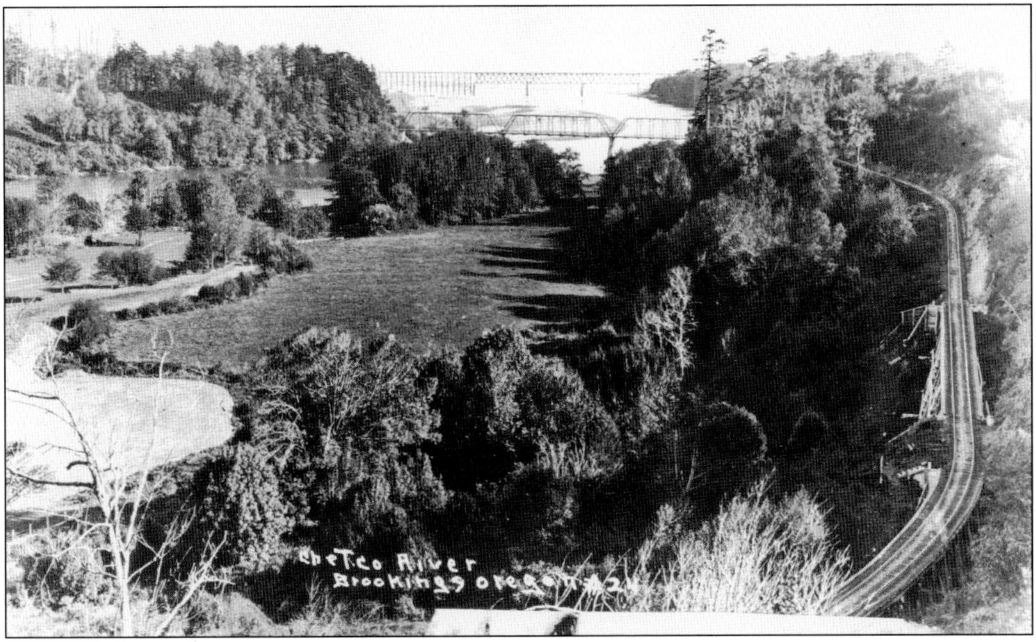

For several years in the 1920s, a railroad bridge and a bridge for wagons and cars spanned the Chetco River; the bridges appeared as such when viewed through the trees on the side of the road. Later, the railroad bridge was torn down and the other one crashed, and so a new bridge was built. Today, it still spans the Chetco River, connecting Brookings and Harbor. (CHS.)

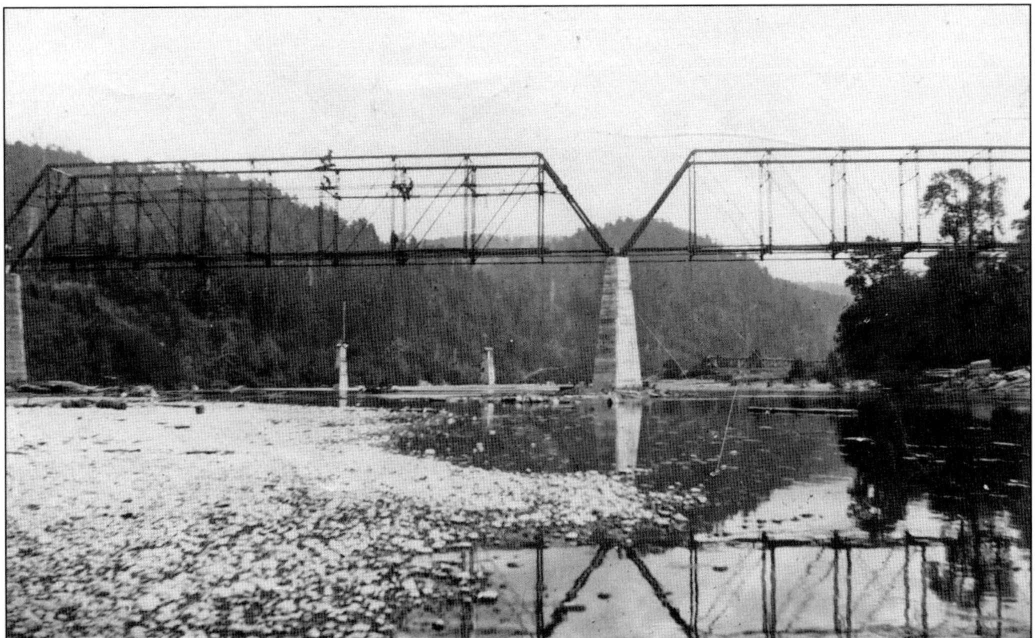

Here is the first bridge connecting Brookings and Harbor. It was necessary to construct this bridge when the ferries were no longer able to keep up with the added traffic of automobiles. It was used until the failure of both the auto and train bridges. At this time, a new auto bridge was constructed. (CHS.)

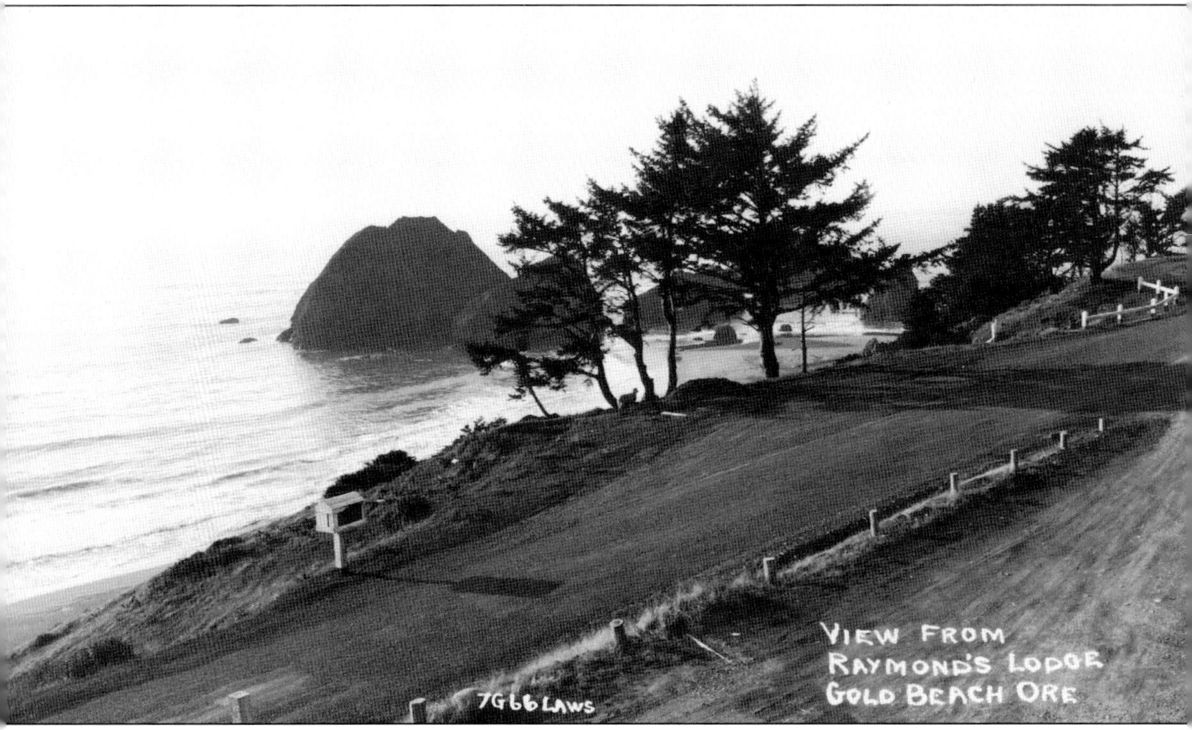

This is the view from the decks of the Raymond's Lodge, also known as Wildwood Lodge. It was a lovely lodge, and the Roosevelt Highway ran right by in the front, with Highway 101 just below it. In later years, it no longer was used as a lodge but was instead rented to two gentlemen as caretakers. It burned to the ground in the 1960s. The nicest part of this area is that the beach is perfect for walking, clamming, making campfires, or just enjoying the views. (CHS.)

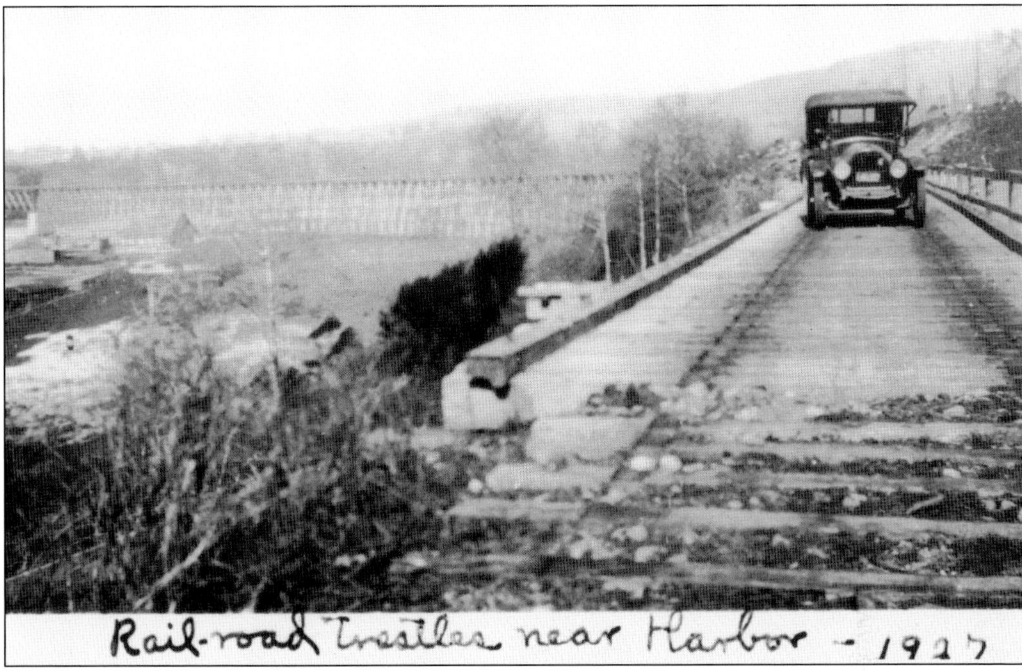

Automobiles are using the train track bridge to travel up the north bank of the Chetco River. The trestle traversed Chetco River about three miles. It was a safe way to transport supplies upriver to the farmers who had their homes in that area. (CHS.)

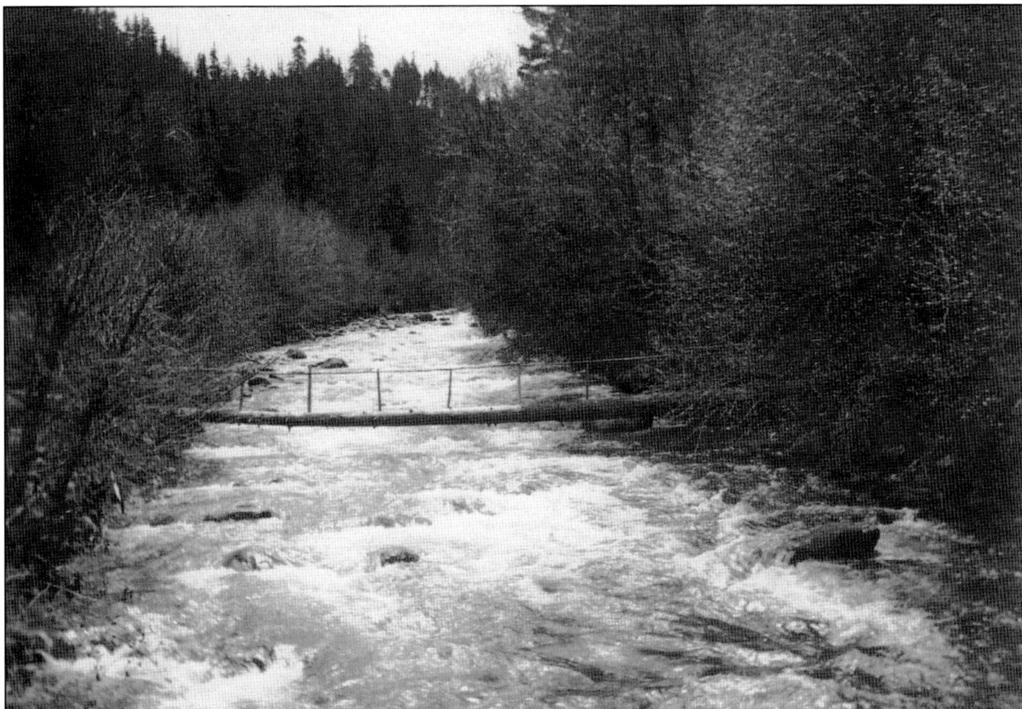

This suspension bridge was used to cross the Rogue River at Marial. This bridge is no longer standing. It was an important part of the lives of the families at Marial. (CHS.)

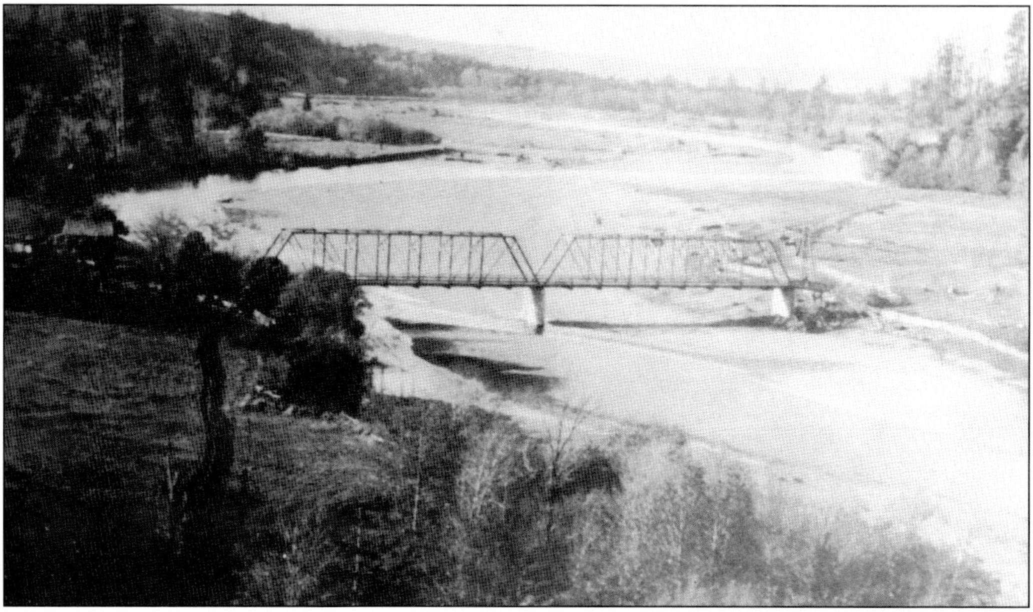

When the Roosevelt Highway was completed, workers built this steel bridge over the Pistol River. At later date, they built the smaller bridge and the bridge on the new Highway 101. The mouth of the Pistol River flows here. (CHS.)

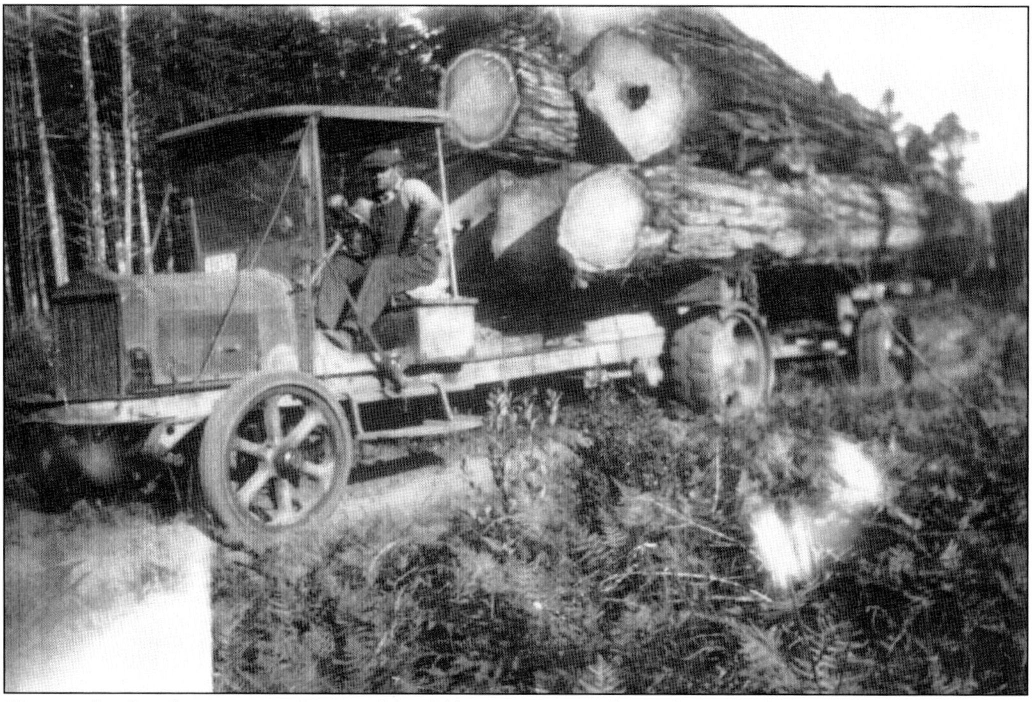

Here is the first logging truck owned by Allen Boice Sr. of Langlois. He first used it as a transport truck from Bandon to Gold Beach. When logging became a new occupation, he turned it into a truck for hauling logs. Soon other trucks were used, speeding up the transport of logs. At one time, there were 102 small sawmills in Curry County, and today, there is just one, which is found in Brookings. (CHS.)

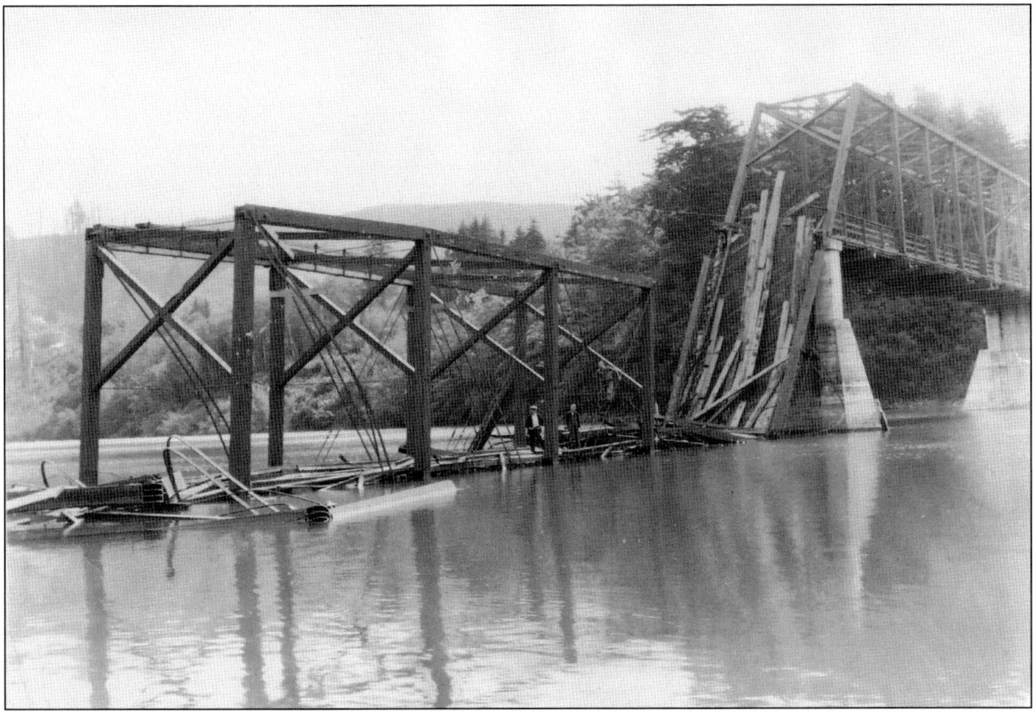

After the automobile came into being, Nick Turner became the mail carrier. When he first started delivering mail in Brookings, he had to cross the first bridge that was built over the Chetco River. Before the second one was built, the original bridge collapsed. He had just passed over it when he heard a rumbling noise and, looking back, saw the whole section he had just passed over crash into the river. (CHS.)

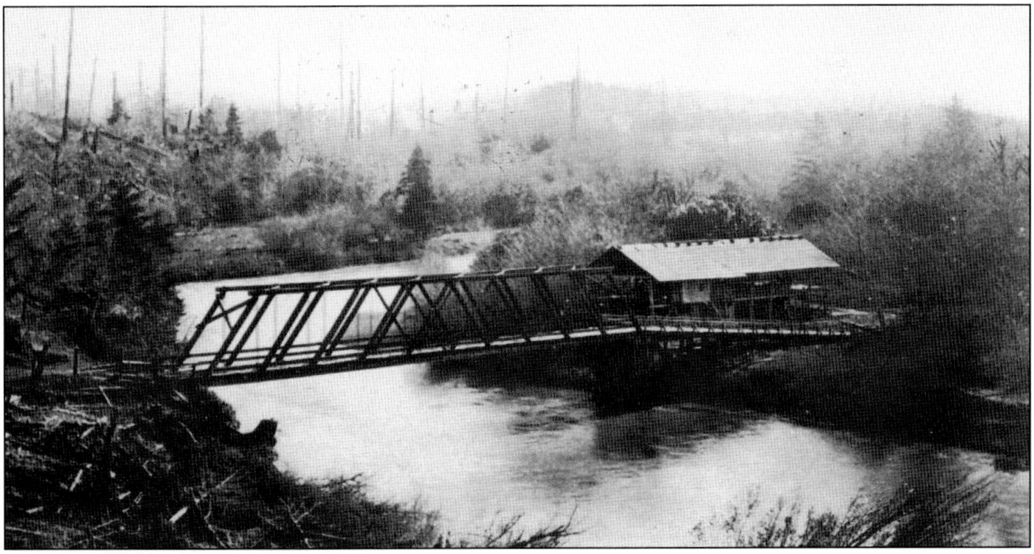

This is the covered swinging bridge in the Big Bend–Illahe area. It was west of Foster Bar at Foster Creek. This creek was where Charlie Foster hid from the Indians and got away to warn the farmers on the lower trail. (CHS.)

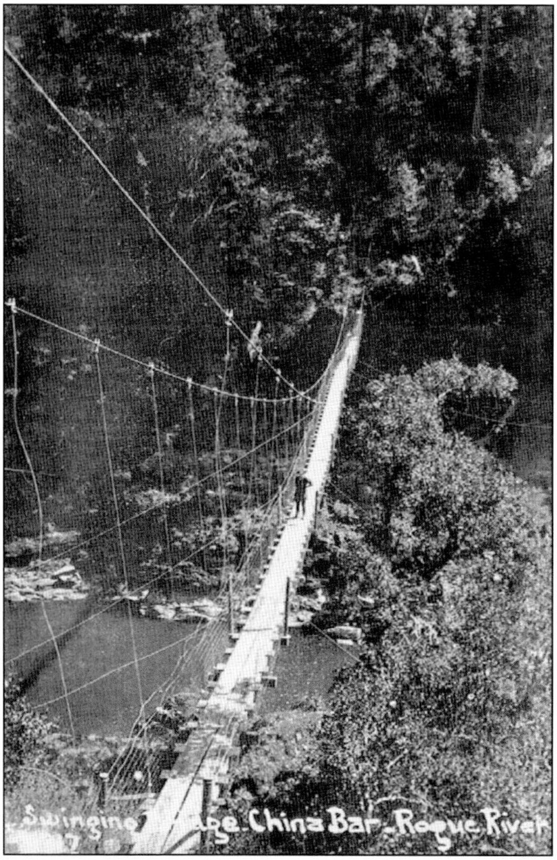

For those on the south side, the swinging bridge at China Bar on the Rogue River was their only option to cross over the river. (CHS.)

This is a portion of the Roosevelt Highway being constructed through the tall fir trees. It was a great improvement over the original road that followed the ocean beaches. It was much safer to take one's wagon or auto on Roosevelt Highway. (CHS.)

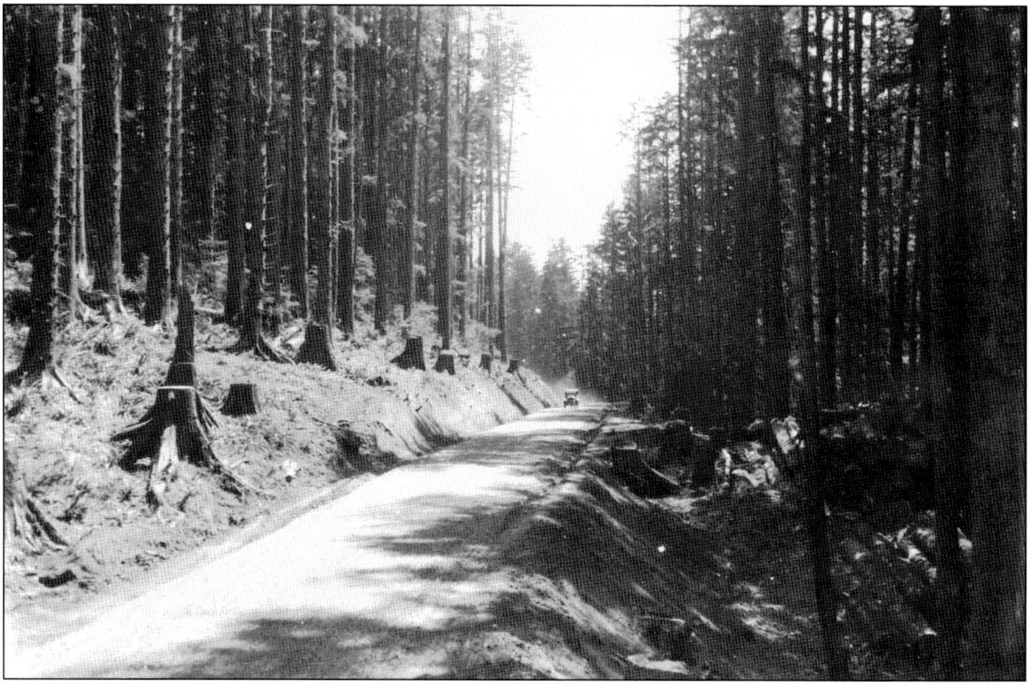

Six

Time Marches On

Here are some samples of the old and the new or the past and the present. Where once there were only three churches, today there are now 11 and one at Nesika Beach. The Peoples store and Leith market are replaced by McKay's and Ray's; they and the Wedderburn are all large stores. In Brookings, there are Ray's, Shop Smart, Bimart, and Grocery Outlet. The town is known as the Banana Belt and is growing fast. It now hosts a population of more than 8,000, while Gold Beach has a population of 2,000. Many retired couples have settled here, enjoying the peacefulness of the ocean and rivers. World War II is long over, and the area where a Japanese pilot dropped his incendiary bombs still stands. He was honored by the City of Brookings a few years ago. The inns and small motels have been replaced, and when travelers arrive, they have many to choose from. Gold Beach is small but growing a little every year.

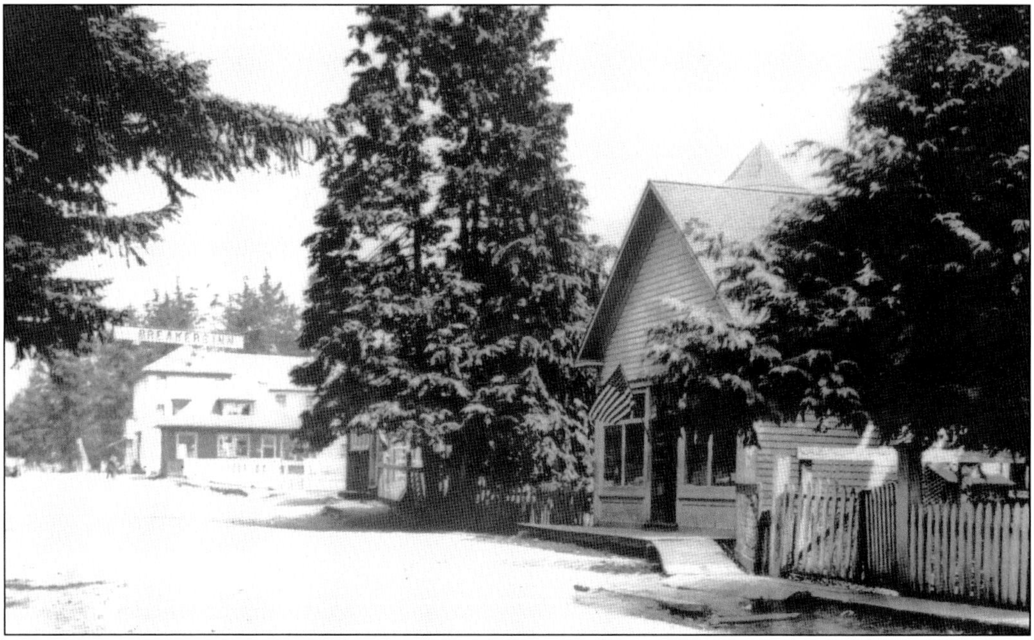

Shown is the front entrance to the Breakers Hotel on Main Street next to the Peoples store. The 1912 courthouse and the first bank of Gold Beach are also visible. There were two major hotels in 1912, the Breakers and the Bishel. The Hickock was later built on the west side of Main Street. Across the river, Hume had built the Bay View Hotel. (CHS.)

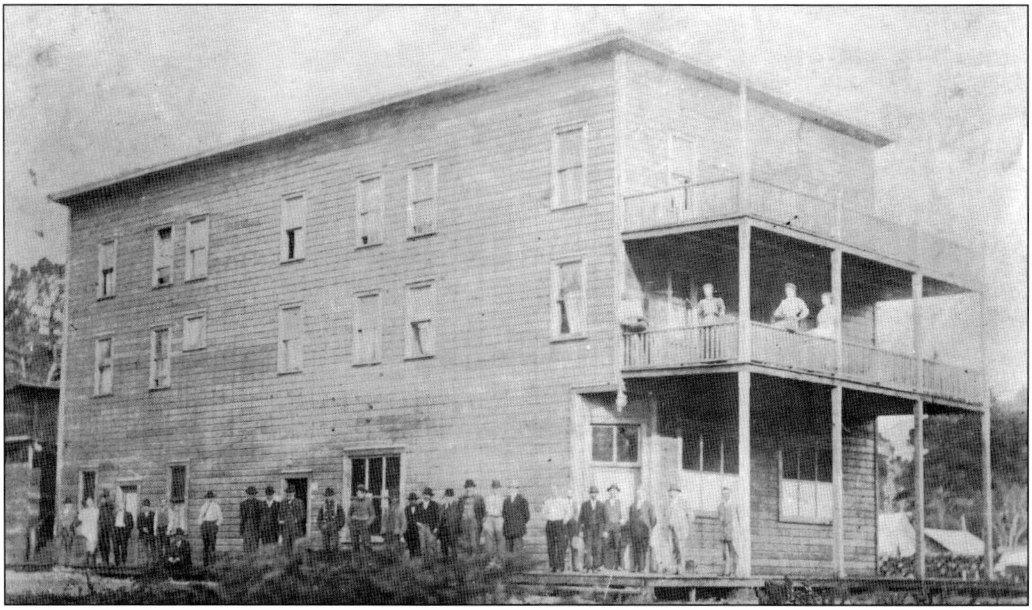

At the end of the Depression, a business group from Portland decided that if Flores Lake were to be connected to the ocean, it would make a great natural harbor. They platted a town and sold lots, and soon many new homes were built, as well as a post office, store, and hotel. When they were preparing to connect the two, they realized the lake was higher than the ocean, and if they were connected, it would drain the lake. The town became a ghost town. This was the hotel. (CHS.)

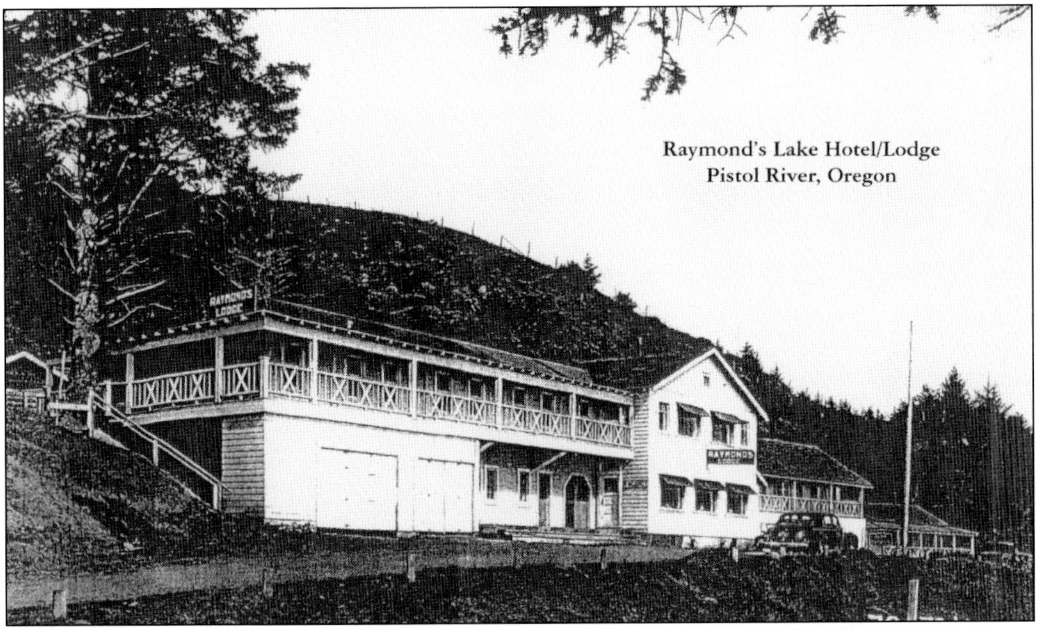

Raymond's Lodge, also known as Wildwood Lodge, was located on the Old Coast Highway above Meyers Creek and across from Hunters Cove. When Highway 101 passed by, it was below the lodge. It was a nice lodge with a wonderful view. In the olden days, the pioneers used to hunt sea lions, and when a storm would hit, they would find safety on Hunters Island. In the 1960s, it was no longer an overnight lodge and was rented. It burned to the ground in the late 1960s. (CHS.)

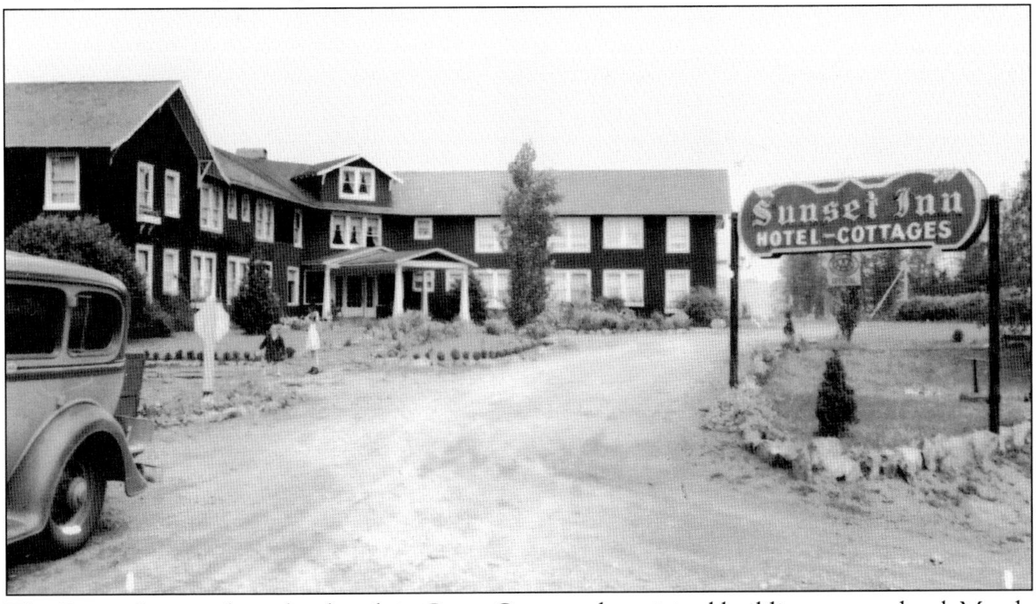

The Sunset Inn was large landmark in Curry County; the original building was a school. Maude Morse and her mother first fixed the smaller building as a kitchen and added another wing to it to make a restaurant. As time went by, she added wings to the main building, and it soon became a lodge for overnighters. Over the years, many famous people have stayed at the inn and spent time sportfishing and enjoying the beach. She sold the inn to Mike Bloomfield and retired; it later burned to the ground. (CHS.)

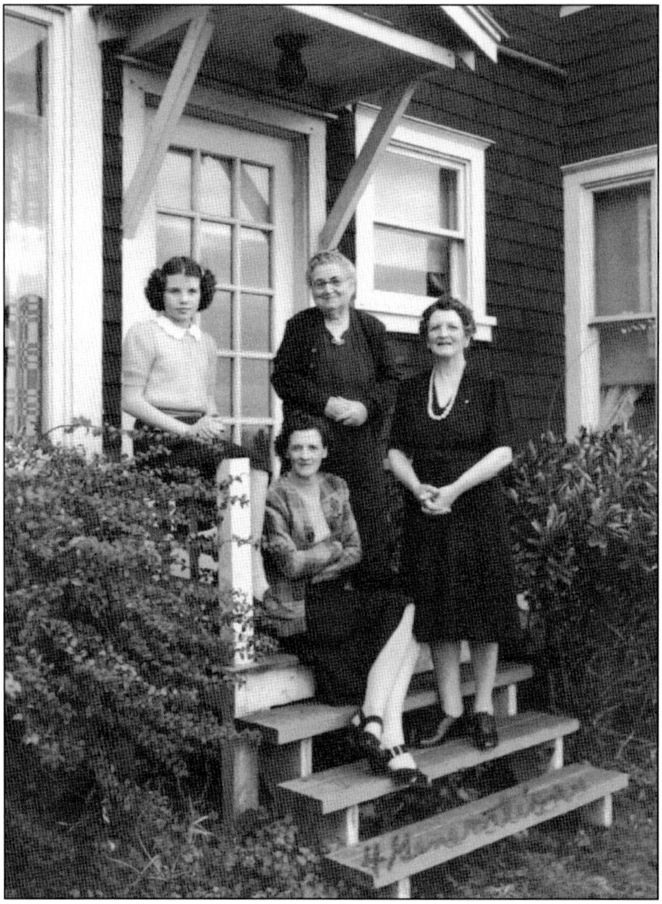

Here Maude Morse (right) stands in front of the Sunset Inn with her daughter Dorothy Lamson (sitting), granddaughter Patricia (left), and mother Alpharetta Walker (center). Maude was a school teacher for years and later built the beginning of the Sunset Inn around the former schoolhouse. She built the kitchen out of the interior of the school. Over the years, she continued to add on until it became quite extensive and soon became an inn. She was well known in the community. When she retired, she built a beautiful home south of Gold Beach past the fairgrounds. She was a member of the Walker family. (CHS.)

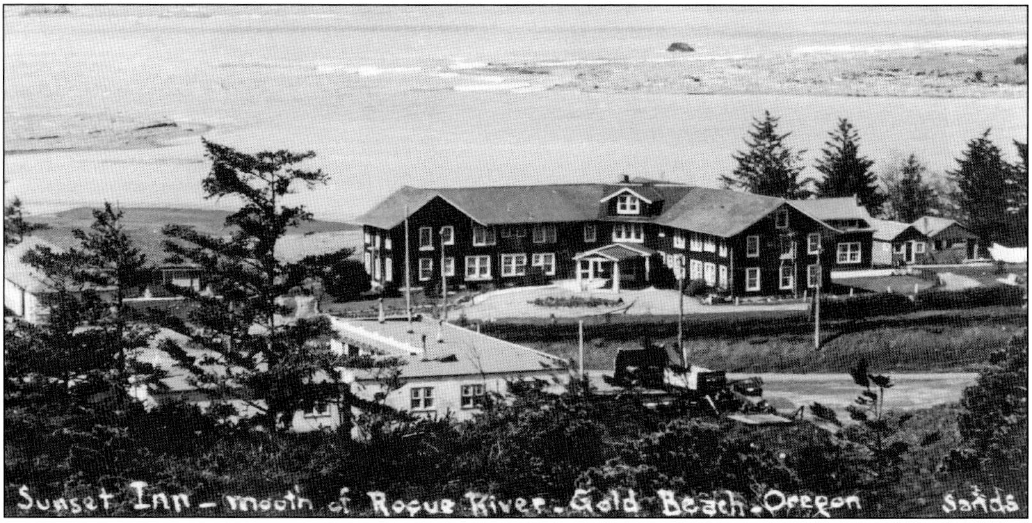

This is the Sunset Inn when Maude finished adding onto the original building. It was a very popular inn, and many famous people stayed here. When Maude retired, she sold the inn to Michael Bloomfield, and only a short while after he obtained the inn, it burned to the ground. It was a sad day, as it was a historical monument. (CHS.)

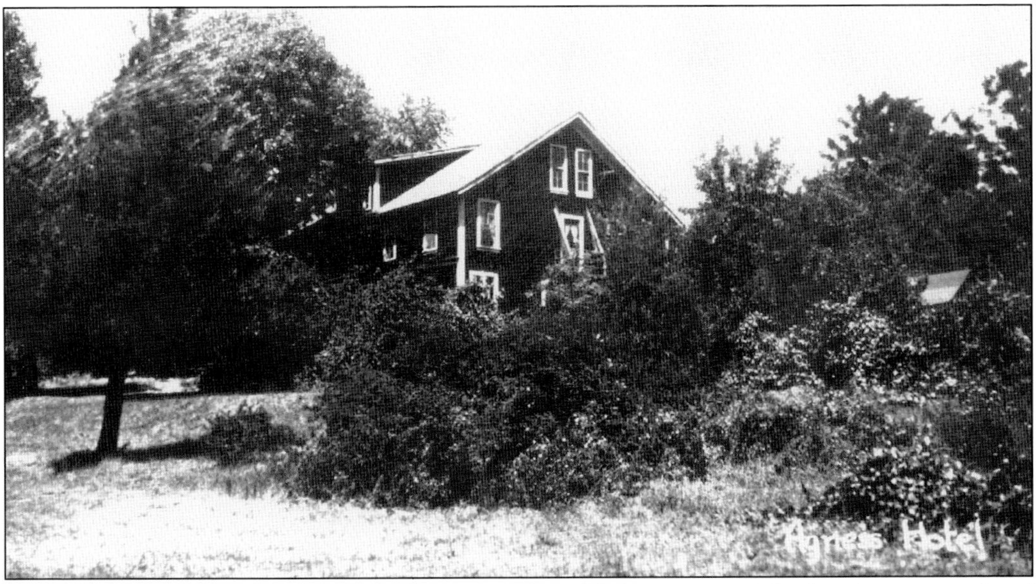

The second hotel built in Agness is the one in the Old Agness area. The hotel accommodated fishermen. Its location is just south of the old Cougar Lane store, and it was later made into the Lucas Lodge. It was first owned by Mabel (Hamm) Lucas, and later, her son Larry added on and made it a lodge to accommodate the downriver fishermen. He later set the lodge up to feed lunch to the passengers of Jerry's Rogue Jets and Mail Boats. It is now the Lucas Lodge. (CHS.)

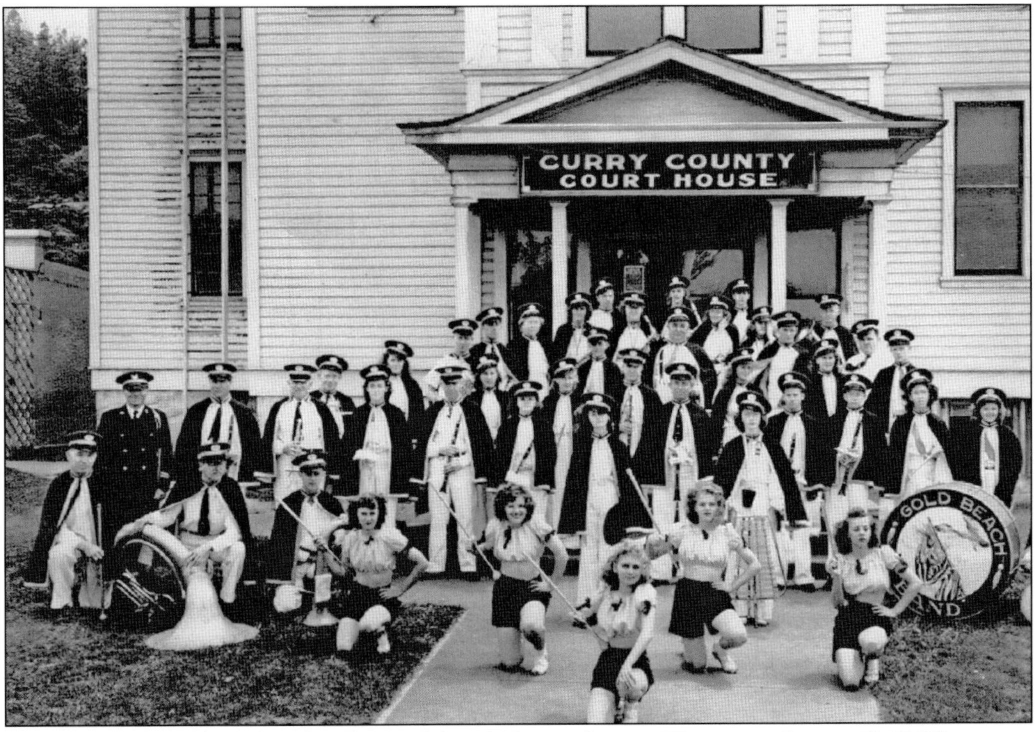

This is the high school band in front of the 1912 courthouse. This was taken in 1940. They were active in the Curry County Fair Parade yearly. The band was a very important activity in the schools. (CHS.)

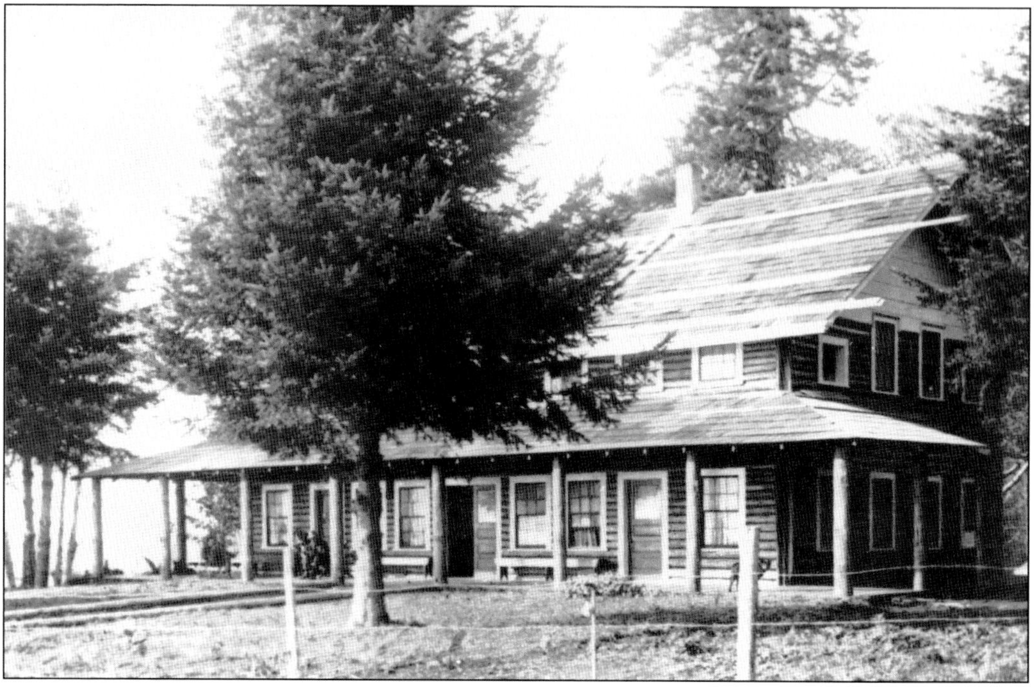

The Antler Hotel in Brookings is shown in the early 1920s. It was one of the first hotels built in the Southern Oregon town of Brookings. (CHS.)

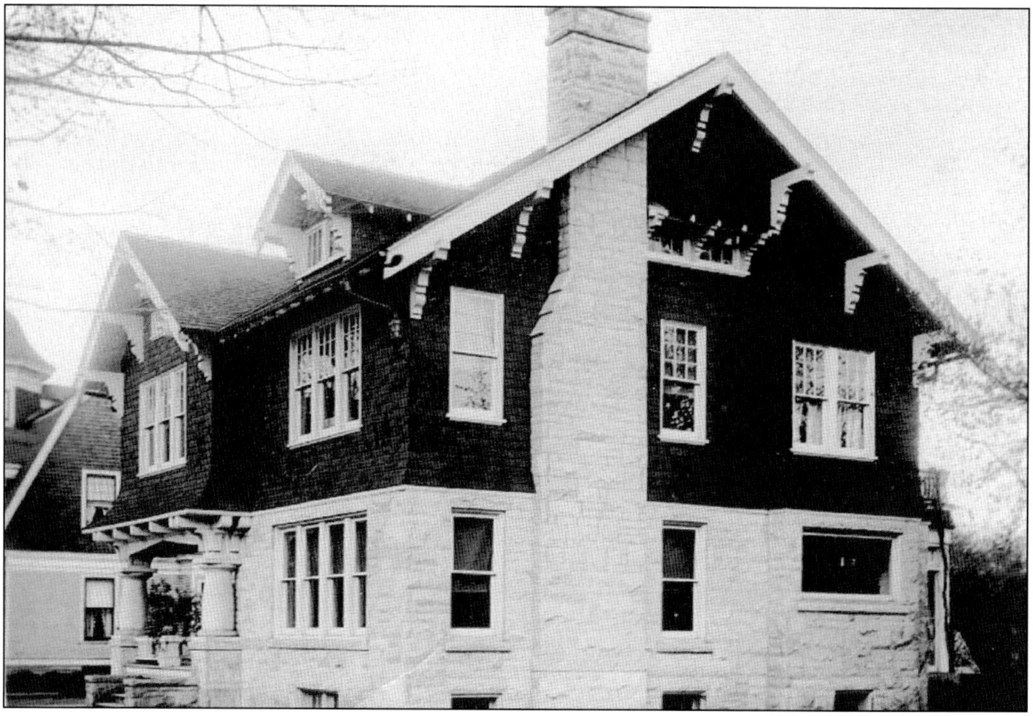

This was the second hotel built in Brookings and was much larger than the Antler Hotel. It was known as the Driskell Hotel. Much later, the Chetco Inn was built up on the hill above Main Street. In the mid-1900s, motels became a way of life for travelers. (CHS.)

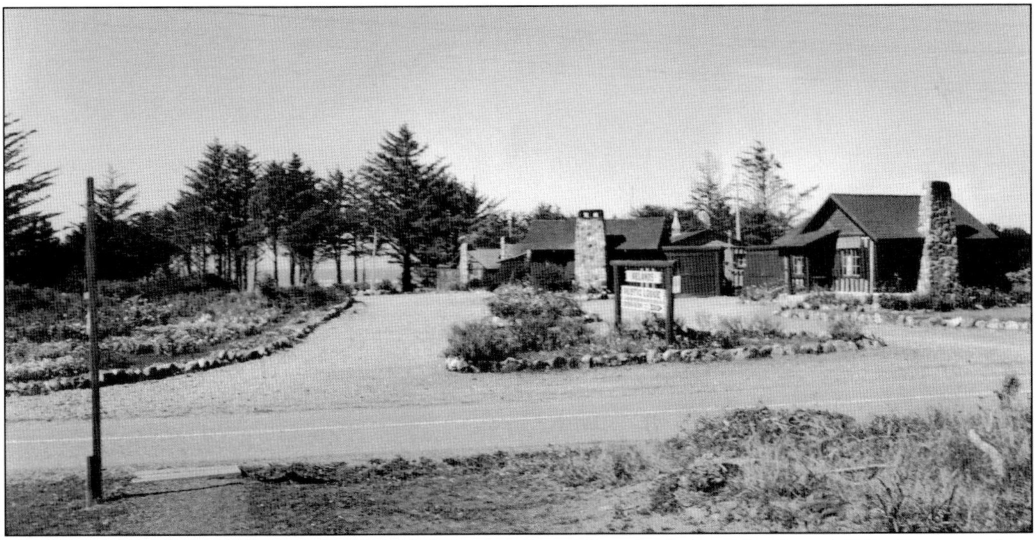

In the 1930s, Mr. and Mrs. Ireland and their daughter Corabelle bought the old Wedderburn Inn on the North Bank Road. They had previously lived in Portland, where they had a restaurant. A few years later, in the early 1940s, they built Ireland's Rustic Lodge in Gold Beach. Each house had a fireplace and a view of the ocean, and all three meals were carried to the cabins daily. After her parents died, Corabelle took over the operation, and she ran it for many years. Corabelle never married. At her retirement, she sold the lodge to the Ralphs and Richmonds. (CHS.)

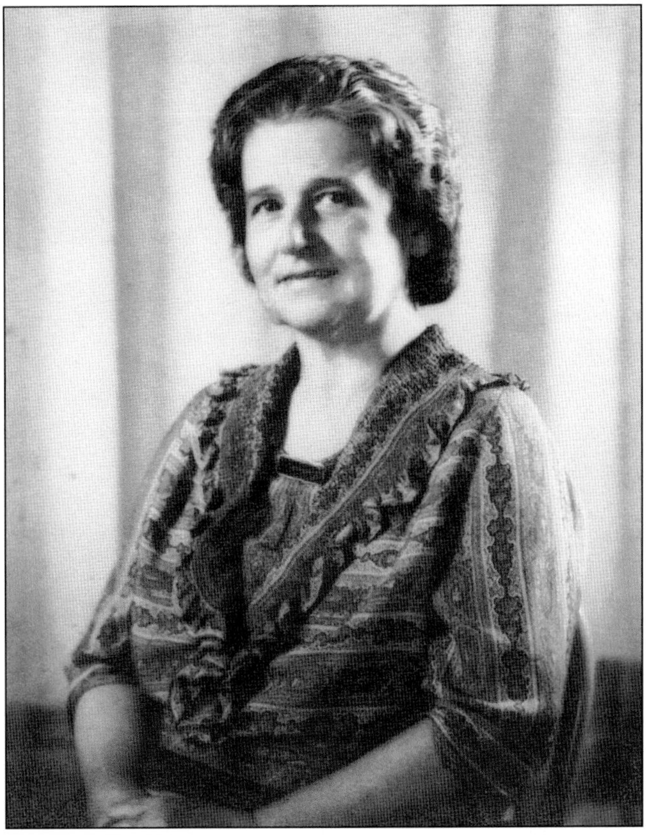

Mary Smedberg was the main nurse in Gold Beach and operated three hospitals before her retirement. She bought the Carl Mack home for her first hospital. When she needed more room, she leased the house next to the James Leith home, later referred to as the Buffington house. Here, she set up her second hospital. As more space was needed at a later date, she sought funding for building her own hospital and received the property from Dennis Caniff on the beach behind the present high school. Caniff donated the land to her as payment for her care of him for many months. She and her husband ended up getting a loan and built her new hospital, the Gold Beach Sanitarium. (CHS.)

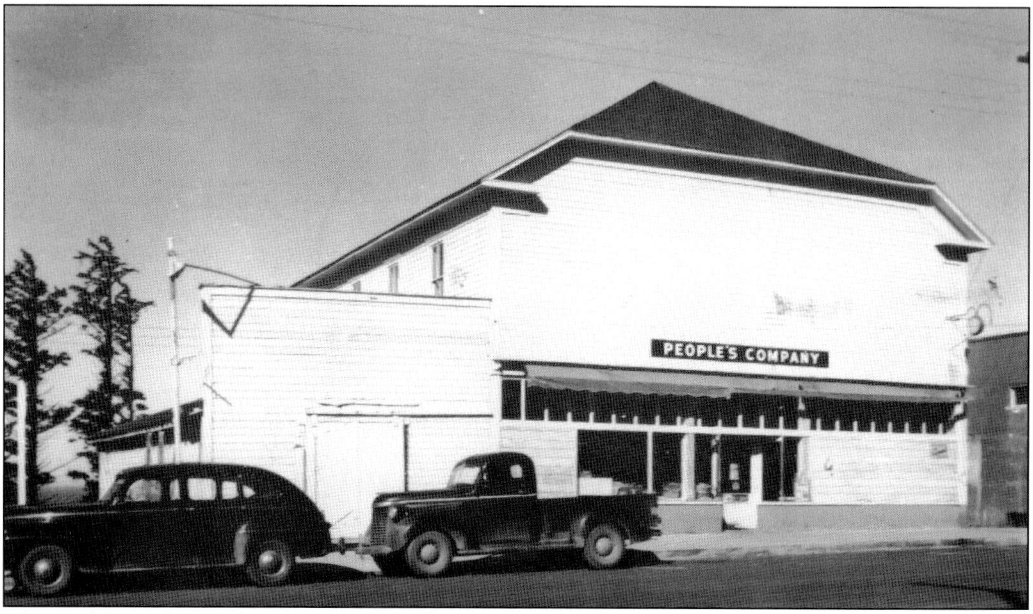

The Gold Beach Peoples store was built and owned by Milton "Bullhide" Moore. His home was located on Gauntlett Street, which was close to his store on Ellensburg Avenue. He received his major supplies from the passing ships that anchored off the mouth of the Rogue River and used boats to bring items to shore. His nickname "Bullhide" was due to his choice of shipping cowhides and other hides to San Francisco. He was congenial and a big help to the local families. When the store was closed, he sold it to the Masonic lodge, and the building was moved to the west of its location on what is now known as Hillcrest Street. In 2009, when the lodge disbanded, the building was leased to the Rogue Theater Group. (CHS.)

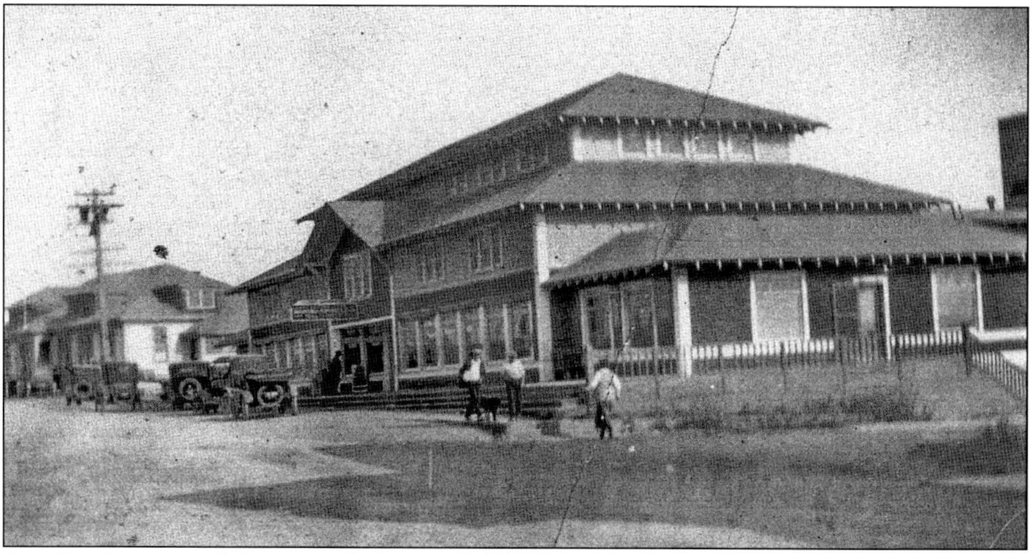

The Brookings Peoples store, now Kerr Hardware, was much the same as the Peoples store in Gold Beach. It was privately owned, and when the town grew and other stores were built and came into competition, the building was sold to Mr. Kerr, who transformed and enlarged it into a hardware store, which it still is today. It is located just off the main street on the west side of Highway 101. (CHS.)

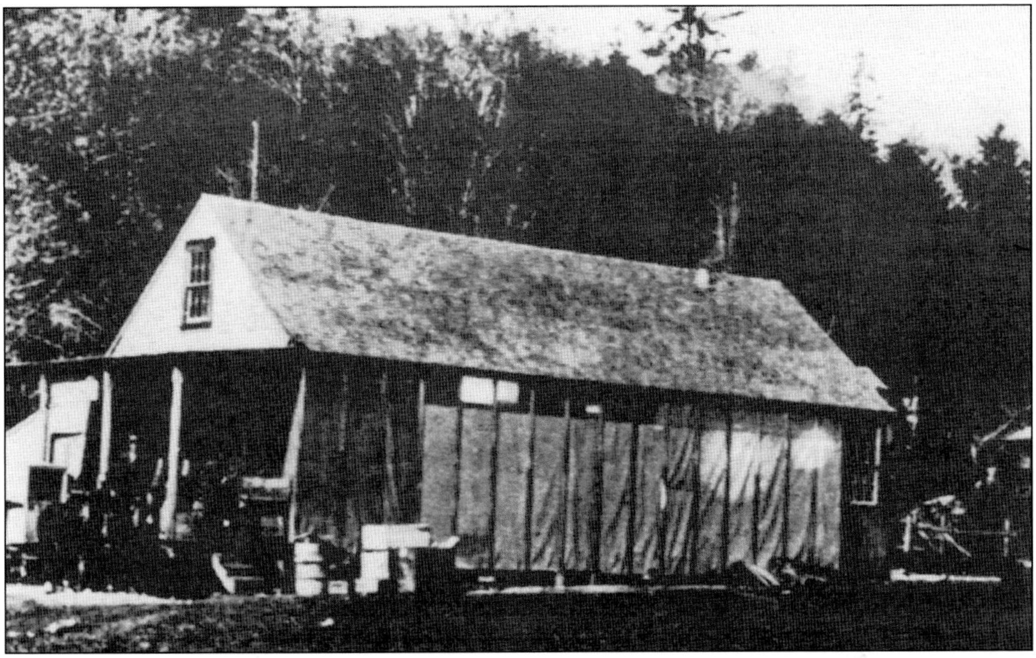

In the early 1900s, the first store was built in Harbor, making it easier for locals to buy their essential supplies, as the only way to buy items up to that point was to go the Peoples store in Brookings across the river, which had to be traversed by ferry. (CHS.)

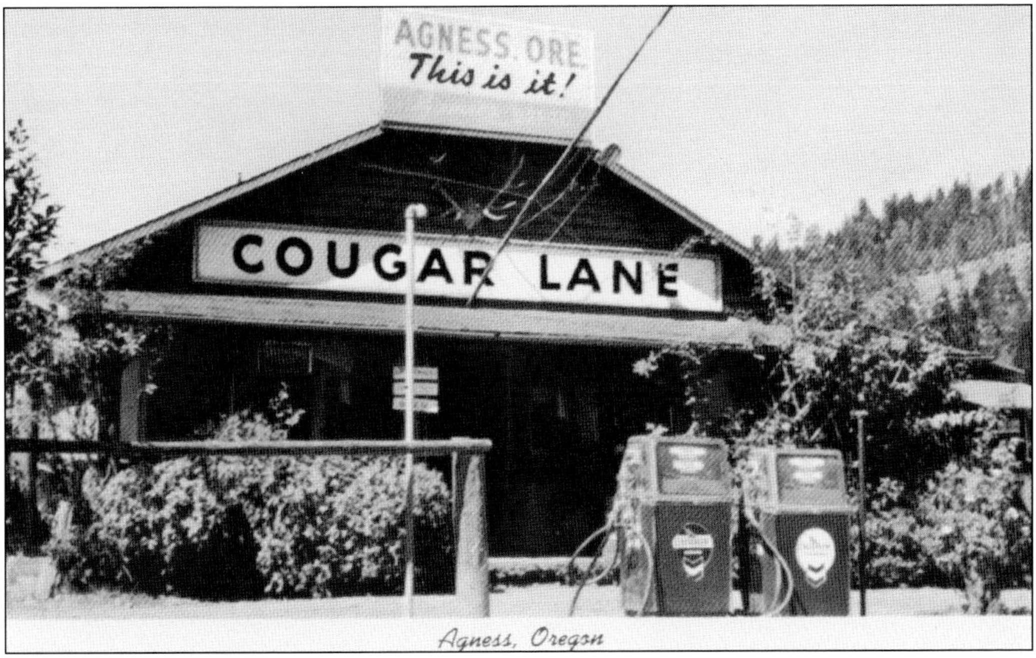

Bernard and Clarice Jackson built a new store in Agness and christened it the Cougar Lane store. Besides groceries and gifts, they sold beer and wine, with Heidelberg being the most popular. Just west of the store stood a huge tree under which those enjoying a beer could sit. As they pulled off the caps, they began hanging them on the tree, thus not only decorating but also naming the Heidelberg tree. (CHS.)

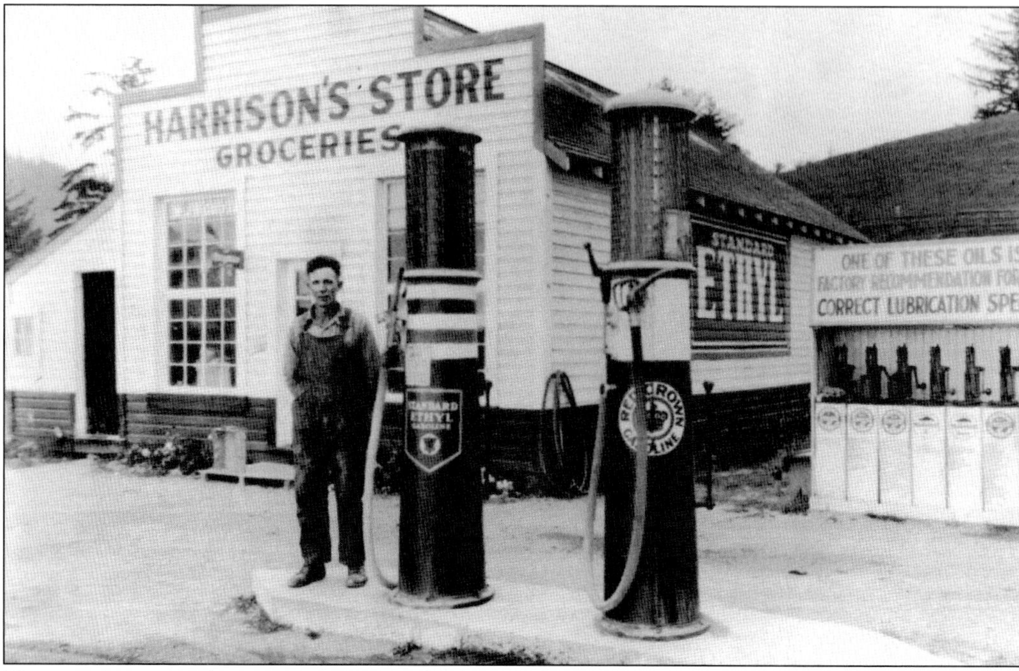

Harrison's store and service station was built at Ophir. It was later sold to Lorene and Mutt Wade and became the Ophir store and post office. It was just south of the Ophir School on the old Roosevelt Highway. Ophir was bypassed by the new Highway 101. The store was also a small garage. (CHS.)

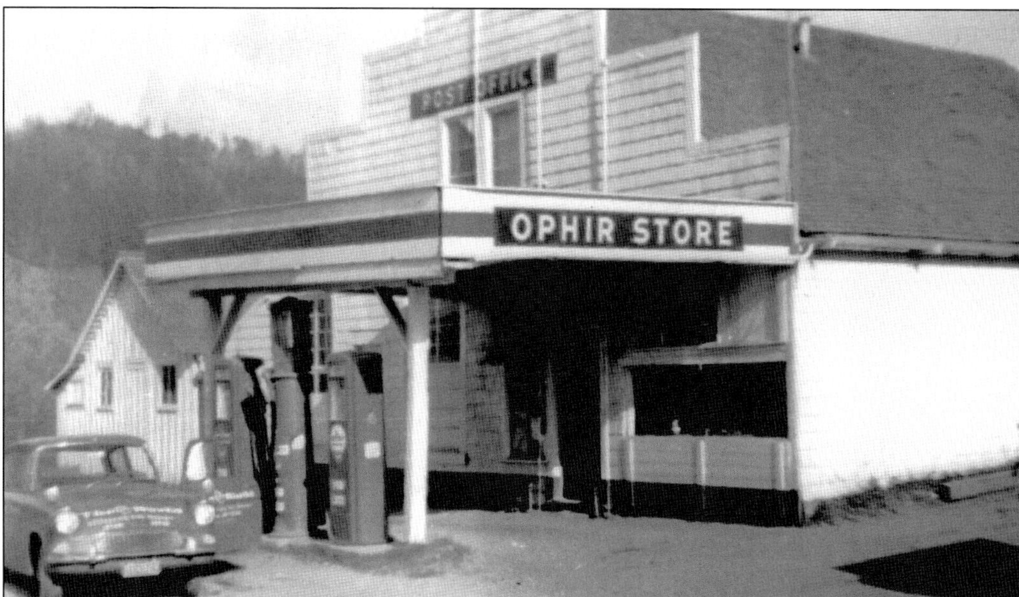

This is the Ophir store and post office that was previously the Harrison's store and garage. Mutt and Lorene Wade owned it; it was located south of the Ophir School. It had remained open for a few years after Highway 101 bypassed the Ophir community. After Lorene's retirement, it was closed, and the post office was moved to Nesika Beach, which is five miles south of Gold Beach. (CHS.)

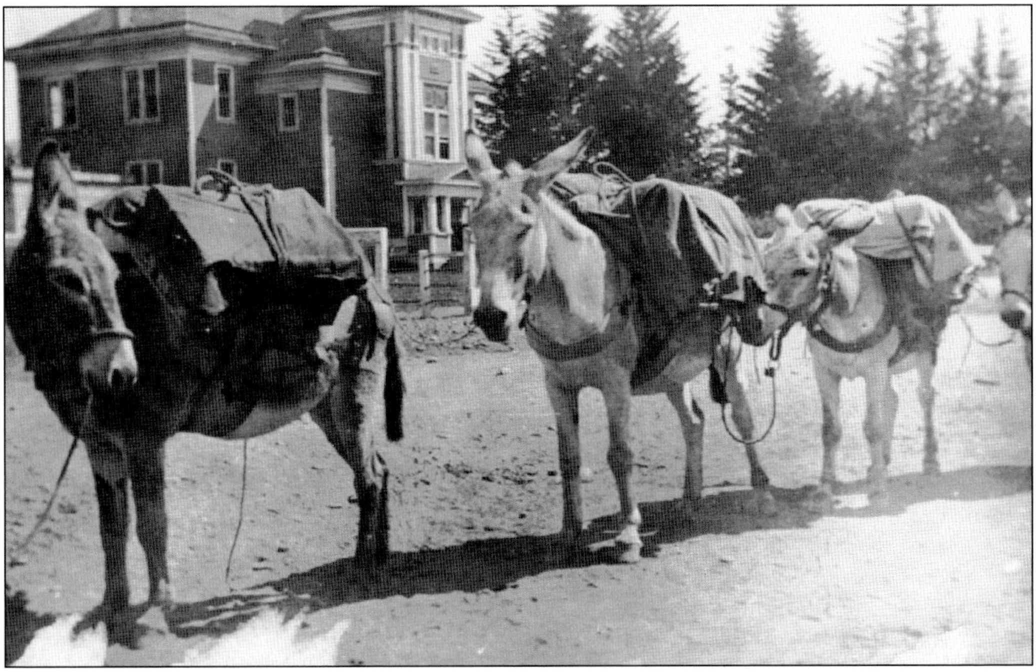

Before the mail boats became the carrier of the US mail, it was delivered once a week by the mule mail train, which connected with Grants Pass. Delivering all the way down the Rogue River, Hathaway Jones was the leader and made round-trips. Here are three of the mules used to transport mail in front of the 1912 courthouse. (CHS.)

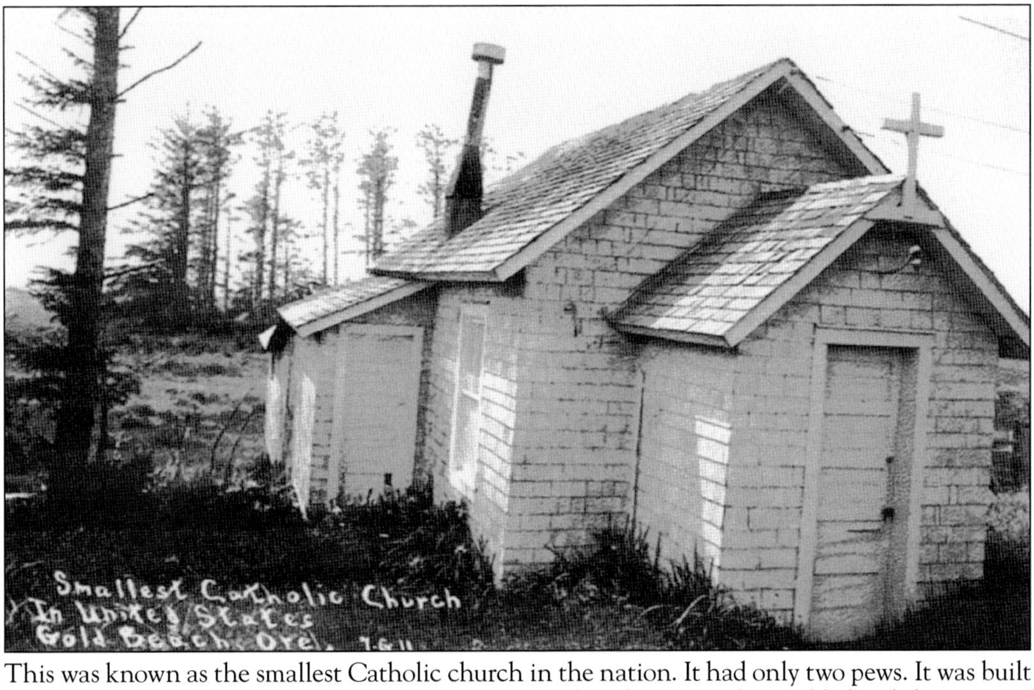

This was known as the smallest Catholic church in the nation. It had only two pews. It was built in 1929 and was torn down in the 1950s; a house replaced it. It was located behind the present-day myrtlewood shop on Hillcrest Street west of Ellensburg Avenue. (CHS.)

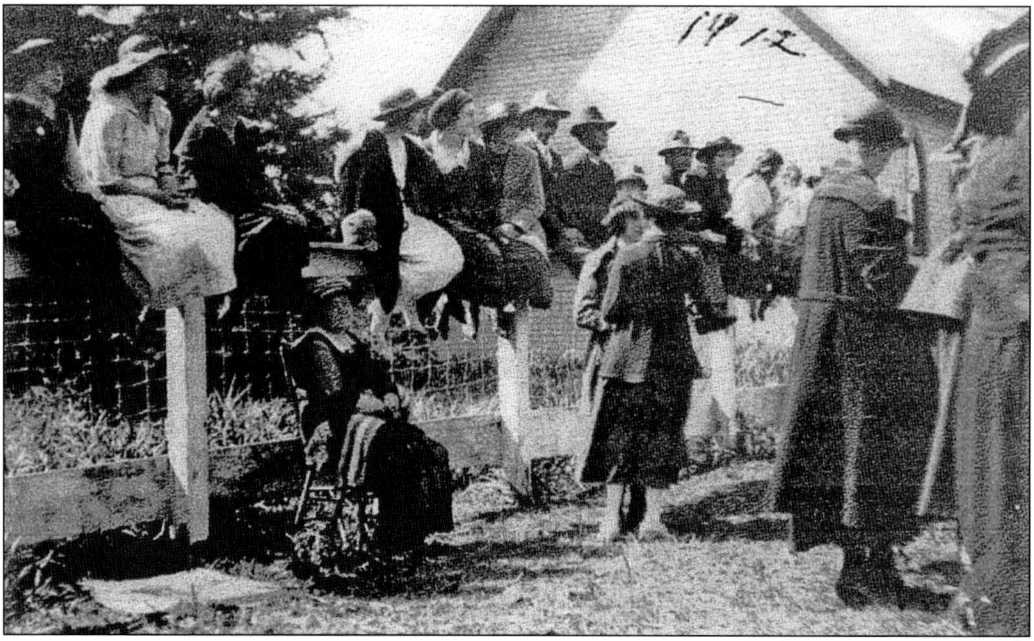

Here is a photograph of the building of the community church and the ladies who were meeting there before construction was finished. They congregated outside for visiting after the service. Later, the community church became the Presbyterian church, and it has been noted for that over many years. For a short while, the Presbyterian, the First Baptist, and the Catholic churches were the only three churches in town. (CHS.)

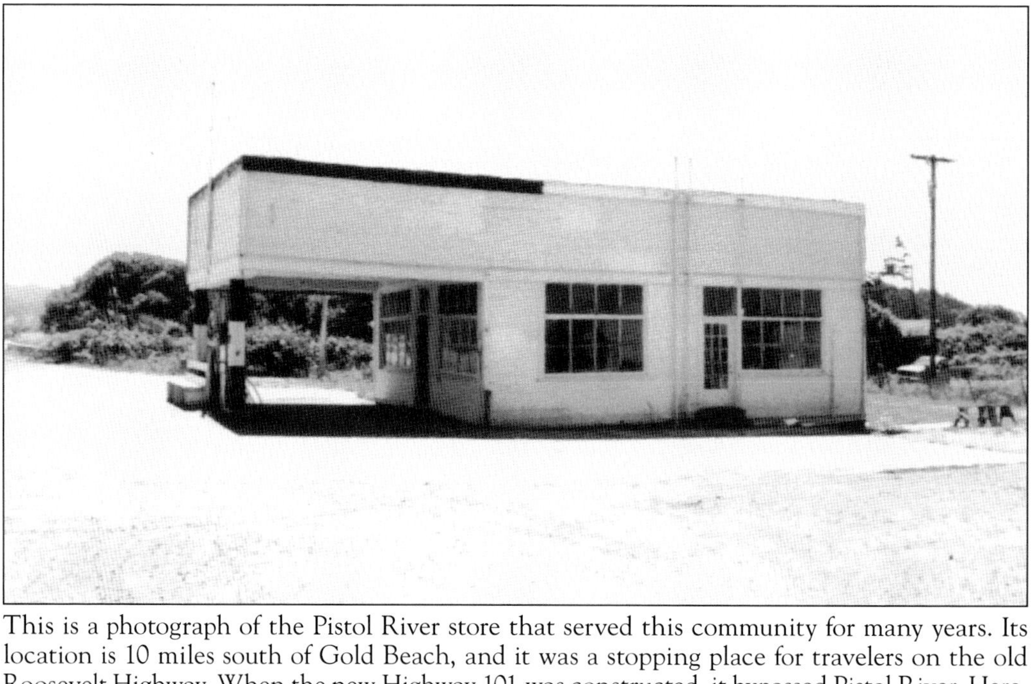

This is a photograph of the Pistol River store that served this community for many years. Its location is 10 miles south of Gold Beach, and it was a stopping place for travelers on the old Roosevelt Highway. When the new Highway 101 was constructed, it bypassed Pistol River. Here, the Pistol River flows into the Pacific Ocean. (CHS.)

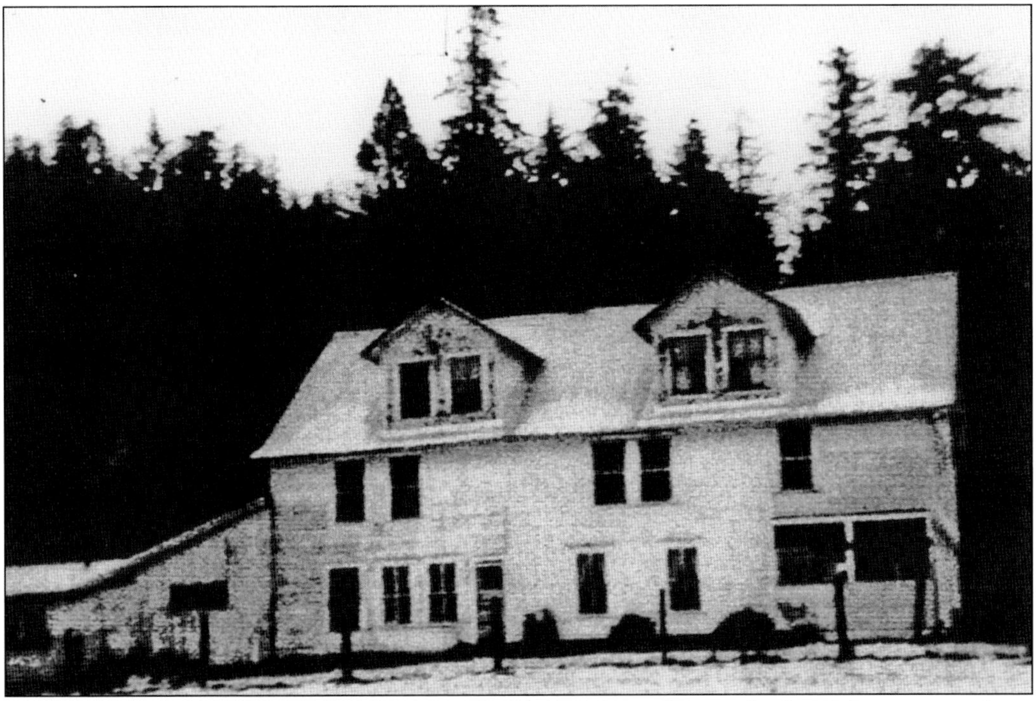

Here is Lowery Inn during the early 1950s. Frank and Anna Lowery built a fishing resort about halfway between Gold Beach and Agness. Anna was a very capable woman and became famous for her hospitality and superlative cooking. Her resort attracted sportsmen from all over the United States and many foreign countries. From her garden, she always had vegetables, and her orchard and berries kept her kitchen filled with fruit. Since they raised their own cattle, there was plenty of meat and fish at their door just for the asking. (CHS.)

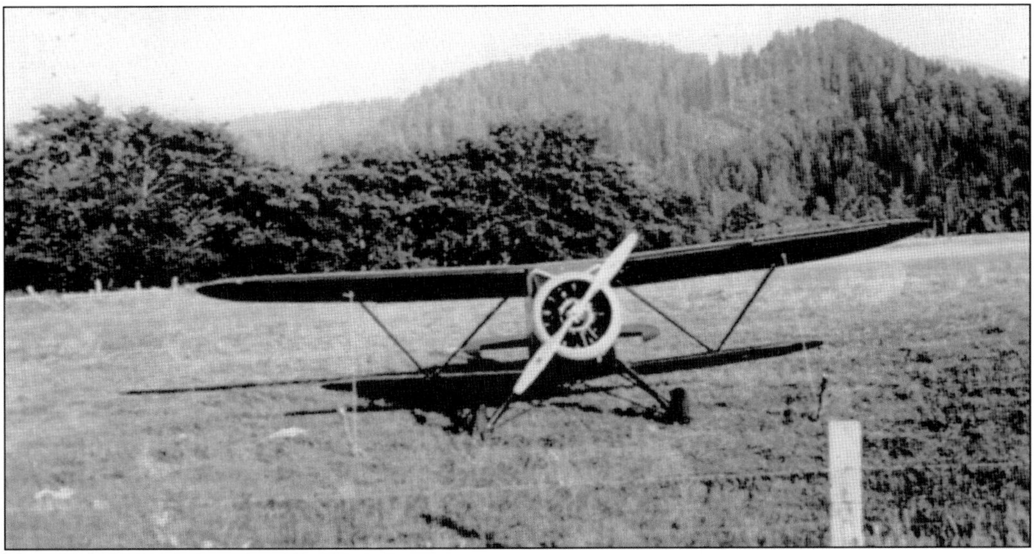

Deak Miller flew his airplane and landed on the grassy strip between Lucas Lodge and the Cougar Lane store. Other planes also occasionally used the small airstrip. (Paradise collection.)

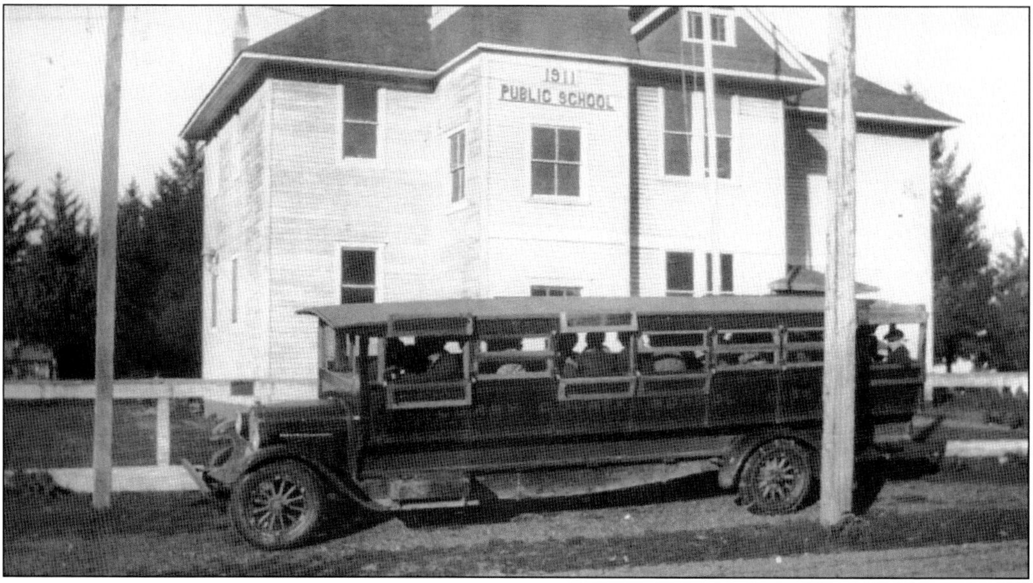

The first elementary school and high school in Gold Beach is shown in this photograph with the bus. The school was two stories, and the top floor had the high school and library, while the bottom floor housed the elementary grades. The bus in front was used for transporting the students. (CHS.)

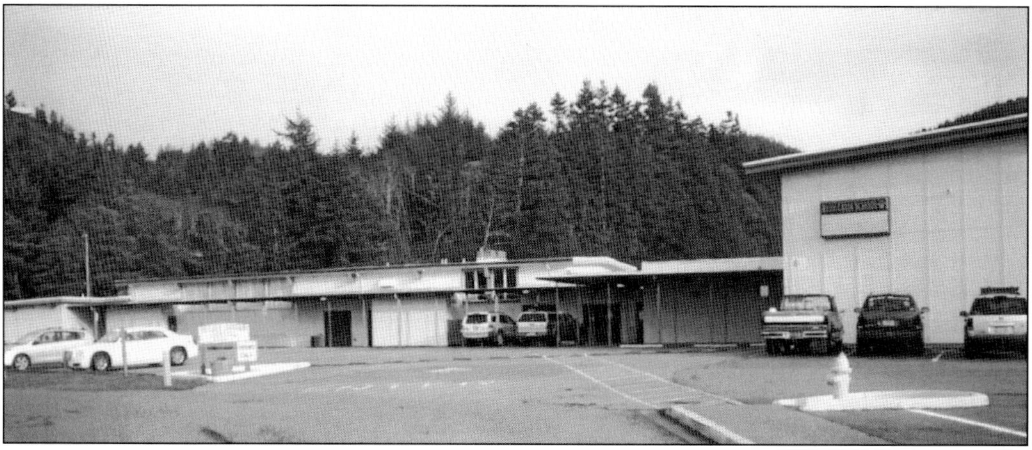

The next elementary school, built in 1960, was Riley Creek School, shown here. When it opened, the students attended fifth through eighth grades here. The younger students, including those in kindergarten, were still enrolled in Gold Beach Primary. (CHS.)

This school was built in Wedderburn and was established for many years. The children were from the families living in Wedderburn, and since there was only a ferry before the bridge was constructed, they utilized this school. Today, it has been transformed into an apartment building. (CHS.)

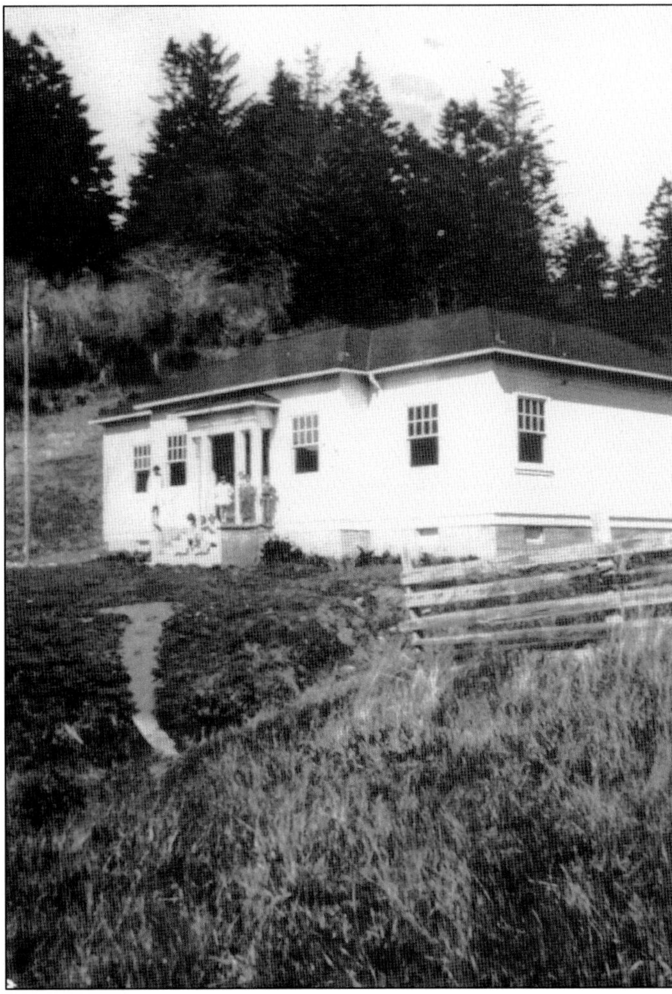

The first Gold Beach High School is seen on the left, and the newer high school is on the right. The first high school was built in 1919. As of 2012, the building is used for the old gym and the music and band room. It now sits directly behind the expanded main high school. It is located close to the football stadium. This photograph was taken in 1939. (CHS.)

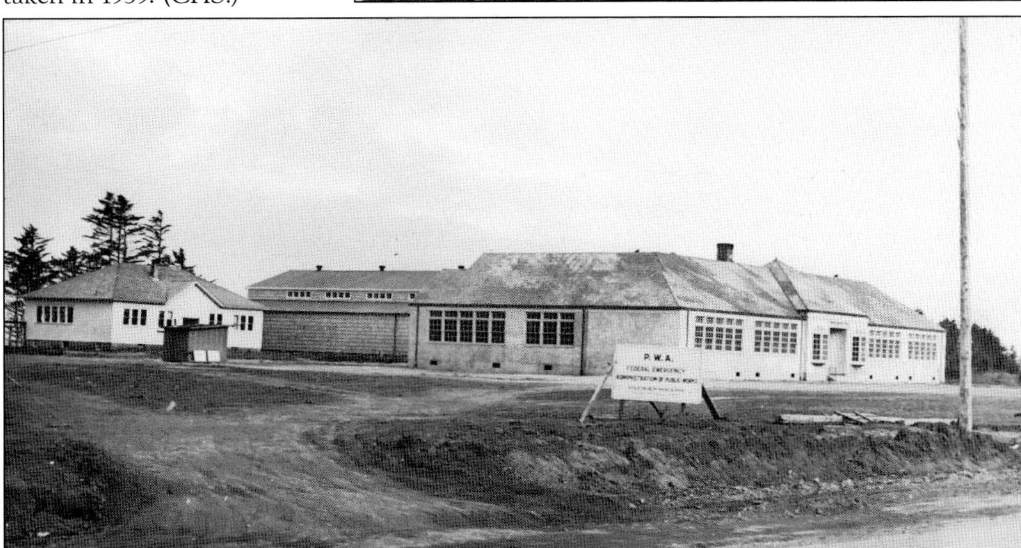

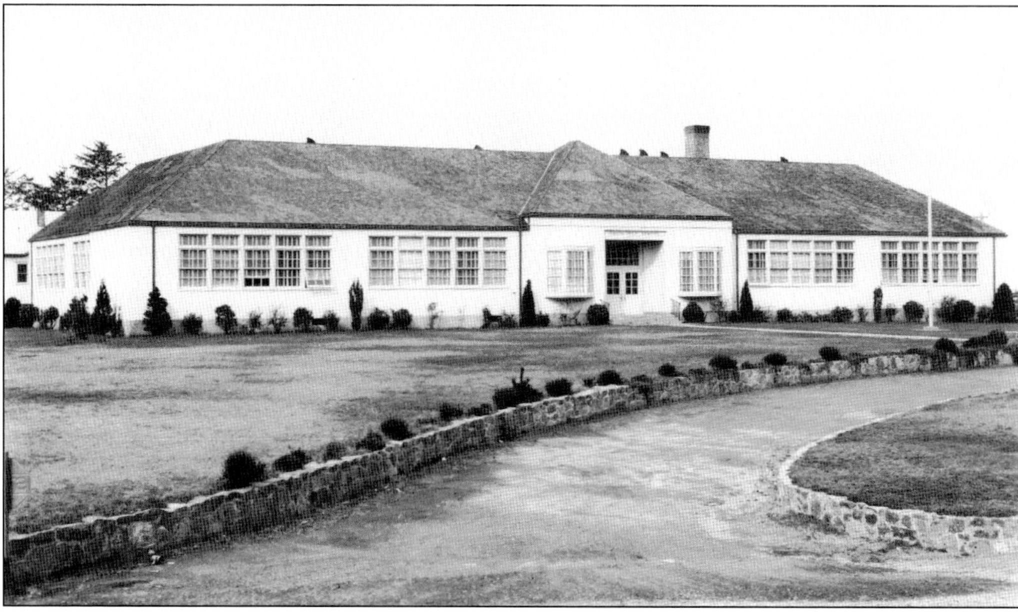

The present Gold Beach High School was built in 1939 due to overcrowding in the old high school, which is now the band room and the old gym. (CHS.)

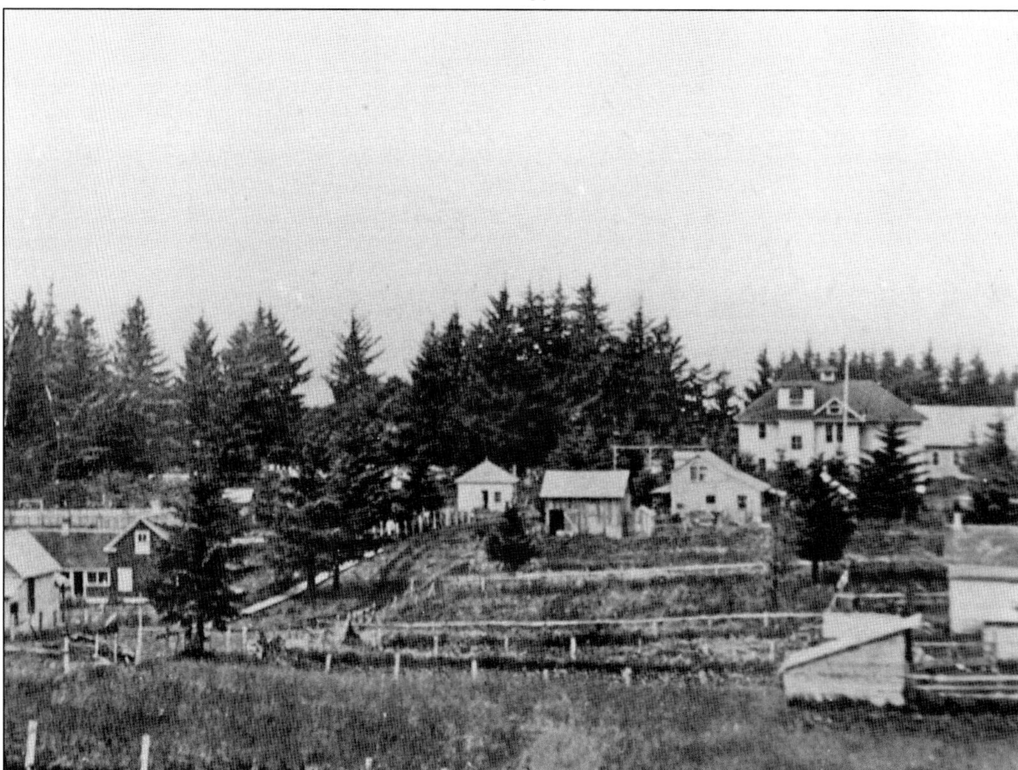

This picture of Gold Beach shows the first school to the right with the belfry on top. This building was located on Main Street between Leith Motel and Moore's Variety Store, where the Rush building was located. (CHS.)

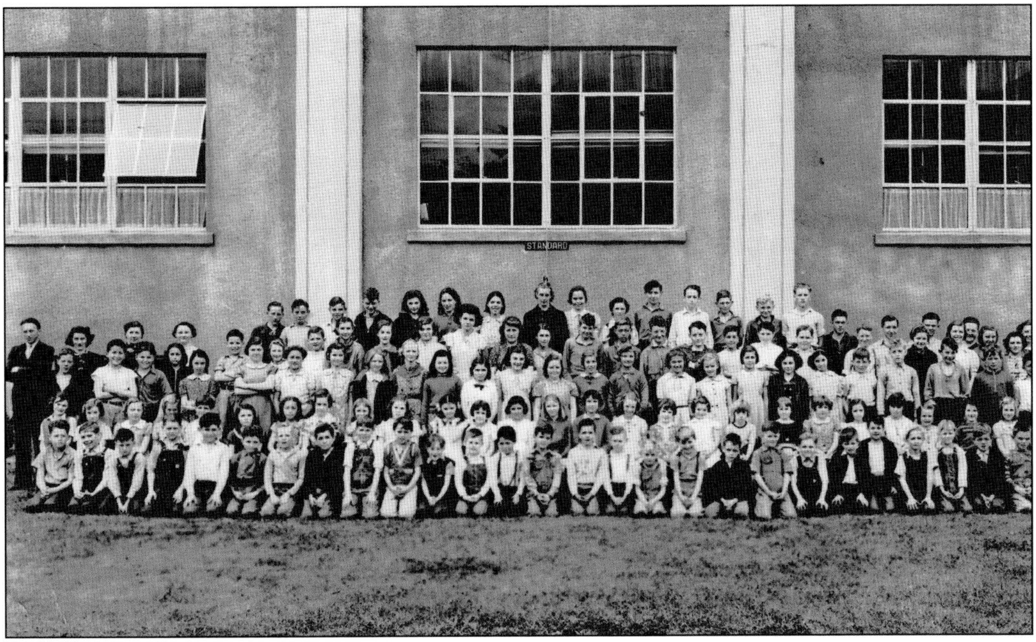

Here are the students at the Gold Beach Primary School from 1936–1937 (above) and 1939 (below). One of their teachers was Georgia Fromm, whose husband, Lex, was also a teacher. This building is on Main Street, and during the 1950s, after the Riley Creek School was built, the curriculum only offered the first four grades. Fifth through eighth grades were taught in the new elementary school. In 1961, the first kindergarten class was started in the Gold Beach School. Flora Chase was the teacher, with the mothers as helpers. Gold Beach Primary School was closed in the early 1970s. (Both, CHS.)

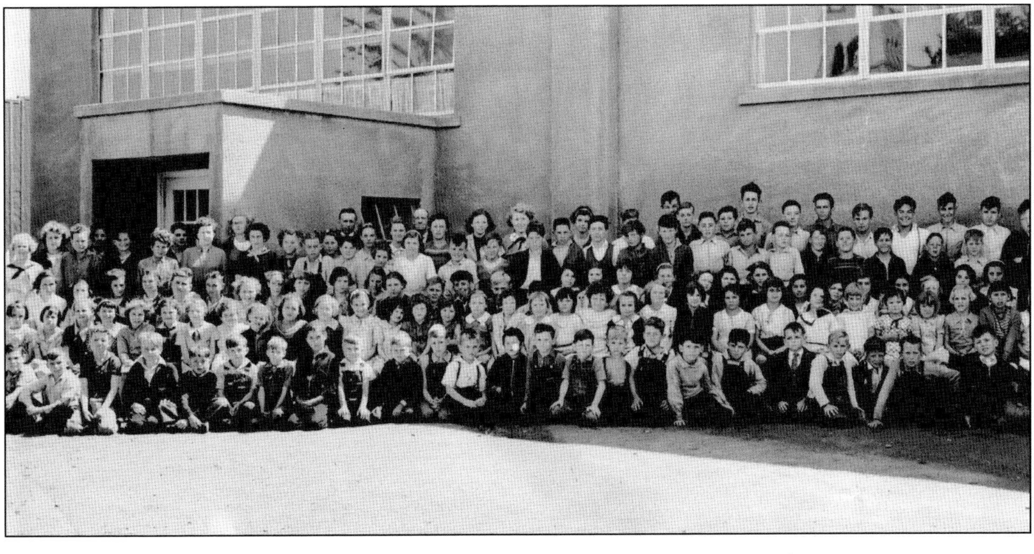

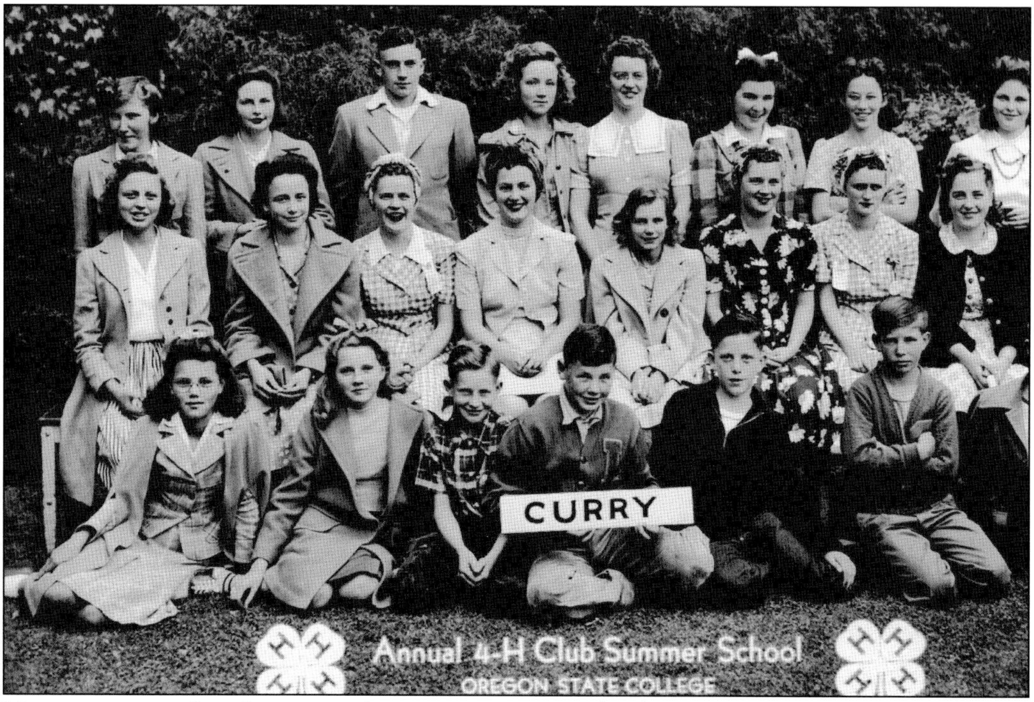

Here is a group of students attending a 4-H summer school in Corvallis. During the fair each year, the 4-H children and teenagers were very active in different activities, such as sewing, cooking, and varied animal shows. They had and still do have a special building to house their show animals for judging. Patrons and especially children love to see all the animals. It is similar to a petting zoo. (CHS.)

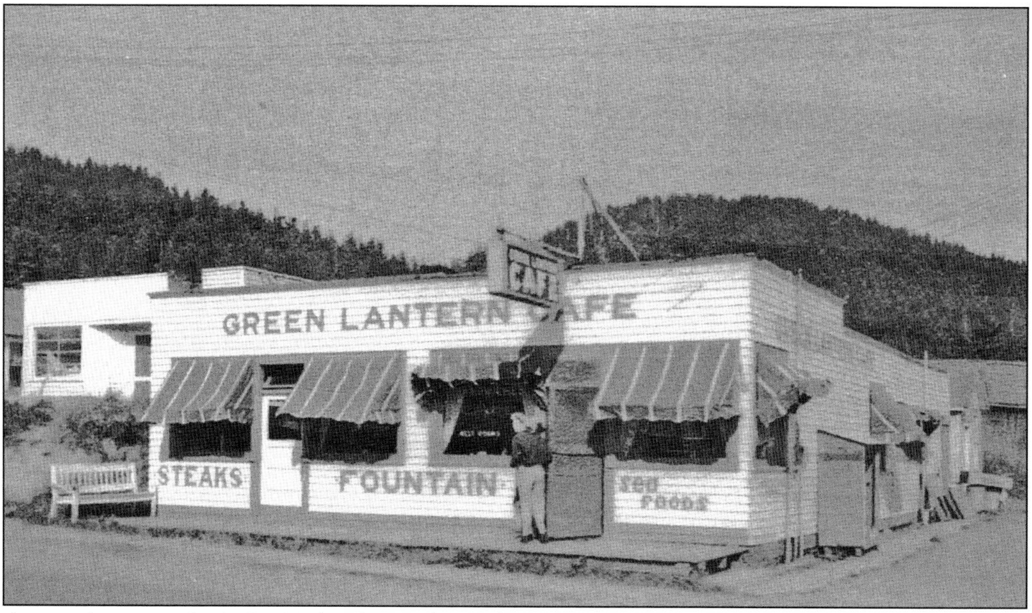

Across the street from the Hickock Hotel was the Green Lantern Café, a favorite place for diners for many years. At the south end of the hotel and across form the café was Bullard's Drugs. This was the middle of Main Street in the 1950s and 1960s. (CHS.)

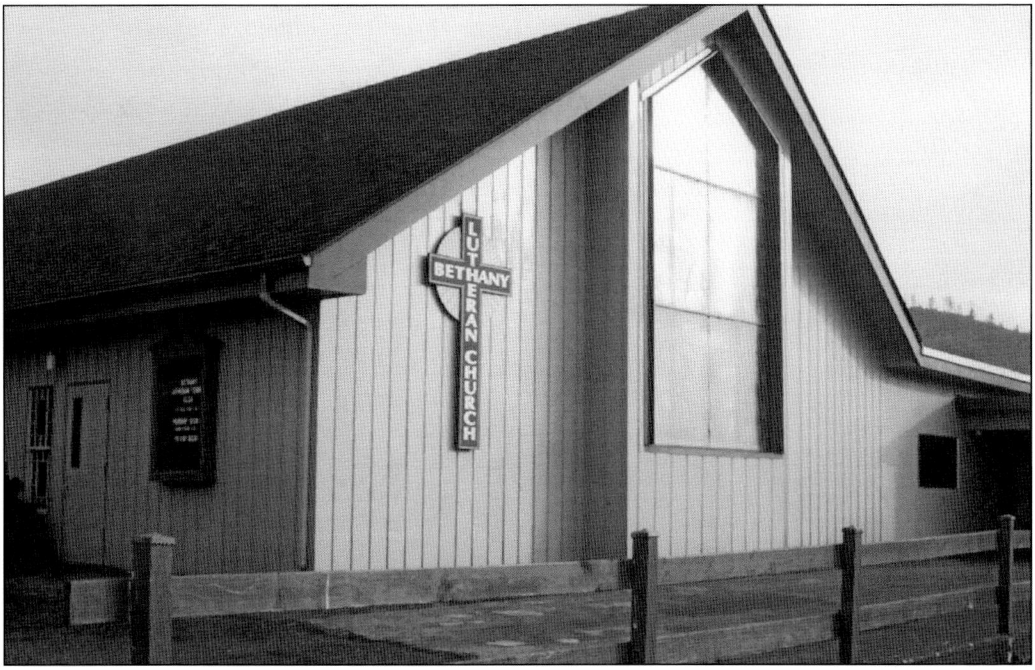

The Lutheran church was built in the 1960s. It is a very dependable church and well attended. Their pastor is Tim Bruckner, and he has been established there since its beginning. (CHS.)

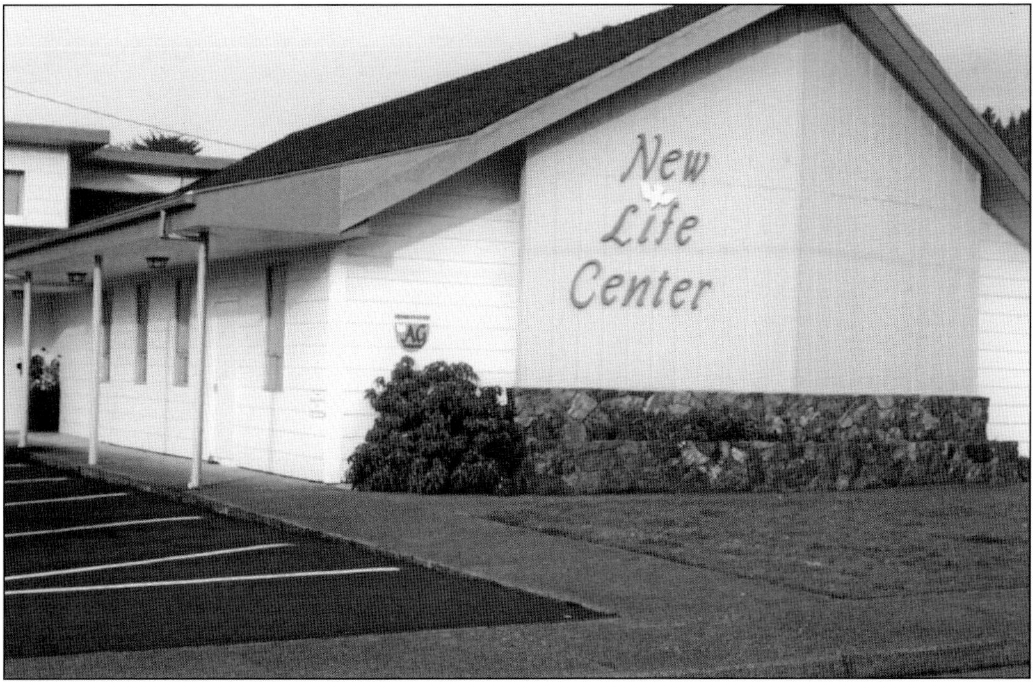

This church is the Assembly of God denomination but is also known as the New Life Center. Established in the 1960s, it has had several pastors over the years. Today, it is still a great church. (CHS.)

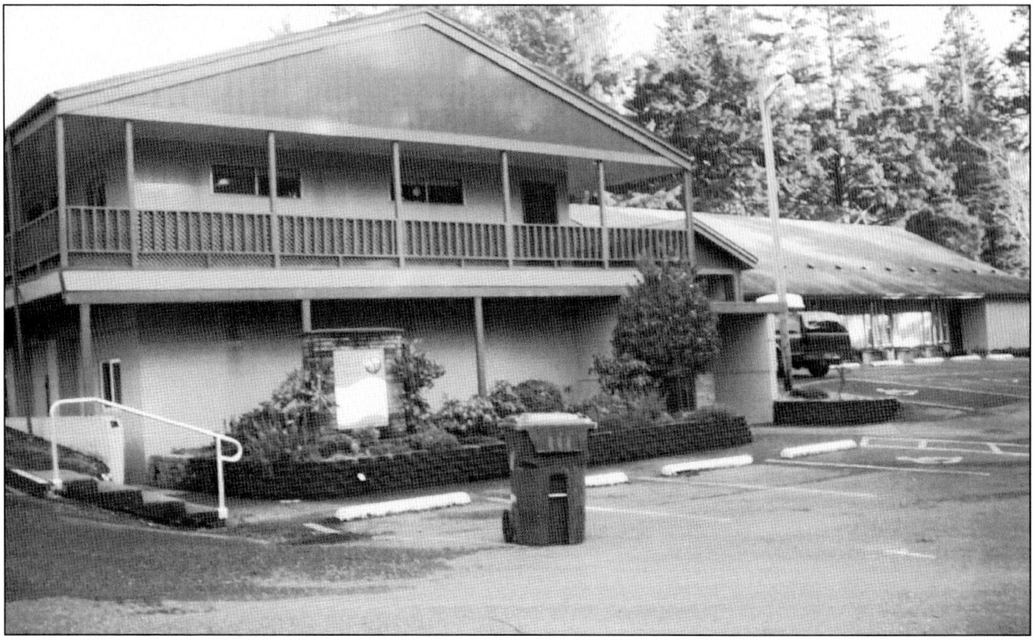

The First Baptist Church was built in the late 1940s and has grown tremendously since its inception. It was necessary to add on to the building twice to accommodate the growing congregation. (CHS.)

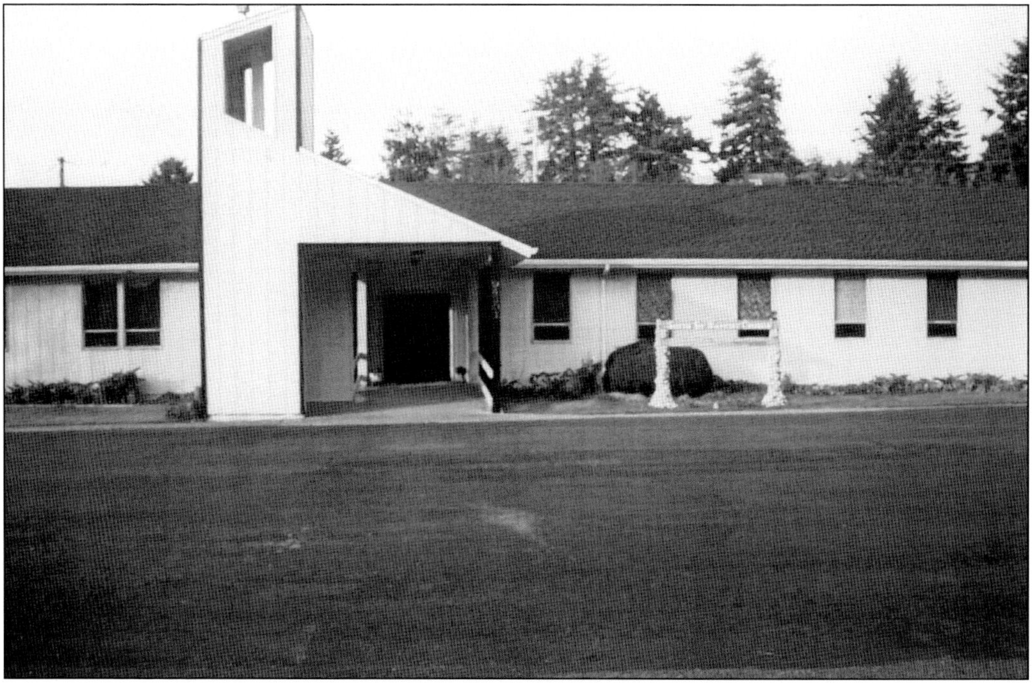

The Sixth Street Baptist Church is located next to the Riley Creek School. The present pastor is John Dawson, a local gentleman who grew up in Gold Beach. It is also a growing congregation. (CHS.)

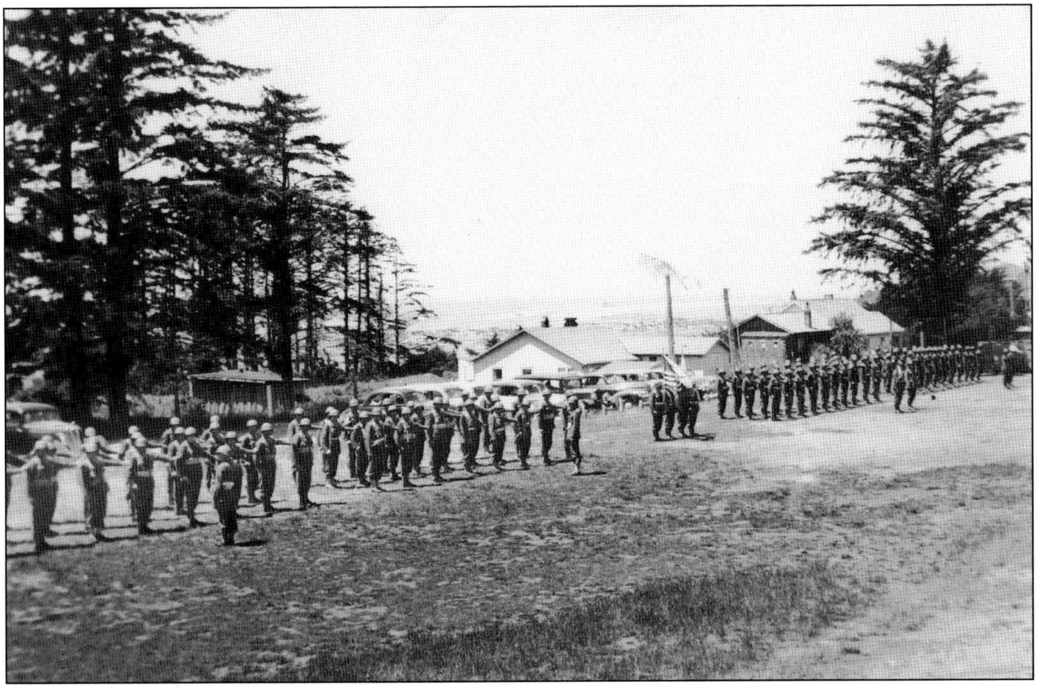

During World War II, there was a platoon of Army personnel protecting Curry County, and they were housed at the Curry County Fairgrounds. They also manned the radar station on Bailey Beach. (CHS.)

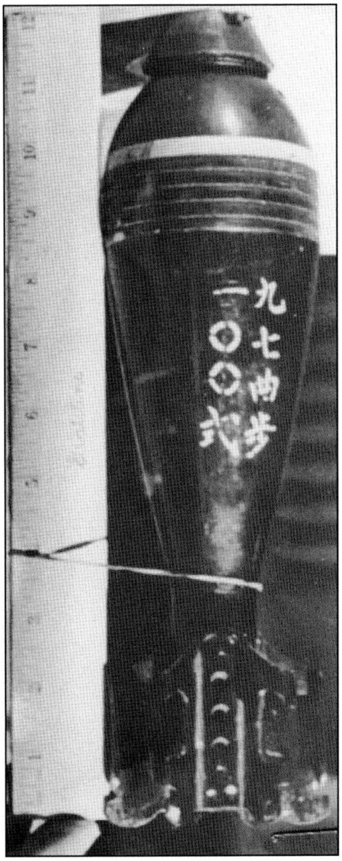

This is a picture of the bomb that a Japanese plane dropped. Japan later sent over balloons with bombs inside, and although the wind carried them past Curry County, they did fall to the ground over by Cave Junction. These were the only Japanese bombs dropped on the continental United States during World War II. It happened on September 9, 1942. (CHS.)

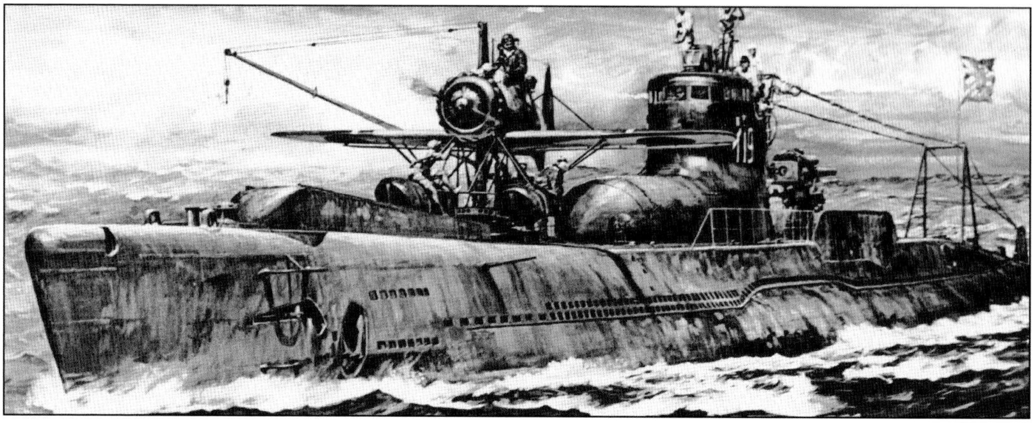

This is an artist's conception of Japanese officer Nobuo Fujita boarding his Glen plane prior to taking off from the submarine *I-25* offshore from Cape Blanco. In 1962, Nobuo Fujita and his family were given the opportunity to be taken to the bomb site by Forest Service official Fred Flynn to see where his bomb landed when it was dropped from his plane. (CHS.)

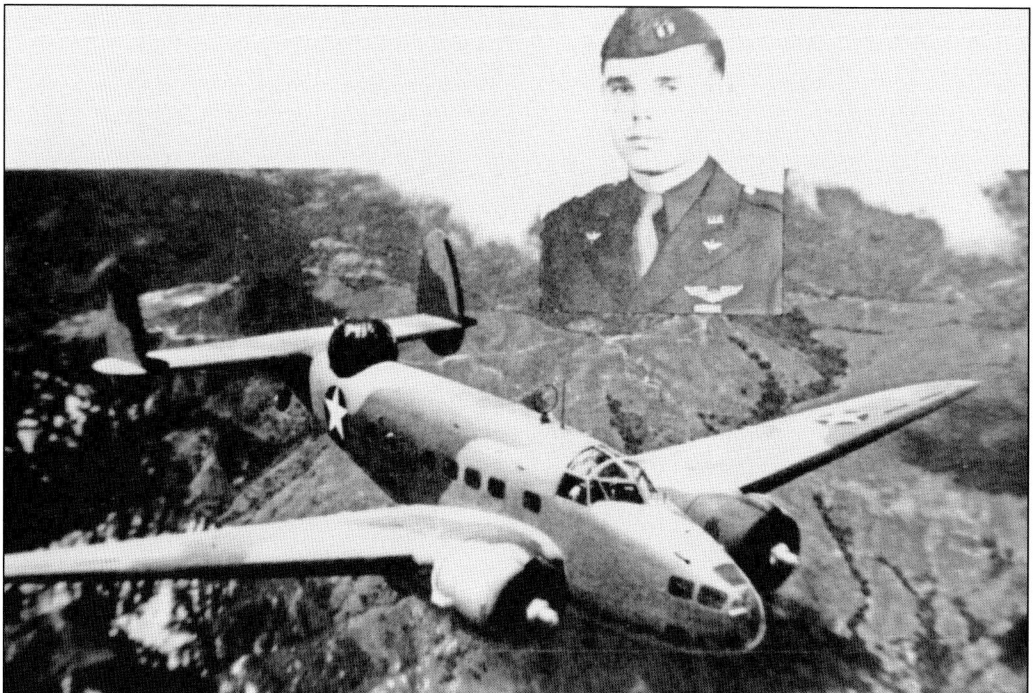

During World War II, Curry County was the only place in the continental United States to be bombed. A submarine surfaced off the coast of Cape Blanco, and a Japanese plane took off with an incendiary bomb, flew over the Kalmiopsis Wilderness, and dropped a bomb at Wheeler Ridge. When it exploded, it left many incendiary pellets in several places. The Japanese pilot was hoping to start several fires to consume the county. Capt. Gene Daugherty was on patrol in an A-29 bomber when his crew sighted the *I-25* beginning to submerge. They dropped many bombs, but the sub was 18 meters underwater. When the first exploded, the sub's lights went out and it rolled sharply. The damage was minor and was quickly repaired, allowing the sub to lay in silence in Port Orford. The Japanese plane soon returned, and they were able to get away. (CHS.)

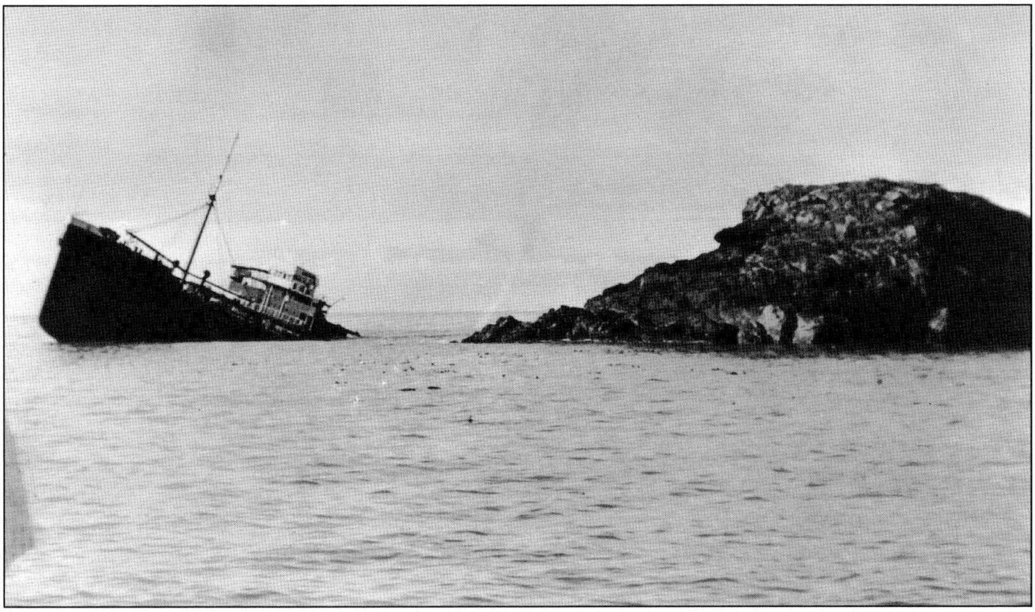

The Japanese submarine *I-25* torpedoed the tanker *Larry Dolheny* on October 5, 1942, and it sunk on the rocks near Cape Blanco. There was a big patrol in Gold Beach, and members manned a radar station on Bailey Beach. The local people also took turns being sky watchers all during the war. (CHS.)

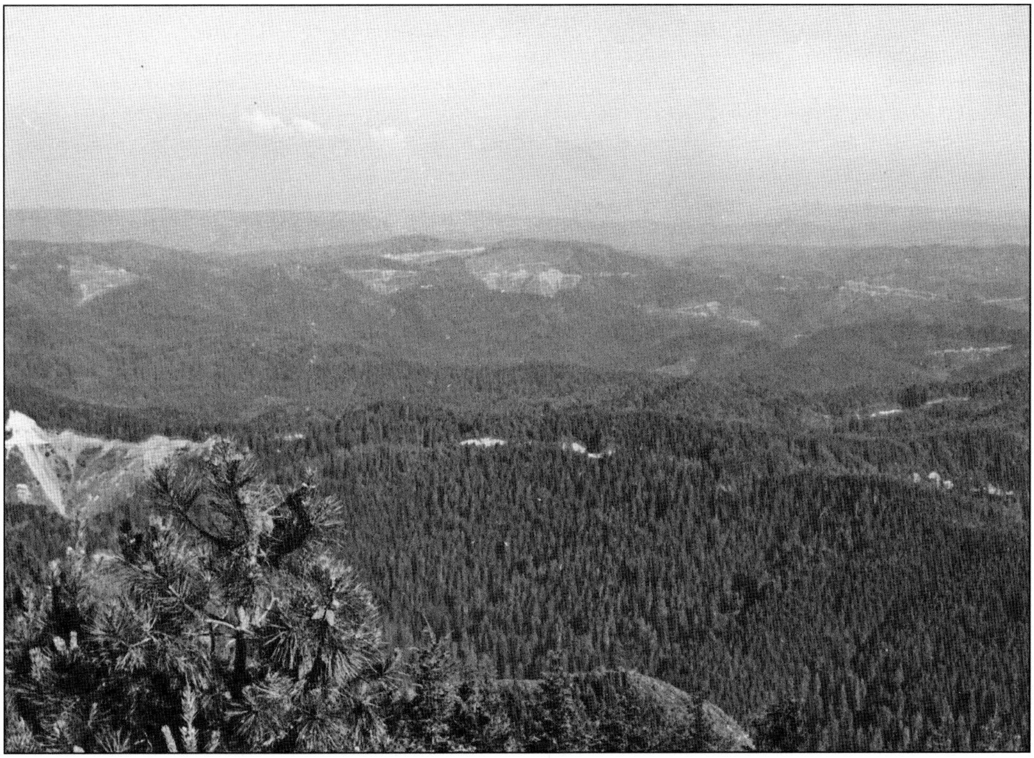

Wheeler Ridge, pictured here, is the area in the Kalmiopsis Wilderness where the Japanese pilot dropped his incendiary. (CHS.)

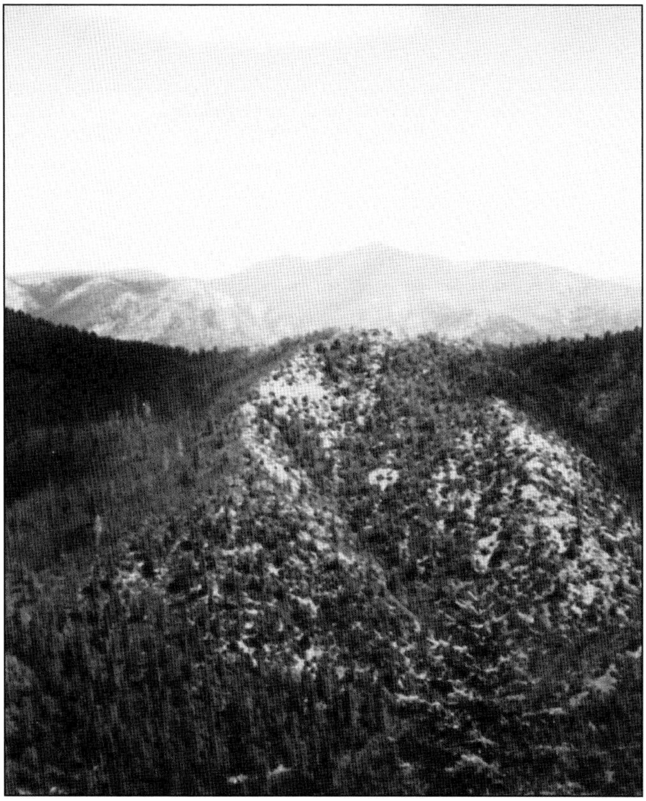

Here is another view of the Kalmiopsis Wilderness. Pearsoll Peak is in the distance. In the winter, it is a fairyland of snow. This is still an untouched part of the southwestern coastal area. (CHS.)

Pictured here is the only drive-in café in Curry County, which was available in the 1960s. It was sold to the Spada family, who redesigned it and made it into a restaurant. When they retired, they closed it down, and as of today, it is a still an empty building. (CHS.)

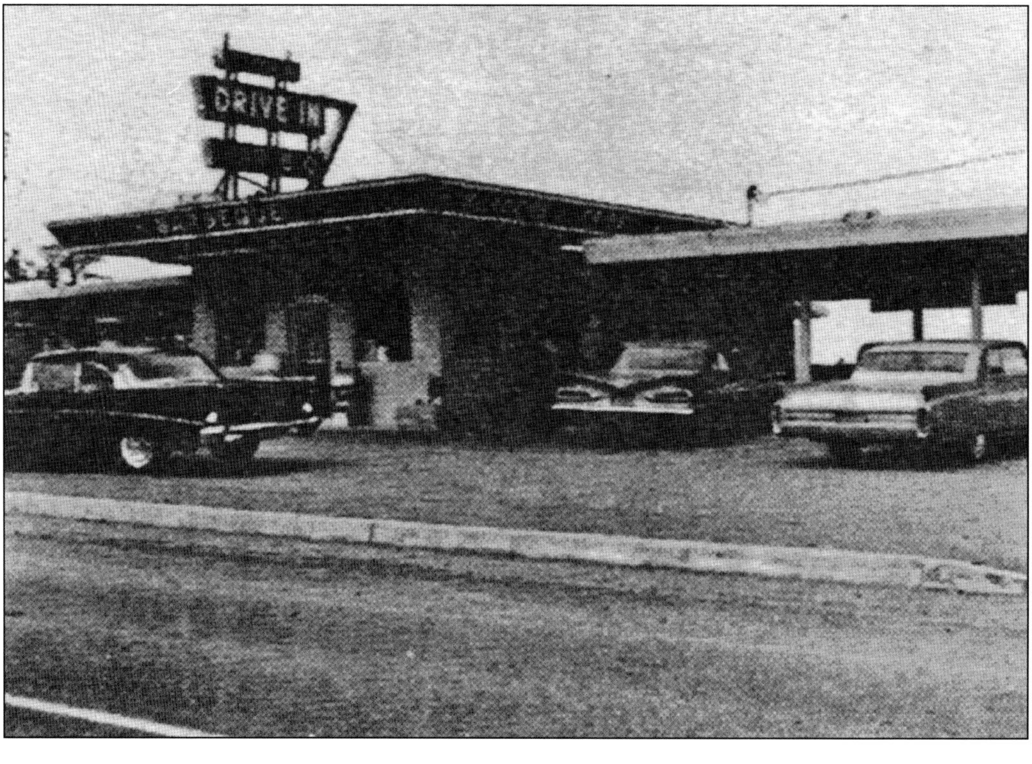

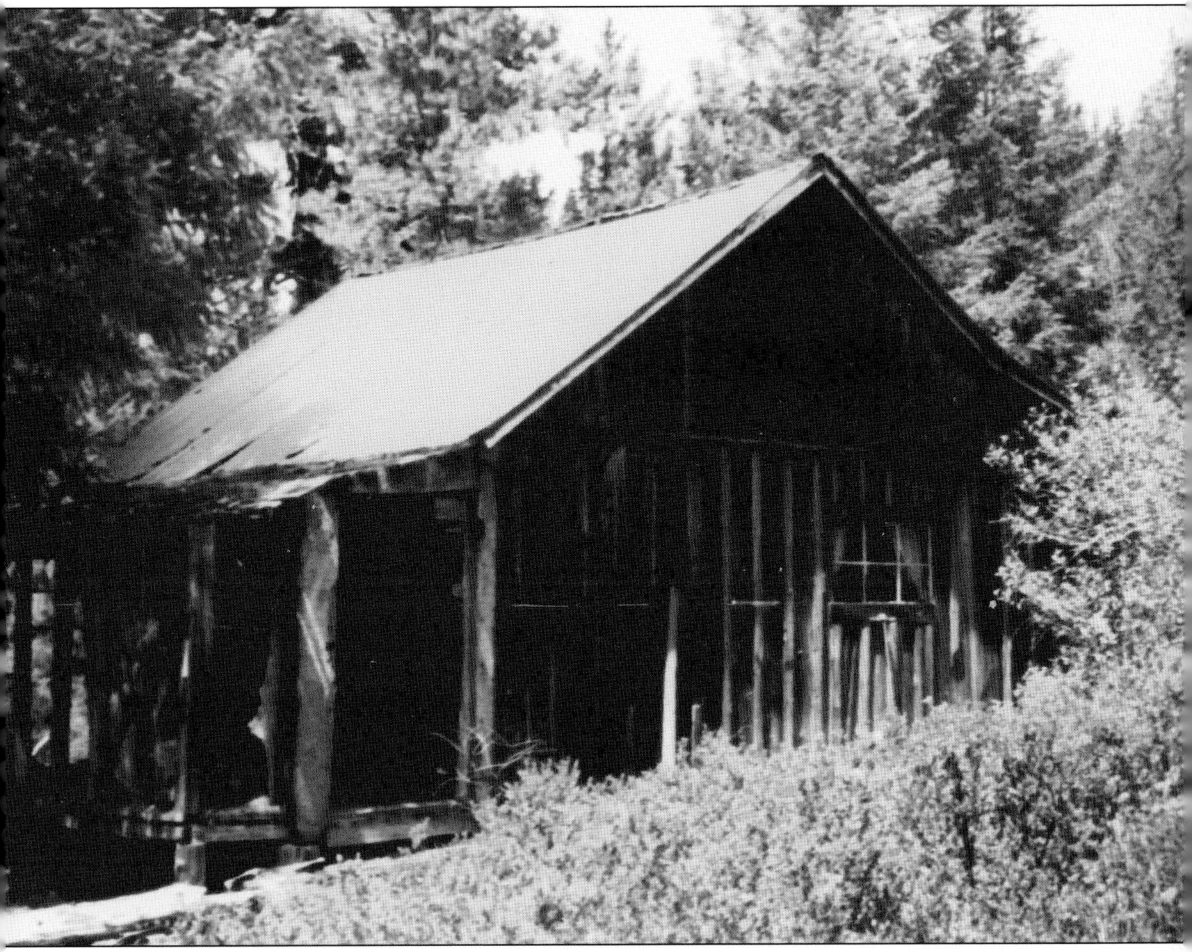

This is a miner's cabin built in the early 1900s in the high area of the Kalmiopsis Wilderness. Other miners built several of these cabins; when their claims became dry, they left, and the cabins remained there. Several hikers used the cabins for shelter, and it was sometimes lifesaving. In the 1960s, the Forest Service tore them down as the area became a government-protected wilderness. (CHS.)

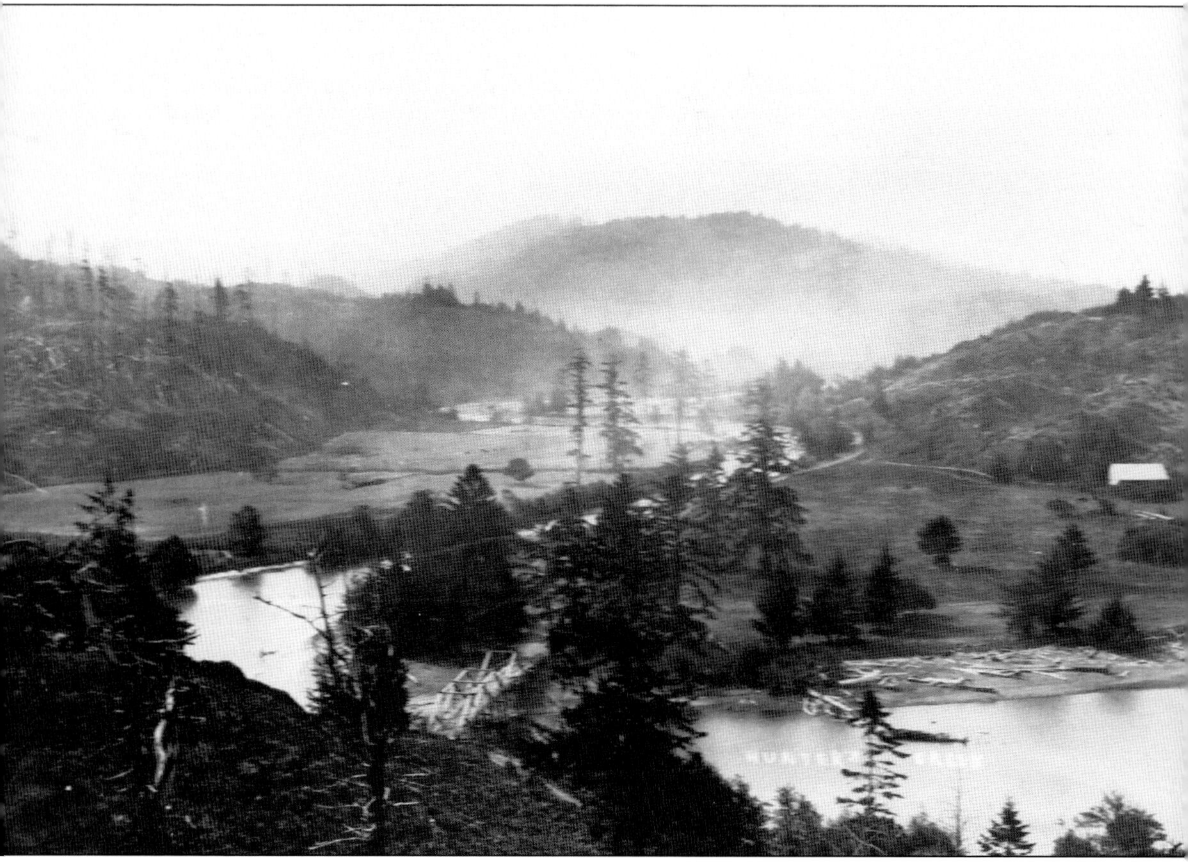

This is the spectacular scenic background to the south of Hunters Creek. It shows a large mountain, which is the location of the Kalmiopsis Wilderness, and the flow of Hunters Creek as it winds down from the headwaters to the Pacific Ocean. (CHS.)

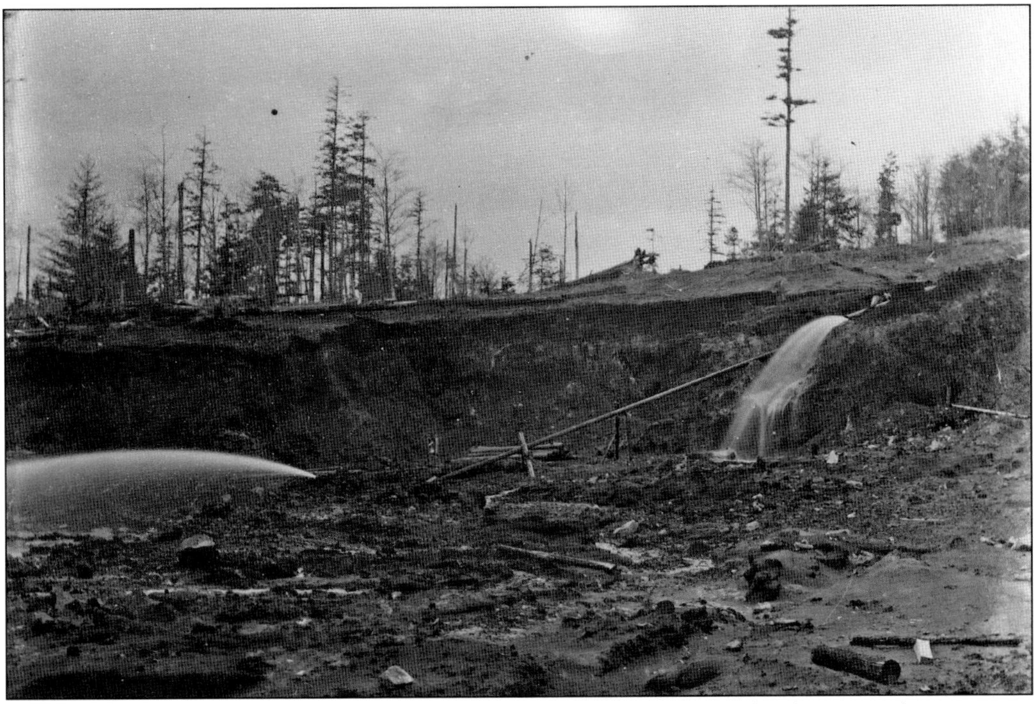

In this picture of the Madden Mine, pressure-washing of the ground is being used to separate gold from tailings. This was just one way the miners used different types of machines to extract gold. (CHS.)

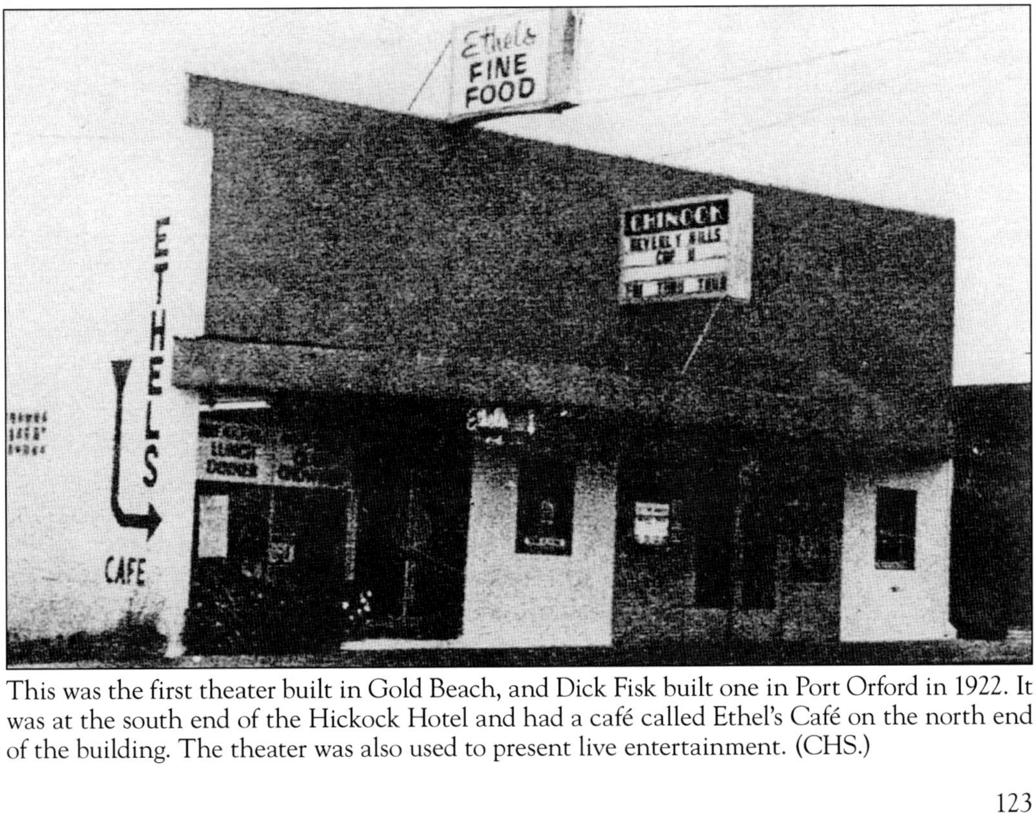

This was the first theater built in Gold Beach, and Dick Fisk built one in Port Orford in 1922. It was at the south end of the Hickock Hotel and had a café called Ethel's Café on the north end of the building. The theater was also used to present live entertainment. (CHS.)

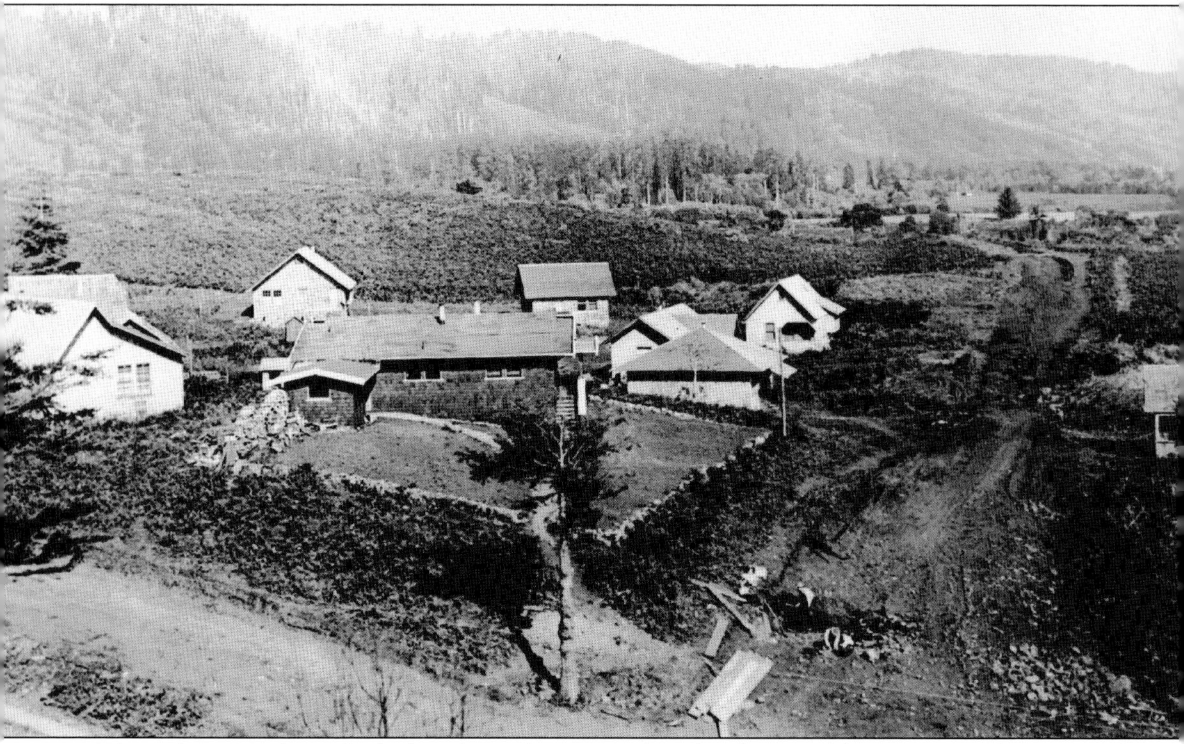

This is how Brookings looked in the early 1900s, after the closure of the C&O Lumber Co. and the regrouping of the town. The population was low, but now Brookings is the largest town in Curry County. Today, there is a population of 6,805 in the city limits. (CHS.)

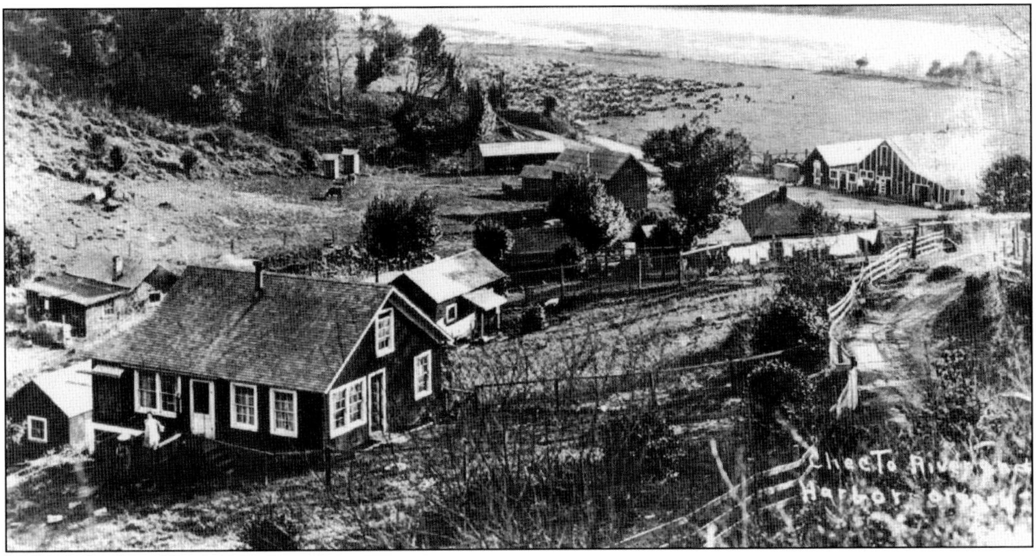

This is a photograph of the town of Harbor in the late 1800s facing the Chetco River. This was taken before the bridges were built; land-based transportation crossed the river by ferry. Harbor is situated on the south of the river, and Brookings is situated on the north. (CHS.)

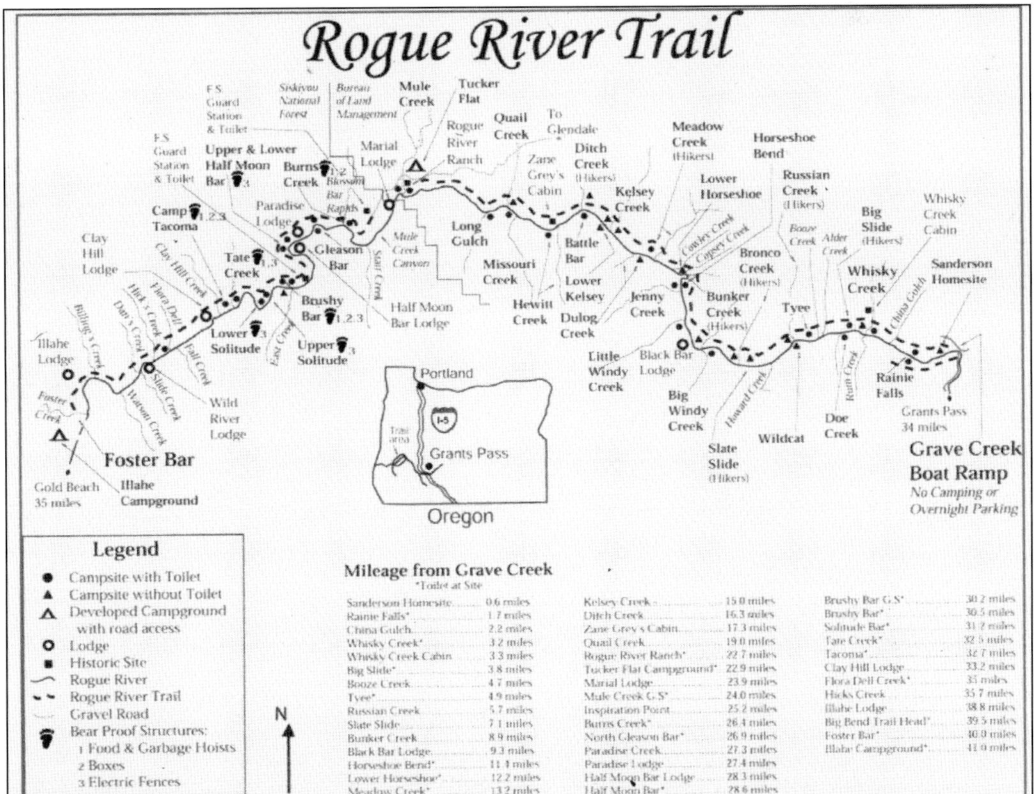

Presented is a map of all the small communities and riffles on the upper Rogue River just above Agness and on up to Graves Creek in Josephine County. It shows the location of the Rogue River Trail. (CHS.)

"The Mighty Pacific"

The roar of the might Pacific,
The low and ebbing tide,
The crashing on rocks on the breakers
Fills me with peace inside.

It's a restless sea that never sleeps,
It must hasten the ships on their way,
It washes the shells on the sandy beach,
And covers the shores with spray.

My cares become so small there,
With the vastness of nature's truth
In daydreams my mind returns again
To the golden days of youth.

Watching the drifting clouds in the sky,
My mind becomes filled with emotion
And once again my eyes are drawn,
Back the shores of the Ocean.

The windswept trees lean Eastward
The boughs tremble slight with the breeze,
The beauty of God's hand in nature
Brings me to thanksgiving prayer on my knees

The mouth of a little creek flows there,
Its banks lined with rocks and shells,
If only it were able to speak,
Think of the tales it could tell

The mornings past of the minus tides,
The clam diggers covering the sand,
Watching the holds for the clams to spurt
In the surf with a shovel in hand.

In the daytime it's a place for playing,
Wading in the waves of the shore,
While at night it's the warmth of the campfire,
Listening to the mighty breakers roar.

The moonlight casts its shadows,
Creating a florescent glow on the waves,
A treasure of beauty to the living,
But to many lost sailors a grave.

From the shore the calm looks inviting,
The beauty leaves a catch to your breath,
But the sight of raging storm tossed ship,
Leaves a mark with its toll of death.

Yes I stand by this mighty Pacific,
Containing creatures of the briny deep,
As I watch this mammoth Ocean,
This restless sea that never sleeps.

—Meryl Boice